The Universe on a Bicycle

The Universe on a Bicycle

TONY WILSON

Illustrated by the Author

Elliott & Thompson

London

To my beloved Pat
who keeps asking the questions even
when she knows there aren't
going to be any answers

Chapters which contain arguments on Dual-Nature Theory

John and I uncovered dual-nature theory during this bike ride; the idea developed as we rode along, it became part of our story. For ease of reference, the following list of arguments gives the chapter in which each one can be found. The essence of the theory in twelve logical steps is given in Chapter 38.

The Universe on a Bicycle

Malin Head

Carrigart   Moville   Portrush

Burt   Limavaddy

Ardara   *Glens of Antrim*

NORTHERN

IRELAND   Belfast

Cavangarden   Strangford
Sligo   Newcastle
Newry

Dromore West

Newport

Leenane   EIRE

Roundstone   Dublin
Galway

Clarinbridge

Cliffs of Mohr   Arklow

Kilrush

Ballybunion   Wellingtonbridge
Waterford
Tralee   Tramore
Dingle   Lismore
Dungarvan
Waterville   Cork
Healey Pass   Kinsale
Toormore

N

0 10 20 30 40 50 miles

ONE

*The Atlantic, the Salmon and
Man's Bad Behaviour –
Cork to Sligo*

1 Morning

I live in a little village in Wiltshire, but I want to make a complaint: Why, I want to know, do we believe everything we're told?

For example, they insist that the earth goes round the sun but that's not true; all you have to do is go outside and see for yourself. It's quite obvious that the sun goes round the earth. Einstein said it all clearly in his work on relativity. If you were standing on the sun, then OK it's the earth that would be going round. But you're not, so don't keep telling me the earth goes round the sun.

People just don't want to think for themselves. When we discuss terrorism, pollution and the destruction of wildlife why does nobody ever state the simple truth that human overpopulation is the root cause of all these horrors?

And here's another one: Why do we believe it when we are told it's right to bomb, shoot and drown other people in what we call war? It might be a good idea, but isn't it going a bit far for Christians to claim that it's morally right?

At about six in the morning I'm tucked up in bed, fast asleep. A vision of humanity swarming over the surface of the earth haunts my dreaming as I wake. But it's not really a dream; it's more like a strident jumble of ideas flicking about in my head. The earth is going round the moon, and terrorists are killing hundreds of millions of people who are standing on the sun. That's what the TV news reader says. But then somebody points out: 'Why do you believe everything they tell you – think it out for yourself – nobody can stand on the sun.'

Which way is up? Why am I in a strange bed? What happened yesterday? In the split second of waking, these strident ideas stop flicking about. They hover in the air like naughty little flying creatures. Then they vanish.

But I'm not in my little Wiltshire village at all. I'm in John's house in Dublin, and today we're off on a bike ride round Ireland. Eventually I'll have to get out of bed.

Look at me. Naked. I smile hopefully into the mirror but it's no good pretending I'm an athlete. The truth is I'm a skinny old man with blue-veined legs. My right big toe looks slightly purple as though it's too far away from my heart to get much of a blood supply. And is that a little pot belly I can see? I thank God we wear clothes and quickly cover it all up and get on with the day.

The first thing is a cup of tea and a session communicating with my sketchbook. It's like a ventriloquist's dummy; I draw and write in it, telling it things, and because I'm still only half awake, it sort of answers back.

We're old friends, John and I. We were at university together; at Trinity College, Dublin. That was fifty years ago. We both rowed in the university crew. John did medicine and then went on to become a professor of salmon biology in Newfoundland. Right now, he's renting a house in Dublin because he's over here for a year doing some research on salmon.

I did economics and eventually qualified as an Irish chartered accountant. After six years working in Paris, I followed a career in British industry.

2   Stream tanks

We load up our bikes and we're off. There really ought to be a small military band to trumpet our departure, or at the very least a bugler, but we just slip away unnoticed.

We catch the midday Dublin to Cork express train. As it inches forward, slowly gathering speed, I look at my watch: it's precisely twelve o'clock on the 1st of August 2000.

Our bikes have been propped with a few others in the guard's van. They look as though they might be damaged when the carriage rocks about. Bikes have intricately adjusted gears, delicate wire spokes, flimsy brake levers and cables. A mailbag might easily fall over and buckle a wheel. The guard says: 'Ah sure they'll be OK where they are, ye don't need to worry.' That makes me worry all the more of course.

The train trundles powerfully down country. We cross the low-lying centre of Ireland. Through Kildare, Monasterevin, Portalington, Portlaoise, Templemore, Thurles, Limerick Junction, Charleville, Mallow. Evocative names! I bet there's a heroic rebel song about each one of them, except perhaps Limerick Junction.

The weather is a bit of a worry. It doesn't look at all nice for cycling. It's wet, grey and overcast. Out of the train window you can see across the flat damp countryside to the horizon. Under the low clouds there's a distant layer of pale blue sky above the land; it's like the filling in a sandwich.

While we plunge southwards down this layer, sitting comfortably in our massive train, I ask John about a stream-tank project he's discussing with the Irish Department of Fisheries.

He has left his hearing aid at home. He's done it on purpose because it's very expensive and he doesn't want to risk damaging or losing it. The trouble is, when he gets going on one of his favourite topics, without his hearing aid he's very difficult to stop, and stream tanks is a good example.

A stream tank is a sort of real-life aquarium. It's built underground alongside an existing river. You walk down into a big room which has a glass wall, say 50ft long, holding back the river. You are in semi-darkness, but once your eyes have become accustomed to the gloom, enough light comes through the watery world the fish live in for you to be able to see very well. The river surface is mostly just out of the picture, just above the level of the top of the glass wall. So you are right there in the river. In with the fish, as it were.

And not only that, John goes on, but you can see the mud, gravel and rock below the riverbed, the 'substrate' as he calls it. What on earth for? I wonder but don't dare interrupt. The whole description is laced with wonderfully fishy scientific terms like algae, larvae, nutrients, gradient, riffles, pools and riparian strips.

It turns out the purpose of being able to look below the riverbed is so that you can see some of what's going on down there in the creepy world of slimy things. This, of course, is where much of the fishes' food comes from: nymphs, eggs, worms, beetles and other succulent creatures.

The glass wall of the tank would be long enough to include at least one riffle and one pool. John explains the amazing discovery that if you let a river flow naturally from source to sea it will always form itself into a series of rapids or riffles, and patches of deeper stiller water, called pools. There is a rather marvellous formula, he says, combining geology, gradient, river width and water flow which says how far apart these riffles and pools will naturally occur.

Riffles and pools mustn't be confused with meanders. I made that mistake to begin with. Meanders, bends and straight sections are sideways movements, whereas riffles and pools are falls in water level.

The only time there isn't a perfect sequence of riffles and pools from the source to the mouth of a river is when it's been messed up by the Great Enemy, the human engineer with his culverts, farm channels, road works, and hydroelectric schemes. Of all these evils, hydroelectric schemes are the worst. Most people think of hell as a raging fiery furnace. John will tell you it's a gigantic hydroelectric scheme.

The stream tank would show indigenous trout and juvenile salmon. The young salmon prefer to nip about in the faster water of the riffles, while the trout like to hover at the point where the riffle water drops down into the next pool. That's where they like to feed.

It would be a tourist attraction where people can watch the fish in their natural habitat. It would also be available for scientific work.

John explains that there are stream tanks in various parts of the world but they invariably suffer from interference by the Evil One. This cowardly creature disguises himself as a civil engineer and hides behind his corrupt side-kicks: the architect and the bureaucrat.

What happens is that the salmon biologist explains how the stream tank should be built according to scientifically published principles of salmon and trout ecology. Then along come the Devil and his smooth-talking assistants. They make it look pretty. They straighten out natural curves and put in a sparkling waterfall where the stream should run into a pool. They create a bend near the entrance to accommodate the Coca-Cola machine. They build in the wrong gradient. They make the substrate out of the wrong sand because they can get it cheap from a builder friend and pocket the difference. They put in the wrong sort of glass, again for backhanders. They put lights in the wrong places, which upset the fish by messing up their daily cycle, and attract algae that stick to the glass.

'Engineers, architects and bureaucrats,' says John, with fiercely compressed air hissing through his voice. 'They're the same all over the world. They can be guaranteed to destroy any ecosystem.'

If his project goes ahead, John will be waiting for the Devil and his assistants with a sharp pencil.

The train slows down. We're coming into Cork. Factory walls, slate roofs and dustbins, houses and streets with shops glide slantwise into view. The midday express clink-clunks over points, drifts into the platform and comes to a stop.

We get our bikes out of the guard's van. The system apparently is that you just wander in and collect what's yours. Mercifully they're undamaged. We look for the guard to thank him but he's gone off somewhere.

We hitch up our panniers, hop on, and head off for Kinsale, which is on the coast about twenty miles due south of Cork.

3   Griffins B&B

The sky is still heavily overcast and it's rather a wet cycle-ride over lush, undulating farmland down to the coast.

We pedal happily along, glad to be on our way. I've got to the age when I have to get off and pee all the time, and whenever we come to a river John has to get off to look over the bridge. He looks for fish, whose behaviour, species, age and health he identifies long before I can see anything at all. I'd be terribly pleased if I could spot a fish in the water before him but I've never yet managed it.

John picks blackberries at every opportunity. So the four-star place to stop for a pee is at a bridge with brambles nearby. And if things are going particularly well, out come John's fishing rod and my sketch book.

But it's getting late so we start thinking about finding a B&B. We ask at a pub in Belgooly and soon we're completely lost. The road signs don't seem to confirm the directions we've been given.

Actually, sometimes I think the whole human race is lost.

We gaze at the map, both thinking the same thing. 'Just look at that coastline,' says John.

'Yes, with those five great peninsulas stretching twenty or thirty miles out into the Atlantic, like a giant's fingers.'

'Can't wait to get out there,' he says. 'Look, see those salmon rivers, the forests and mountains, the sea and the offshore islands.' John's the naturalist on this trip.

I, being more the urban type, am looking at the villages and roads along the route we hope to take.

We go silent. Then John says, 'You know a map is really a sort of model of the landscape. Clever really. We can see the whole jagged south-west coast of Ireland laid out for us in detail, and yet it's only just a piece of messily folded paper.'

'D'you mean the way we try out alternative routes on a map like testing an aeroplane in a wind tunnel. Is that what you mean by a model?'

'Yes, a model or a paradigm.'

I hate those long words beloved of academics, and poncy journalists. They come and they go. As soon as the common herd has mastered one it goes out of fashion because it's no longer obscure. Other intensely irritating examples in vogue at the moment are eponymous and palimpsest. I'm about to pounce on paradigm saying I don't know what it means, but I can sense that John's got more to say. So I keep quiet.

'I've been thinking recently. The plight of the Atlantic salmon here in Ireland is a paradigm too; it's a paradigm of man's destructive behaviour. We're driving the salmon to extinction, we know we are doing it; we know full well it's wrong and yet we seem quite incapable of stopping ourselves. It's like all our appalling behaviour: war, terrorism, global warming, pollution and genocide, only on a smaller scale.'

'Yes. I see what you mean,' I say; glad I didn't make a fool of myself with paradigm.

After half an hour wandering about we eventually find our way back to the main road.

Just before Kinsale we come to a nice looking B&B. The landlady is very kind but she's full. She suggests we try Griffins down the road and off to the right; she's heard they still have vacancies.

At about eight o'clock we find Griffins B&B. Mercifully they do have room for us. It's modern and luxurious. We're sharing a room. Everything is frilly and brand new. Very neat and tidy and we feel embarrassingly scruffy and out of place. The only thing we can do is just get on with it and, above all, act normal. Act as though we've just got back from the office.

There's a huge conservatory looking down over the town to the hills beyond. The hills slope down into the sea. Kinsale is a popular holiday resort and yacht haven.

One of the problems facing the touring cyclist is dinner. When you've found a place to stay you're usually totally knackered and quite hungry. But B&Bs don't do evening meals. The last thing you want is to have to get back on your bike after a shower and change of clothes, and cycle miles to find a pint of beer and somewhere to eat. And then, to make it worse, have to cycle miles back again, in the dark, slightly drunk, getting your 'smart' clothes splattered and wet. So the best thing is to find a B&B near a restaurant, and Griffins B&B is well placed for the weary cyclist.

4 Light bulb in Leenane. The pucai

The idea to go on this cycle-ride came to me the previous summer. My wife and I were staying in a little Atlantic village called Leenane. It is a mystic, magic place in the far west of County Galway. The dot com city life hasn't got there yet. Maybe it never will. In Leenane it's easy to believe in spirits and the supernatural; difficult not to in fact.

There's a mountain right above the village, and I had noticed indications on maps pointing to a neolithic burial place high up under a cliff near the summit. So one day I went up to try and find it. The going became very difficult and precipitous and I never did find anything that looked like an ancient burial site. It was disappointing.

When I was halfway down again the sun came out and the view, sweeping in a great panorama, was magnificent. There were green mountains, lakes and rivers as far as the eye could see. I sat for a while, and as I became intoxicated by the beauty of the place, I thought wistfully how marvellous it must be to bicycle all the way round the coast of Ireland.

But for me that was impossible. At sixty-eight I was too old for that sort of thing, and anyway, I couldn't think of anyone really suitable to ask to go with me, and it would be too lonely to do it alone.

Then, as though a light bulb in a comic strip had gone on above my head, I thought of my old friend John. I felt that the spirits, in Ireland they are called the pucai, had steered me away from the burial site, guarding its sanctity. But then, noticing my disappointment, they had offered me this suggestion as a consolation.

Later I phoned him in Newfoundland. 'How about a bike ride round Ireland, next summer?' There was only the slightest pause, then: 'Yes, OK,' he said.

5 Crispy dried seaweed. Ice age and salmon history. *Human behaviour raises an Awful Question*

In Kinsale we shop for a picnic lunch: cheese, salami, tomatoes, bread, bananas, a raw onion, beer, nuts, black chocolate – that sort of thing.

We find a lunch-spot just off the road looking out over a broad estuary. It's windy but the sun has come out. Seagulls are swooping and crying around the rocks out to sea, and there's a wind-surfer skittering across the waves like a dragonfly.

John goes in for a swim wearing his sandals. He steps over great beds of mussels in the mucky, brackish, estuary water. The very idea makes me shiver.

Then we have our picnic lunch on the sand under a sea-wall. We're surrounded by crispy dried seaweed, broken mussel shells, plastic bags, old flip-flops, sand hoppers and jagged pieces of fibreglass from the wrecks of small craft. We are watched by crows and a heron and ignored by a brigade of small, long-beaked black and white estuary birds, which leapfrog over each other in low-flying formations as they forage along behind the receding tide.

Our picnic is delicious. Warmed to perfection in the morning sun.

Over lunch John talks about evolution, the Ice Ages and salmon. He's a walking encyclopaedia on this sort of thing and I could listen for hours.

Unlike painting, which everybody is familiar with and has opinions two-a-penny, this salmon stuff has vitally important lessons for mankind and most people know hardly anything at all about it.

Ten thousand years ago Ireland was covered by vast, mile-thick ice sheets which wiped out virtually all animal life. However, due to the Gulf Stream, there were patches, mainly in Kerry and west Cork – where we are now in fact – that were never completely iced over, and some hardy animal species managed to hold on – and still live here today. The best known of these is the Natterjak toad. St Patrick, alias the deadly ice, banished all snakes and toads from Ireland. But the Natterjak is one he missed.

All the rivers and lakes were frozen too, of course, so all the freshwater fish were wiped out.

It never occurred to me till John pointed it out, but it's obvious really that when the ice eventually receded and the rivers started to flow again, there were no fish. The rivers were empty.

The only way fish can come back naturally to an island that's been under ice is by sea. There was once a theory that fish could spread overland by having their eggs carried on birds' feet. But that's now been proved to be untrue says John.

European freshwater fish such as pike, carp, gudgeon, roach and perch survived south of the limit of the ice. But because they can't live in the saltwater, none of them could swim across from France or England to recolonise Irish waters.

But, John explains, there are a few freshwater fish that can also live in the sea. The main ones are the salmon family, which include salmon, trout, smelt, char and pollan. Others are shad, which is a type of herring, eels, sticklebacks, flounders and lamprey. So these were the fish which reoccupied all the accessible Irish rivers and lakes, though each in their own way.

Having little or no competition, this small handful of fish species flourished abundantly for about ten thousand years.

It's all quite fascinating, and by popping in the odd question I manage to steer John into the areas I know least about. It's just like dipping into an encyclopaedia. Could the humble little stickleback really swim all the way over from France? I want to ask. But never do because there are more important questions.

He explains that the salmon family are particularly quick to adapt to local conditions. They do this by throwing out a wide variety of characteristics in each hatch. They have evolved this technique to cope with the problems of breeding in fresh water. The thing is that the conditions of their rivers, the habitats in which they breed and mature, change much faster than those of sea-breeding fish. This is because erosion and climate change are much faster on land than they are at sea. So salmon and trout have had to become particularly quick to adapt to changing conditions.

John says, 'In their chosen environment habitat change is pronounced and this is responsible for the variation in their life history strategies.' Scientists talk like that.

So over the centuries salmon and trout, which are mostly migratory and return to breed where they were born, have developed an impressive array of subspecies and tribes to fit the particular ecology of every different river and lake. Some became landlocked, some specialised in fast-flowing, flash-flooding mountain streams, others occupied the bigger slower rivers. Each tribe became recognisably different in physique and lifestyle. They became as they are today; specialists in the art of surviving and prospering in their own specific waters.

Things went very well, says John, until man, the great monster, came along and messed it all up. First, medieval monks introduced all sorts of edible continental freshwater fish like pike, carp, perch, rudd, dace, tench and barbel. These species of fish then steadily spread all over Ireland, and the indigenous trout and salmon had to compete with them for food, habitat and breeding grounds.

New varieties of fish, particularly roach, have recently been introduced by French coarse-fishing clubs.

The next assault on the salmon was made by farmers. They straightened up riverbeds to rationalise field shapes and farm boundaries, and to prevent flooding. This destroyed the natural sequences of riffles and pools which salmon and trout require. And they recklessly poured their waste into the rivers. The most poisonous to fish were slurry, insecticides and fertilisers.

Finally, as John has already said, the Devil disguised himself as a civil engineer and built trunk roads and hydroelectric schemes which systematically wrecked the salmon habitat of every river they touched.

Each 'improvement' was more deadly than the last. So that now at the end of the twentieth century most of the indigenous trout and salmon tribes are extinct. Their habitats have been destroyed, and their waters poisoned.

There used to be magnificent salmon in all the big Irish rivers: Shannon, Boyne, Liffey, Lee, Blackwater, Slaney, Barrow, Suir and Nore, Bann, Suck, Foyle, Lagan, and in the countless smaller rivers and streams too. Even in the 1930s these rivers teemed with salmon and trout.

Year after year they returned to their own rivers to spawn and restart their life-cycles. But now most of these specialised tribes have been wiped out and it would take many hundreds of years of evolutionary natural selection to recreate what we have destroyed in sixty.

Aren't we clever.

John points out that people have recently realised that it's very difficult to restock a river with salmon because it's almost impossible to find the right fish to match specific river conditions. It's like trying to repopulate northern Siberia with a vigorous tribe of Australian Aborigines. Rivers differ from each other far more than I had realised. They can be peaty, which is acid, or chalky, which is alkaline. They can be fast or slow, rich or poor in nutrients. They vary in amounts of shade, sand, rocks, soil, frequency of flooding and so on. Ironically great harm was often done by restocking. What typically happened is that well-intentioned fishery owners introduced the eggs of a vigorous Norwegian strain of salmon. The new fish being strong fast growers, take over the breeding and growing-up grounds. In this way they completely kill off what little remains of the indigenous fish. But then after a few years they themselves die out because they haven't evolved the specific skills, inbred instincts or physical features needed to cope with the actual conditions of their new surroundings.

Of course Ireland still does have tribes of indigenous salmon and trout in many rivers and lakes and these could be saved and built up again. But it would require intelligence and money and John thinks modern man is too stupid and too greedy to do it properly. So the great diversity and abundance of the old is almost certainly lost and gone for ever. Destroyed by the crass stupidity of man, says John: 'Wiped out by civil engineers.'

By now he needs calming down. His face is pale with anger and he's talking in a quiet murderous monotone. His eyes, like a deadly sniper's, are narrowed to evil slits.

One of John's slimy monsters is big business. He has a clear academic's view of the matter. The big multi-nationals like Coca-Cola, Monsanto, McDonalds, Honda and Shell, supply world markets with ruthless efficiency. Taken together they have eased and improved the lives of countless millions, but why, he wants to know, do their side effects have to be so destructive? They pollute the air, poison the water and devastate the land, and as though that's not enough, they also interfere with the economics and politics of the world.

With my degree in economics and my career in big business I do feel somewhat on the spot here.

'Well that's the outsiders point of view,' I say, 'but when you are working in a big company it's not at all like that, not really.'

'How do you mean?'

'Well for a start I've never known a big business executive who had what one would call evil motives. Most are very moral upright citizens. Lying, cheating and greed are frowned on and stamped out. IBM, Marks & Spencer, John Lewis and many others are renowned for their highly moral corporate ethos. There are some corrupt companies of course but they are the exception. A bad reputation in the marketplace can do a lot of damage. For a start it makes it difficult to recruit top people.'

'Hmm,' he goes, clearly not convinced.

'Well of course there's fierce competition; it's a real hot-house. We compete internally for promotion and with other companies for market share, but the business jungle has its own very clear rules of morality.'

'So why do you callously seek to put small companies out of

business, set up monopolies and secret pricing agreements, pour poisons into the watershed and cut down rainforests? Why do you kill trees with acid rain and pump battery hens full of hormones, which accumulate in the human children that eat the hens? Why do you create unemployment in whole communities, ruin beautiful coastlines with high-rise hotels and theme pubs for lager louts . . . '

'Well yes,' I interrupt with difficulty, realising that with salmon in mind he's quite capable of going on like this for ever, 'but we don't actually do these things, not on purpose. That's just progress, it's what people want. If we didn't supply the market, the Japs, Germans and Americans certainly would. They do already.'

But there's something wrong here, my words have a hollow ring. As I finish my lunch amongst the crispy dried seaweed I realise I've fallen into the trap of playing the Nazi officer's defence: 'Everybody else did it, and anyway I was only obeying orders.'

So what's the real answer?

Well, what exactly is the question? Better get that right in the first place.

When it comes to human behaviour I always find Darwin puts things in perspective for me. I fancy he would have said that no matter how evil it may have been, Nazi behaviour was perfectly natural; it has happened countless times before and will happen again countless times in the future. And furthermore, no matter how moral and incorruptible I may believe myself to be, I would be a fool to think that I would have refused Hitler's orders.

John breaks the silence. 'Evil monsters believe themselves innocent too you know. Vile dragons have friends, families and loyalties, and they lead domestic lives, so did Gengis Kahn, but that doesn't make them any less evil.'

Eventually I'm going to have to admit I'm wrong about the innocence of big business, and my part in it, but it would be too humiliating to do so right now. Also, the trouble is, I can't quite work out why I actually am wrong. And if I'm wrong what does that mean?

There's no getting away from it though; what John has just taught me is that the description of an organism cannot be used as a moral defence of its behaviour.

'I do see what you mean about the plight of the salmon being a model for man's appalling behaviour. It's a very big, awful and depressing question.'

'It is indeed,' says John, and from here on it gets referred to as the Awful Question.

Well . . . And so what? Old men are allowed to complain about what the world is coming to. That's mainly what we're here for.

6 Varicose vein

After lunch the wind drops and the sun shines hot. Soon I'm feeling really fit and well. That's cycling for you. You gather strength as you go. It seems to come from nowhere and I spin along, free as the breeze and happy as a song.

The scenery is lush with grassy roadside clumps of flowering montbretia splashing a startling bright red into the air. Its red turns to a hot orange at the edges. I've never seen montbretia so vibrant as it is here on the Atlantic coast of Ireland, and it's beautifully accompanied by the acid yellow of ragweed and the soft white of meadowsweet.

It's about five o'clock when we swoop through Schull and start wondering should we be looking for a B&B.

We take a little coast road shown on the map as a short-cut to Toormore. The road goes by the sea. It's very pretty with masses of wild flowers, but it's not a short-cut at all. More like a detour in fact.

We stop for a pee and blackberries. The blackberries are excellent here, John says; fat and juicy. Must be the soft Atlantic climate.

Then he goes and spikes his bare shin on a fierce bramble. We never wear trousers when riding along, they'd get wet and dirty. Of course, your bare legs do, too, but they dry off quicker and are easier to wash.

Well, a thorn pierces a varicose vein. The result is rather amazing. Instead of bleeding normally and pouring down his leg, a neat little spout of blood streams steadily out. It shoots about three inches horizontally into the air before turning into little droplets and curving down on to his foot. It's rather like a small pin-hole puncture in a water pipe.

Being squeamish I quickly look away for fear of passing out. John the biologist, using a handkerchief, wraps it tight with the detached air of someone doing up a parcel. And we cycle on.

We discuss the ageing body and how it's liable to disgrace itself and let you down when you least expect it. 'Ah well!' says John. 'In Canada they say you are not really happy till all your teeth have gone and you have lost your interest in girls.' I don't want to tell him I've heard it before, and anyway an old joke in the right context is so much better than a new one which isn't.

We come to a B&B sign. The house looks bleak and there's no village with restaurants but it really is getting late now. So we go up the path. There's an obsequious dog wiggling about. We ring the bell. She has one room left. But it turns out she's offering us a double bed.

She must think we're a couple of aged weirdoes; too old perhaps to be IRA terrorists, but wild looking, stubbly-bearded, dirty and damp, one with a blood-stained handkerchief wrapped round his leg. The wiggling dog, too, obviously has its doubts.

With formal dignity and prim good manners we decline, and pedal on till we get to Toormore.

Toormore is a nice little village. A few houses at a crossroads, not much more really. It's right by the sea. The Fastnet lighthouse is about ten miles offshore. We ask a lady is there anywhere to eat near here. She tells us about the Altar; a very good restaurant right in the village. People come from miles around to eat there. So that's promising.

And to our great relief there's a B&B. The sign reads: 'Sea Front B&B. Margaret and George Whiteley. Vacancies'. Margaret answers the bell, doesn't flinch at our appearance, shows us our room and offers us a pot of tea.

She installs us in the living room, which looks out to sea. Tea then comes with two pieces of homemade swiss-roll and a big plate of chips. This is a much more healthy response to our dishevelled appearance. I do a little drawing of the view. John goes off to have a shower and to deal with his varicose vein.

While I'm drawing and finishing my tea and chips, I hear John calling me from the room, his voice is anxious. This isn't like him at all. He usually floats mildly across the switchbacks and potholes of daily life. So I stop drawing immediately – not like me either – and go to help.

He's tried to fix his leg with an elastoplast and some tubigrip bandage. But it's started to spout again. His two hands aren't enough to inspect the puncture, wipe, wash and dress it, and to mop up the constant stream of blood all at the same time. There's blood all over the lovely, brand-new, pale yellow, deep-pile carpet. It's quite a mess.

We spend thirty minutes mopping and wiping with cold water to

Looking out to sea at Toormore. The Fastnet rock is ten miles beyond the tower

remove all signs of blood. It's amazing how densely red and copiously staining a drop of blood actually is. Worse still, some of it is on the plush, pink and pale-green bedspread too.

At last, except for one bloodstained towel, it's all mopped up. The carpet and bedspread are soaking wet but clean.

Should we confess and risk disgrace, or pretend nothing has happened? Too tired to decide, we leave it till tomorrow and stroll round to the Altar restaurant where we have a superb meal.

The man who owns the restaurant is from Yorkshire. He does the cooking, which is excellent; gastronomic in fact. There are some beautifully coloured stained-glass panels around the place. They are for sale and it turns out he makes them; that's what he does in winter when the restaurant is closed.

We totter back to Sea Front B&B for a good night's sleep.

During the night the loom of the Fastnet Lighthouse sweeps mesmerisingly at ten second intervals across our bedroom window lighting up the curtains. I've bought a postcard of the lighthouse and on the back it says: 'Fastnet lighthouse Co. Cork. In 1854 a cast iron tower was built to replace the Cape Clear island lighthouse, which was often shrouded in mist. Present tower started operation 1904.

Converted from vaporised paraffin to electricity in 1969. Automated in 1989, it has a range of twenty-eight nautical miles'. Quite a long way, that.

The Fastnet lighthouse from a postcard

John's leg didn't bleed any more in the night, thank goodness!

We have breakfast looking out towards the lighthouse. Beyond that there's no land till you get to South America.

Nasty weather is forecast for today and huge clouds are arching overhead, but it looks quite nice and it seems possible that they won't be turning to proper rain till they get further inland.

Nothing's been said yet about last night's blood on the carpet and bedspread. So maybe we've got away with it. Except for a slightly rumpled look, it was all clean and dry this morning and apart from the towel it looked perfect, really.

Nervously we pay the bill. This is the moment of truth.

But no, all is courtesy and best wishes.

As we cycle away I feel a lingering guilty fear that Margaret Whiteley did indeed notice but was too kind to say. Women do have extra-sensory perception when it comes to the detection of domestic misdemeanour. When I was a little boy I once came home with a dead rat in my raincoat pocket. My idea was to give it a good inspection when I next got a private moment. I wanted to see how it 'worked': its legs, whiskers, fur and so on. I was particularly interested in its tail which seemed to be jointed. But I never got the chance. My mother immediately said, 'Anthony! What's that you've got in your pocket?' There was a dreadful fuss. But what still mystifies me is; how did she know?

That taught me to respect women in authority. They have a sixth sense in these matters. So it was a relief to get away unscathed from Sea Front B&B.

7   The pucai appear. River inspection and lecture

At ten to twelve we stop in Durrus; a nice little town on its own river, with a post office and several pubs. We do some picnic shopping and then settle down for a coffee in the Old Mill Bar.

Next thing is we are minding our own business quietly enjoying our coffee, bright sunlight is slanting in through the window, when some pucai appear in my sketchbook. This is quite unexpected. Must have been daydreaming with pen in hand.

I'd better explain what little I know about them. The pucai are the little people and they appear when you don't expect them. But you have to be in the right frame of mind, which is sort of alert but calm

Coffee stop at the Old Mill Bar, Durrus

and reflective. Dawn and dusk are good times, they often consort with swallows and they'll come into your drawing imagination if you let them. They are everywhere if you can recognise them. Matisse painted excellent pucai. They are all over the world and very common in the west of Ireland. The correct spellings for the Irish ones are: singular *puca*, and plural *pucai*.

The pucai are like fairies but they aren't pretty. Paedophiles find them disgusting. They are mischievous but not particularly evil, however they can be quite dangerous if provoked. For example, they are known to steal sheep, human babies and so on, and they can cause accidents and start fires. The main thing is that they will ignore you if you don't bother them, make fun of them or get in their way.

Like all Irish children, I've known about the pucai since my first fairy stories and I know how very important it is not to disturb or provoke them. So after letting them on to the page in a little drawing I look away as though they don't exist.

But they do.

Pucai appear at the Old Mill Bar in Durrus –
remembering Matisse

After our coffee we go and look over the bridge to see does the river look promising. John gives it his usual inspection. Observing the depth, flow and clarity of the water he looks to see if it has been 'canalised' between unnaturally straight, steeply walled banks or does it flow freely through its riffles and pools as God intended? Is there a buffer strip of trees, grasses, and riverside vegetation on both banks? Are the waterweeds the sort that thrive in dirty polluted water or are they the ones which indicate the healthy clean water that supports an abundance of river life? Is the water chalky or peaty? Are there any fish moving? He takes all this in at a glance. Occasionally there'll be an exclamation of disgust or approval, and he'll point things out to me.

The river here in Durrus looks promising so we prop our bikes under some trees in the corner of a field and out come fishing rod, and sketchbook.

John has to wade out in his sandals and bandaged leg into the middle of the river because it is so overhung with branches that he can't cast properly from the bank.

John with bandaged leg fishing in the Durrus River

He catches several little fish, including two 6-inch juvenile salmon. Each one gets unhooked and put back with the deft touch of the ecologist but not before it has been examined for size, markings and parasites. He fishes in the rapids, under trees, behind rocks and in promising looking pools.

Then, while he's putting his rod away, I get a fascinating lecture on the riverbed and the many things which live in it. These are the creatures which the fish feed on. They include caddis flies, mayflies and dragonflies with their extraordinary metamorphoses and life cycles.

How, for goodness sake, can natural selection have developed creatures like these which first live happily under water, then become pupae and finally turn into a totally different flying and mating machine? But interruption seems impertinent because now he's on about worms, snails, molluscs and crayfish. To John the whole river is teeming with life from algae and sponges to otters, herons and king-fishers. He explains the importance of dead leaves which give sustenance to the humbler aquatic creatures, and of overhangs that offer shade and hiding places.

But when he starts talking about something called biomass ratios I know it's going to be more than I can absorb right now, so I shuffle about and then excuse myself to have a pee. The weak bladder does sometimes have its advantages.

8   Dirty smelly hotel in Glengarriff. Recumbent bike

When we get to Bantry it's grey and a chilly wind is gusting again. A heavy shower is imminent. We're hungry. It's a quarter past two. We buy pasties, a baguette, and some salami and take them into Murphy's bar.

Murphy's is in the big square, which is on an inviting sea front, but soon it's slashing rain and inside a pub is the right place to be. They do their own pub lunches so John tentatively asks is it OK to eat our sandwiches here while we shelter from the rain and have a pint. It's a picnic really but 'sandwiches' sounds more acceptable.

'Ah sure, that's no problem,' says the barmaid. So that's what we do and all's well.

Then to underline the gastronomy of the occasion we have a second pint. So it's Murphy's stout in Murphy's bar, bikes leant against the wall outside. No problem indeed, and God bless Murphy.

Finally the call of the road gets us back in the saddle and on into the afternoon we go, pedalling towards Glengarriff via Ballylickey. This coast is bathed in the warmth of the Gulf Stream, the winters are mild and frost free so it's a horticulturalist's paradise. The beautiful coast road skirts around Bantry Bay. Up and down it goes, over hills and valleys past majestic Scots pines, well kept gardens, palm trees and monkey puzzles. There's abundant growth everywhere.

But unfortunately it's drizzling wet and grey, and cars have their intermittent windscreen wipers on.

At about five o'clock we arrive in Glengarriff. I'm tired. John says he is too but I think that's just to make me feel better.

It's my suggestion that tonight we'll try and find a hotel in the middle of town instead of a B&B. This is just for a change and to be more in the centre of things where there might be some boisterous chat and laughter and possibly a singsong or maybe a fight to liven things up. The B&B's are excellent but they're a bit genteel, and they are usually in the outskirts and that's never where the action is.

That's my excuse anyway and I certainly do need one because it turns out to be a big mistake. We get a nasty uncomfortable room with a neon sign right outside the window. We don't realise it yet but this is going to flash on and off all night. There is no excitement or local colour. In fact there's nothing to remember at all, just a few very tall German backpackers.

Once installed John does some running repairs to his varicose vein.

I have a large gin and tonic in the bar hoping for a chat with the locals. But it's deserted. Then I wander out to see what Glengarriff looks like.

Opposite the hotel, propped against the wall of some tearooms, I notice a recumbent bicycle. It clearly belongs to the couple sitting proudly beside it, so I say hello. They are Dutch, aged about thirty-five. The recumbent is a strange and rare sort of bicycle. This one is made in Holland by Bram Moens. It's a long, low, two-wheeler, which you ride with your feet sticking out forward as if you were sitting in an armchair.

They look dramatic and unusual. I rode one briefly some years ago and found it difficult to balance on take-off but I'm sure one would quickly get the hang of that. Being so low, it must be hard for cars to see them in traffic, so safety could be a bit of a worry; and they must get more than their fair share of petrol fumes, not to mention splattering from the wet road. But recumbent bicycles do look terrific fun.

It's the woman who rides the recumbent, the man has a conventional bike. But they seem to be a bit precious. She says she has to have a recumbent for her bad back. That might be OK but then she follows up with strong advice not to go round the Ring of Kerry 'because of all the traffic'. And anyway what are they doing in a teashop when the pubs are open? I bet she's a vegetarian.

The Ring of Kerry starts at Kenmare, probably the day after tomorrow, and we are most definitely looking forward to it. It's seventy miles and said to be spectacular. We're not going to be put off by a couple of Dutch pinkoes, recumbent or conventional. I smile insincerely through my disreputable growth of new beard, wish them well and continue my stroll round the nice little town of Glengarriff.

We have dinner at Caseys in the main street. Then we call it a day.

I wake up early after a perfectly dreadful night's sleep and creep down to the main rooms of the hotel. Breakfast is being served in a dimly lit rear section of the huge public bar. Certain unlit parts of this cavernous room haven't yet been cleaned this morning despite the fact that it's already half-eight. In the gloom you can't actually see last night's debris. But a smell of stale beer, soup-stained carpet and cigarette-butts interferes with the bacon and eggs.

This is one of the dirtiest hotels I have ever slept in. The kitchen, which we have to squeeze through to collect our bikes from the yard behind, is dark, dirty and grim beyond description. And the yard is filled with the acrid stench of filthy dustbins.

Not coming back here again that's for sure. At least not till it gets the face-lift it so badly needs.

During the night the neon sign outside our window flashed remorselessly. But every now and again all the lights in town went out. That was a relief while it lasted; probably caused by thunderstorms inland knocking out fuses in the local electricity sub-station. The weather, according to the TV, is wild and there is bad flooding 60 miles away in Tipperary.

Actually it's not too bad out here on the Atlantic coast. There is the occasional wet spell but it's OK for cycling.

9 Mix 'n' squash gastronomy

A better day is forecast on the radio this morning. You can hear the weather-man willing it to improve. He's urging it on. Like a football commentator criticising the referee; he knows he ought to be impartial but can't quite manage it. So you are not totally convinced by his optimism.

Today we'll go out along the Beare Peninsular. It's about thirty miles long and seven miles wide.

At a quarter to twelve we stop for coffee in Trefask. We buy some bread and cheese for lunch to supplement what we've got left over from yesterday. There's three quarters of a whiskey cake, some bread, black chocolate, a couple of apples, a tin of sardines opened and wrapped shut again in plastic but oozing oil, half a raw onion, and some salami. It all gets squashed together and bounced around in a plastic bag strapped tightly on to the bike with shock cord.

Doesn't sound very appetising, I know, but in fact it's quite delicious when eaten out in the open after a morning's cycling. I'd go further. It matures. After all, cheese ripens doesn't it; well that's exactly what happens to the twenty-four-hour cyclist's picnic.

Perhaps we're on to something big here. A completely new branch of cookery. A delicious field of gastronomy, which requires no oven, saucepan, grill, or frying pan. No heat at all in fact.

The secret is in the bouncing around and the squashing together. The raw onion with the cheese, squashed into salami and bread, with sardines and their oil, plus half an apple and some whiskey cake. How could it fail to mix into a unique blend of flavours and fragrances after several hours of jolting in the warmth of the sun?

The instructions would be something like this: 'Take each item half out of its wrapping. Puncture sardine tin. Place gently together in plastic bag alongside what's left in there since yesterday. Leave to "rest" overnight. Next morning put it on your bicycle carrier to bounce around and warm up in the sun. Add salt and pepper to taste and eat outdoors. Goes well with a beer such as Guinness or Murphy's or with red wine.

Much more exotic than 'place in oven, for forty-five minutes, gas mark 3'. Cheaper too, and more, well, ecological . . . ? Ethnic . . . ? What's the word I'm looking for – recycled? Something like that.

Like all the best things in life it would be banned by Brussels.

'Mix 'n' Squash Bicycle Gastronomy' by Gibson & Wilson. I can see it now. It's in 'all good bookshops' in the cookery section.

10 Healey Pass. John's campaigning

At half-twelve we get to Adrigole and decide we won't go down to the tip of the Beare Peninsular. We'll cut over the mountain at the Healey pass. So we wind our way up and up. It's quite a long way and our panniers full of luggage feel extra heavy. But the gradient is kind and the views are wonderful. Soon we reach the top, which is at about fifteen hundred feet.

At the pass there is a tourist shop and high on a pedestal there's a splendid fifteen foot dazzlingly white marble statue of Jesus carrying the Cross. He's facing down the road we have just come up. Having just wound the pedals laboriously all the way up here we sympathise with Jesus. His cross must have been extremely heavy.

At this point we cross the county boundary out of Cork into Kerry, which is a nice little morale-boosting milestone.

Just over the pass we select a rock to sit on for lunch. We are perched high above Glanore Lough looking north towards the Ring of Kerry and the majestic MacGillycuddy Reeks. The ground is wet and there's a strong wind up here but it's warm and the sun is trying to come out. Our mix 'n' squash picnic lunch has matured nicely. We start with tinned Guinness, salami and dry bread.

The view up here is magnificent. The mountains, forests and lakes, the islands and the sea, the clouds and the huge sky; it's intoxicating. You could even believe in God up here. God of the wind, forest and mountain.

Over lunch I ask John about his conservation work. He was recently given several prestigious awards by Canadian environmental bodies. These include the Government of Newfoundland and Labrador, and the Guenther Behr Trust. The honour he is proudest of is a salmon fishing fly designed for him by the Salmonid Association of Eastern Newfoundland, and named the 'Gibson Special'. Much of this was in recognition of the fact that he spearheaded the preservation of threatened trout habitats right in the centre of St Johns, the capital of Newfoundland and Labrador.

View from the Healey pass looking north over Glanore Lough

Until recently there had been a thriving trout population living right in the middle of the city but it was being systematically des-troyed by all sorts of development schemes; schemes to straighten and beautify the banks, schemes to make new super-highways, new buildings, installations for sewage and industrial waste. These were threatening to wipe out the trout for good and all.

Before it was too late, John coordinated a public campaign which succeeded in halting the more foolish and deadly aspects of this 'progress'. Proper arrangements were made to accommodate the fish and their natural requirements. The result is that St Johns now proudly boasts the biggest trout population in the middle of any modern city anywhere in the world.

During the campaign, John's adversaries were the usual baddies: politicians, bureaucrats, engineers, architects and big business interests. What shocked him most was the indifference, bordering on obstruction, he received from his colleagues at the Department of Fisheries and Oceans. These were the very people who were actually supposed to be responsible for the preservation of fish stocks. He quickly learnt that they were completely unequipped to stand up to the powerful, ruthless and sometimes deceitful methods of big business. It's the old story about the crass stupidity of man.

John's back in the driving seat. Hearing-aidless and unstoppable, he's off in his quiet determined voice which he wears like a steam-roller driver wears his earmuffs.

I sit back and listen.

He's into his stride now. 'Of course behind all this is big business seducing politicians as it chases "the bottom line"; bringing about progress for all mankind.'

'Yes OK,' I interrupt with difficulty, 'but what about better housing, clothing, better food, more comfort, entertainment, better medicine? These are the positive aspects of progress; you can't ignore people's needs. It must surely be possible to educate people so that they'll elect politicians who will do the right thing; politicians who'll respect nature and work in harmony with it?'

But that doesn't calm him down at all. Quite the reverse, in fact. 'That'll take ten or twenty years by which time the Atlantic salmon will be extinct. Big business is evil, politicians are corrupt and bureaucrats are spineless. And quangos, they're the worst of all.'

11 *Ideas arrive in 3-D. Is there a connection between morality and cooperation? What does bad mean?*

I try to pay attention to his monologue but I've heard a lot of it before, and inevitably I start daydreaming along in parallel with him. Bits of ideas flit around my head like pucai vying for attention. There's the awful question about Hitler, big business and morality. These get mixed up with Darwin who's whispering in my ear that we are a cooperating animal.

And then in an involuntary sideways leap, probably brought on by the altitude up here at the Healey pass and the wonderful views, I wonder: Instead of asking why do we behave so badly when we know it's wrong, perhaps we should be asking why do we distinguish right and wrong in the first place? Is there any purpose to this deep-seated human instinct?

What's so different between the loving family and the nasty big wide world? It's all human behaviour after all, and if Darwin was right, this behaviour is neither good nor bad. It has simply been evolved as part of our lifestyle.

But it's all a bit of a pucai muddle, and I don't know where to begin. That's the trouble with ideas. They don't come in logical sequence, step-by-step in proper order ready to be written down.

A new idea is more like the formation of the solar system. When you first notice a possible idea it's like interstellar dust collecting under its own gravity into a ball. Gradually it whirls around, gathers speed and spins off extremities which form into planets while the core concentrates into a sun. And there, if you're lucky, is your new idea.

The next problem is that words on a page are not even two-dimensional; they come in a single line, one after the other, whereas ideas, especially new ones, are three-dimensional like the solar system.

Getting a new idea down on paper isn't easy. First it has to be turned around and around till you have found the right angle to approach it from. Then it has to be beaten flat to reduce it to two dimensions. You can use a page of your sketchbook for this stage; jotting down arguments all over the place, rubbing them out and joining them up with arrows. This is the time to look for flaws and illogicalities. Finally the different elements have to be arranged in a straight line of nicely connected one-dimensional writing starting at a beginning, the best one you can find, and ending when you've said everything.

And even that's not the end of it, because then your reader has to put the whole process into reverse to get a full understanding. She – my imaginary reader is a fiercely intelligent Scottish feminist – has to recreate her own three-dimensional structure out of this one-dimensional stream of words; a structure which she too can turn around and around for criticism, improvement and use.

It would be simpler if someone could invent three-dimensional books and maybe the first step will be to start writing in two dimensions. James Joyce had a good try, but it doesn't seem to have caught on. I blame the novel and the modern habit of recreational light reading.

I come back to that awful question. Maybe . . . maybe there is a distinction to be made between how we behave to each other within a tribe, and how these 'tribal' units themselves behave towards the world around them. There seem to be ideas here which, by taking cooperation into account, could turn the awful question upside down and inside out.

In my excitement I interrupt John, who is now going on about weed-killers and culverts. 'Do you think there could be a connection between cooperation and morality?'

'How do you mean?' He looks completely baffled.

'Well you know . . . You've been talking about man's thoughtless destructiveness . . . '

'Er . . . yes,' he says, obviously still totally perplexed.

Shamefully I realise that my gauche interruption has revealed that my attention to his lecture has been less than total. In fact, having started it all off in the first place by asking about his conservation work, I haven't been listening properly at all. John's expression relaxes as he pretends not to notice this.

I try to explain. 'I've been wondering, could there be a connection between cooperation and morality . . . ' But my thoughts are only half formed so I don't make much sense.

Anyway he was the one who was talking; I've rudely interrupted him by going off sideways. So I shut up and listen.

As he gets back into his stride I realise that he is of course doing exactly what my beliefs suggest he should. To get things changed in a democracy you must first change public opinion, and John is a redoubtable one-man public opinion shifter. He talks at conferences, publishes articles and lectures relentlessly on man's crass destruction of nature and on the wiping out of the Atlantic salmon. Right now I am his public, and the subject for today is weed-killers and culverts.

Soon, both being full of thoughts which require further examination at the rhythm of the pedals, we get back on our bikes and we're off again.

The sun is out now and it's a lovely freewheel spin down from the pass; it goes on for miles. John hurtles down as fast as his bike will go. I take it much more cautiously, and watch the distance between us increase as he sweeps around bend after bend way below me; getting smaller and smaller until he's completely out of sight.

We meet again at the bottom and I explain that I go slowly to prolong the lovely views and because I'm nervous about punctures. But really it's because I'd be terrified rattling along at the breakneck speeds he goes at.

Soon we come to Lauragh. It's a little cross-roads with post office, pub and church. The lovely Derreen gardens are nearby. There's a beautiful river that sweeps round the gardens down to the sea, which is about a mile away. The river banks down here, below the mountain, are lined with big mature beech trees, also some oak and larch. On the woodland floor there are ferns and small rhododendron saplings.

Big beech tree on the bank of the Lauragh River

The river flows fast and clear. The colour of weak tea, it runs over a rocky riverbed. It twists along in plaits and plunges and then subsides into calmer deeper water.

'You can see it's well managed,' says John, but he doesn't need to point out the series of riffles and pools that succeed each other as far as the eye can see, because I've become a fully qualified R&P spotter by now.

He gets out his rod and I find my sketchbook.

John fishing in the Lauragh River

A kingfisher flashes down river emitting its piercing cry. The cry harmonises with the electric blue of its feathers. We watch it streak in and out of the sunlight. A little while later it flashes back up again.

John catches a juvenile salmon, a six-inch sea trout, and then several brown trout of varying sizes, the biggest is eight inches. He puts them all back, but first each gets the usual scientific once-over. He also identifies various insects and finds a bright green freshwater sponge. The slightest pollution he says kills these sponges, so they're a good sign of clean unpolluted water.

At about half-five we reluctantly leave this idyllic spot and pedal on towards Kenmare and the famous Ring of Kerry. But that's quite a way and it's getting late so maybe we won't make it that far tonight.

13 Dutch cyclists. Ring of Kerry. Purple-arsed lady

We spend the night in Feormore and make an early start.

Quite soon we pass a small group of cyclists. We stop for a pee and blackberries. They pass us and then, lo and behold, we pass them a second time.

Now this is a major triumph because, since we left Cork, we haven't actually passed anybody at all yet. Other cyclists keep passing us all the time. We save our pride with excuses like: 'But we're long distance travellers', and, 'We could go much faster if we really wanted'. We're particularly snooty if they aren't carrying heavy panniers like us. But if they're loaded up and come whirring by, and especially if they are young women, which is quite often, well, then we do have to admit that we're just a couple of scruffy old men with knobbly knees and pink elbows. So it's a big moment when we pass this little party of cyclists.

We're keen to get out on to the Ring of Kerry today so we ride through Kenmare without stopping.

At half-eleven we start thinking how nice a steaming mug of coffee would be, and at the psychological moment we come to Pat Spillane's bar by the roadside six miles beyond Kenmare.

In charge are two big strong healthy-looking twenty-year-old lads. Working in unison they are clearing up after last night's fun and games. One is tidying off the table-tops which are crowded with beer cans, bottles, glasses and ashtrays. The other follows behind wielding the brush and dustbin. Judging from the trophies, photos, a signed hurley stick and a framed sports jersey, this pub is owned by a sporting family. And it doesn't take much imagination to conjure up last night's story-telling, the post mortem on Saturday's match, the boasting about the exploits of yesteryear, the laughter and the deafening music.

Anyway these two lads cheerfully switch on the coffee machine and install us nicely at a clean table outside.

Almost immediately along comes the little cycling party we passed earlier. So of course we have a chat. They are Dutch: mother, father and three small girls. The youngest is a little racing demon aged eight. She is wearing all the latest and most lurid cycling clothes; skin-tight and luminous. They started at Killarney and are going to go round the ring of Kerry. Judging by the girls' outdoor look and their 'catch me if you can' attitude, there's not the slightest doubt that they'll make it. Not bad for a little girl of eight.

The road to the Ring of Kerry at Pat Spillane's Bar in Templenoe

The Ring of Kerry is the coast road around the fattest of the five fingers which stretch out into the Atlantic on the south-west corner of Ireland. The distance from Kenmare, on the south side, round to Killorglin on the north is seventy-four miles. The MacGilliycuddy Reeks, the highest mountains in Ireland with Carrantuohill at 3,414 ft, are within the Ring. And Killarney which, God love it, has inspired one of the most sugary sentimental songs in the English language, is just inland to the north-east.

As we ride out along the south shore it's getting more and more scenic. Soft Atlantic air is coming off the Gulf Stream. There's no rain but there's not much sun either.

There are coach-loads of tourists 'doing the Ring'. Their number plates and livery declare them to be German, French, Dutch, Spanish, Italian and English. These enormous coaches tower over us. Their great shoe-box bodies are carried on wheels which are set about eight feet inboard from the front and rear bumpers so that there is a huge overhang at both ends. On main roads you don't normally notice this, but on these small roads the overhangs sometimes stick out alarmingly as they hiss-and-go, brake-and-hiss slowly around a tight bend.

The rule is that to prevent traffic jams, coaches must all go round the same way. Some years ago it used to be clockwise but then they changed it to anticlockwise: coming against us, because apparently the views are better that way round. A coach load comes by about every five minutes. Thank goodness they are coming the opposite way to us otherwise we'd be boxed in by them as they prepare to swish past in frightening manoeuvres. That must be what the Dutch lady on the recumbent in Glengarriff was trying to warn me about. Maybe I should take back those rude thoughts I had about her. I certainly wouldn't have enjoyed coming round the same way as these coaches on a recumbent.

At around lunchtime we get to Sneem. It's a tourist-conscious place with lots of pubs. We go into Dan Murphy's Bar for a pint of Guinness and another delicious 'mix 'n' squash' picnic lunch.

Bikes leant against the window of Dan Murphy's Bar in Sneem

We are operating the 'kitty' system of cash control. All shared expenses such as B&B bills, meals and pints of stout are paid for out of the kitty. It's kept in a wallet in John's pocket. Being a retired accountant I'm trying to avoid the responsibility so I never look too closely in case he might try and pass it to me. Anyway, whenever it looks like running out of cash we both contribute equal shares to replenish it.

This traditional system works well. It's simple and effective, and Kitty money being joint property is somehow easier, less painful to spend than personal money.

But today John effortlessly invents the branch kitty. It's actually quite a sophisticated development. This is how it happens. Like I say, we're in Dan Murphy's Bar. The nice barmaid has said 'sure of course it's OK' to eat our mix 'n' squash here. We order pints of Guinness. But John has gone and left the kitty in his smart trousers packed deep in one of his panniers, and he's not sure which one. However he does have his own money with him, so with a brilliant stroke he puts a £20 note into a new pocket, which he calls the 'branch kitty'. He buys the drinks with it and puts the change back in the new pocket. Then when he finds the proper kitty again he gives it the change out of the new pocket and tells me to put in £20 to even up.

Very impressive. That must be part of the story of how banking started, way back before the Bible was written. If he hadn't become a salmon biologist, John could have been an international banker.

We hope to get to Waterville tonight. It's quite a way still. So on we go pedalling and winding our way up and down hills, in and out of trees through the beautiful coastal scenery. Across Kenmare Bay on our left we can see the Beare Peninsular, that's where we were yesterday. And the MacGillycuddy Reeks are on our right.

Suddenly, heavenly vision, we are passed by a lovely sporty young woman wearing skin-tight, purple licra pants. She is with a man. They look athletic. No panniers. They come whirring past on an uphill stretch.

From directly behind you can see right through under her saddle, which is surrounded by her perfectly shaped bottom and thighs shining like a well-groomed race-horse.

'Did you see that?' says John, who is up ahead.

'Nearly fell off,' I say.

Then about three quarters of an hour later they pass us again – must have stopped for a rest after going by the first time. We exchange cheery waves as cyclists do, and she becomes known as the Lady with the Purple Arse.

On the way out to Waterville we have several piddle and blackberry stops and these two must be doing the same thing, only in their case it's probably that modern athletes' carbohydrate and glucose juice they drink from a plastic clip-on bottle. And they must be stopping at times that are syncopated with ours because they pass us twice more during the ride. Apart from her perfectly shaped bottom she also has a charming smile and wave. Didn't notice what her man looked like.

This lovely vision sustains us during the final climb before Waterville, which goes on for longer than expected.

And so, at long last, we free-wheel down into Waterville. Totally knackered again of course.

There are no B&B vacancies in town, but we get kindly advice from a middle-aged woman. As she peers at us her facial expression reads: 'What these two old wrecks need isn't a B&B, it's the local hospital more like.' After a cup of tea we'll be right as rain again but she can't be expected to know that.

Anyway, she sends us a couple of weary miles back and up a side road to Lakerise B&B, which does indeed have vacancies. She's right, but how did she know? Is there a sort of bush telegraph amongst local B&B's?

Lakerise is a substantial Victorian house owned by Mrs Breda McAuliffe. She installs us in a nice big room with steaming cups of tea.

14   Pucai at Lakerise. Art talk, fishing talk. Purple-arsed lady again

In the early morning light I can see that Lakerise B&B is on the shore of a lake. Lough Currane it's called. While we're having breakfast Breda McAuliffe tells us about the many little songbirds which come to feed at her bird table. She says that hawks often swoop down and carry them off. She's about sixty-five, tall, slender and good-looking; she must have been very beautiful when she was younger.

There are some unframed oil paintings propped against the wall in the dining room. Must be by a member of the family.

Breda admits in an offhand way that they are hers. In fact they are excellent; masses of character, colour and verve shines through a fresh amateur touch. But many's the talented amateur who could be a successful painter if only they had the single-minded motivation to paint all day, every day.

We chat about painting. Boring for John, but it makes a change from fish. Anyway he doesn't have his hearing aid so he can blank it out if he wants to.

Breda would like to have a local gallery to take her work, but the whiff of insincerity she gets from the whole art-selling world puts her off. The exaggerated enthusiasms of framers, gallery folk, and the buying public seem to contrast so falsely with the actual struggles and thrills of making a painting. 'Ooh, Aah, Jeremy come and look at these.' And people seem to praise the pictures she considers failures. All hype and puff, she says. Finally, to cap it all, she loves her best paintings and, when she sells one, she hates the empty sadness when it's gone. That's the amateur's dilemma.

Of course it's only human that there should be a lot of bullshit in the art world. Making money out of painting isn't a straightforward business. The deal an artist makes with society is a colour story in exchange for a living wage. Naturally hype and puff helps to make it all go round. If your paintings are good enough, and if you don't have a gift for the bullshit or the artistic persona, then you can leave all that to the galleries, collectors, dealers and journalists. But only if your paintings are good enough. And what is 'good enough'? To know that you have to go back to the bullshit, the hype and the puff because it's all in the eye of the beholder.

After breakfast I'm reviewing my sketchbook and thinking about the eye of the beholder, when it occurs to me that rather than hawks, it's probably the pucai that are taking the songbirds. So I try putting them into a drawing and they seem to fit the scene allright. Naughty little devils.

We say goodbye to Breda McAuliffe and hit the road. Or perhaps wobble gently away is a better way of putting it.

We cycle on along the north shore of the Ring, still under the Mac-Gillycuddy Reekes. The Dingle Peninsular is now clearly visible in the distance as we look out across Dingle Bay. It's the last of the five fingers that stick out into the Atlantic. We'll be over there tomorrow if all goes well.

The Lady with the Purple Arse passes us once more. Truly up-lifting. We speed up but it's no good, she and her man eventually vanish into the distance never to be seen again. I'm left imagining the

Pucai raiding the bird table at Lakerise B&B

dreadful chaos she would cause if she entered for the Tour de France. That must be why it's a men-only event.

Wonderful wild flowers flourish here all along the coast; luxurious and beautiful. We're drenched in their lush colour. The real dazzler is again montbretia which even on dull days radiates orange-red light in great massed banks. There are also hedges of fuscia, and the poisonous ragweed whose acid lime-yellow contrasts so explosively with the montbretia. Then there's purple loosestrife and fluffy, creamy-white meadowsweet.

Of course, these all flower inland too but here on the soft and mountainous Atlantic coast they seem extra plush and radiant. They pulsate with colour in the bright pearly seaside light. It's a light which I always think seems to have an extra magic ingredient; akin perhaps to St Elmo's fire and the aurora borealis. My belief is that it's caused by seaside ozone reacting somehow with the ultraviolet end of the spectrum. You get this bright pearly seaside light all over the world when conditions are right.

As we spin along free as the breeze I start thinking about morality. I've finally admitted to myself that John's right about big business being immoral. And yet I know from many years of experience that chief executives are usually moral and upright people. This needs to be thought through.

Daydreaming in the saddle, I find myself thinking about Political Correctness. I'm not really sure why; perhaps it's because I find the idea of business immorality too difficult to explain. PC is almost a new religion, a new moral code for industrial society. It might be the answer to managerial immorality, but where has it come from?

There seems to be a promising line of thought somewhere here, but I can't quite pick up the trail.

We cycle on into the afternoon until, at about four o'clock we cross a little bridge over a fast flowing brook. A sign on the bridge says it's the Behy River. Looking inland you can see that its valley drains the northern slopes of the MacGillycuddy Reeks.

After a pee and blackberrying out come sketchbook and rod.

John gets into the river bare-legged, wearing sandals. He wades up and down casting left and right. He fishes out and releases about fifteen salmon parr. If perhaps a little confused, they'll be glad to have escaped alive, and maybe one day they'll come back from the sea as fine big adult fish.

He casts most expertly between the bushes and overhanging branches. It's amazing that his flies and line don't get badly tangled.

He says he's hoping to pick up a bigger trout under the bank: 'A nice one for dinner.'

The montbretia where he's casting his fly is orange and red. Like flames.

Now he is after a bigger trout which he has spotted. He must have X-ray eyes to compensate for his deafness. But the trout eludes the hook.

'Extremely wily; these Irish brook trout,' says John. 'In Canada they are quite different, they're easy to catch. They're thick as two short planks over there. Most probably a case of natural selection. Centuries of fishing in Ireland having made sure that only the canny have survived. As soon as you get within a hundred yards the Irish trout says, "Watch out chaps here comes another damned fisherman." While in Canada they've never seen one till recently.'

John fishing in the Behy River

Eventually John slips and half falls in. His shorts get wet and his rod comes undone in a royal muddle. But luckily his bandaged leg doesn't start bleeding again. I've finished sketching, the sky has gone overcast and grey and the wind is getting cold. So we pack up and go.

The next town is Killorglin, and it's time to find a B&B for the night. It's the second weekend in August and Puck fair is on. This is

The Behy River valley looking towards the MacGillycuddy Reeks

one of Ireland's great traditional fairs. It's a huge tourist attraction with international TV crews taking all the best hotel rooms, and televising the decorated ram in his cage, the big horse fair, and the singing, drinking and dancing all night. Stories will be told and music will be played till morning, the Murphy's will flow in Killorglin tonight. It exhausts me to think about it.

I wonder who Puck was? I suppose he must have been related to the pucai, perhaps he was their king. But that's not the point; the point is that all the B&Bs will be booked up for miles around.

For some reason we seem incapable of planning ahead. I suppose it's because planning is so boring. It gets in the way of fishing, sketching and talking. It makes life so predictable. Planning ahead is what you do in the office.

Everywhere is full. Our hearts sink. After an anxious hour plodding wearily round the countryside, following local advice, and making phone calls we strike lucky at Hill Crest B&B.

It's half-six and as we unpack and have a cup of tea, several people are turned away. The noisiest of these is an angry French family with little children. We've got the last room. John feels sorry for them. He can well imagine how they feel and wonders should we let them have our room? After all, we have been brought up to give our seats to old ladies on the bus. But I tell him not to worry; they have a car. 'And,' I say, 'you should see how they treat tourists in their own country. It's no harm for them to be on the receiving end for a change.' In fact, I'm quite embarrassed by the pleasure it gives. Schadenfreude they call it.

16 Puck Fair. *PC might replace Christianity*

At breakfast next morning we're chatting to Kathleen O'Neill the landlady. She asks where we are going today. We say we are hoping to get to Dingle.

'I hope you don't mind me asking but are you booked in somewhere?' she wants to know.

'Well not really, no,' we have to admit.

She's worried about the hit and miss way we go about finding B&Bs. Particularly since it's a Sunday in the middle of August. So she very kindly insists on ringing around.

She phones four or five places she knows of around Dingle town. They are all full and they each tell her that everywhere else is full too. We see what she means.

Eventually she finds us a place out by Ballydavid Head some miles beyond Dingle.

Kathleen has to shoot off to get mass; phoning around for us has already made her late. We wave our grateful farewells as she goes off down the drive. Ten minutes later we go too.

It's Sunday morning, and at about ten we come to Killorglin where the town is still rubbing its eyes after a heavy night of Puck Fair festivities.

There are sleepy looking people drifting about; hung over and not yet fitting into their clothes properly. Crowd barriers block off several streets and the Gardai are out in numbers. You can see horses and ponies everywhere, some are being ridden bareback as if in a children's book illustrated by Jack Yeats, others are being led along, excitedly rolling their eyes and focusing their ears. Horses are grazing where they shouldn't be. Some are standing about with semi-erect penises. We jerk our front tyres to avoid a huge smelly puddle of urine where one has just peed. There's a pungent smell of excited horse.

We don't see the goat in its cage nor do we go looking for it. We just cycle on through the town feeling a bit prim.

It's another sign of getting old. Years ago we would have joined in the fun with gusto; immersed ourselves in the drinking, singing and dancing; the boasting, laughter and naughtiness. Ah well.

Castlemaine comes next. That's where Jack Duggan, the legendary wild colonial boy, came from. He robbed the rich and saved the poor, and his boisterous song will have echoed forth from the pubs of Killorglin last night.

We cross the River Maine and go west again; out along the Dingle Peninsular. The road is straight and flat as we cycle along the shore. It's a change from the hills and mountains we've been in for the last week.

After what seems a very long time, but was probably only three quarters of an hour, we come to the Phoenix Vegetarian Cafe. It's tastefully decorated with Thai printed cotton fabrics and tasselled Bedouin tent hangings. Not at all what you'd expect out along the Dingle Peninsular but very nice. The two elegant women running it are English, they seem to be in a vague sort of vegetarian trance, possibly brought on by the wafting smell of incense that pervades their little cafe. Come to think of it the whole of Kerry seems half asleep this Sunday morning. Disgraceful really. Anyway they bring us lovely coffee with organic biscuits.

We stretch out in comfortable wicker chairs.

Maybe it's the sudden contrast of finding ourselves in an English vegetarian café with Buddhist overtones that starts us talking about political correctness. This feminine little English nest seems a million miles away from the rude, Irish, wild horse bustle of Puck Fair. And we guiltily remember how difficult it was to think politically correct thoughts about the lady with the purple arse.

There are so many different ways of behaving in this world; it's bewildering sometimes. All a chap wants to do is fit in. Well, nearly all.

'A bit "holier than thou" in here,' I say.

'How do you mean?'

'Well you know; the vegetarian things on the menu and the refined hint of transcendental meditation in the decorations; that sort of thing.'

'Yes, I see what you mean. It is a bit genteel. I do often wonder why does there always have to be some busybody around telling you what to do, and what not to do.'

He's right. What is it in people that makes them want to tell others how to behave? I used to think it was the power and authority a preacher gets. But that doesn't explain why we're not allowed to tell them, 'Oh just piss off,' in the politest possible way of course.

'It seems we have a sort of built-in obligation to listen and even to respect preachers,' says John. 'That's what I don't understand.'

But then I point out that with his own dedicated campaigning for the welfare of salmon, John himself is a preacher. Everybody's at it; after all why do people write books and, come to think of it, why does anybody read them.

Political correctness seems to have arrived like an urban myth. It's a sort of thought movement, a spontaneously created code of behaviour. A whole list of new rules about how to behave runs like electricity through our lives. Furthermore there seems to be no high priest or written text of PC.

'If there were, it'd be a woman. A big one; Jewish or maybe black,' says John.

'But,' I insist, 'it really is like a new religion. Maybe the thing is that Christianity is so out of date that it's lost its grip.'

'How?'

'Well look at the outrageous mysteries and miracles we were taught at school. There's the crazy idea of drinking the blood and eating the body of God. It's a wonder we don't believe in cannibalism. And then there's all that "three in one and one in three" stuff: "God the Father, God the Son and God the Holy Ghost". These beliefs collapse along-side simple A-level science. The real wonder is that Christianity has survived for so long.'

'Yes,' says John, 'and there's the appalling cruelty of the crucifixion and all that baloney about original sin, which is supposed to make it better. I tried very hard to accept all that when I was a teenager, but it never made any sense so I gave up.'

'Me too, but the fact that we tried so hard shows how willing we are to soak up this sort of stuff, logical or not. When it comes to belief we're all like blotting paper.'

We go silent.

'Well maybe John, that explains it.'

'What?'

'Well, maybe we suddenly found that we no longer had any rules to teach our children and PC has grown to fill the vacuum. Some of the rules are daft, others only apply to young men roaming the streets looking for a party or a fight, but most are sensible and civilising.'

'Yes and come to think of it, Puck Fair better watch out, they'll sanitise that next,' says John.

'But what fascinates me,' I go on, 'is not so much the rules themselves, or even the fact that PC has no God – not yet anyway; it's the spontaneous way in which it has caught on in the West, and been introduced into law. You know, like demonising smoking and other enjoyable ways of living dangerously. It seems that if you erase a religion without imposing another, people will quickly conjure one up; by common consent. PC may die out but it could equally well coalesce into a great new religion for the electronic age.'

'Could we include something about salmon?'

'Well yes, we could, because from what you say the destruction of salmon habitats is a comprehensive example of man's bad behaviour.'

'Oh good.'

*John having coffee and organic biscuits
in the Phoenix Vegetarian Cafe*

17   The cycling helmet. Private and semi-private. Arrival in Dingle

Touring cyclists I notice, nearly always go at slightly different speeds, and soon John is about a hundred yards up ahead but he's easy to spot because of his bright yellow helmet. It is important to be visible to motorists but cycling helmets do look so utterly silly. I feel like an overgrown schoolboy in mine. I'm not exactly hoping for street cred. as I cycle along but I'm well aware that my helmet is distinctly naff.

And of course it doesn't help if you've forgotten to take the stupid thing off when you appear hopefully at a B&B. You're trying to put on your most charming and sophisticated persona. It's already a handicap that you're in shorts, wearing no socks, with knobbly legs and varicose veins, looking exhausted in a scruffy beard. You are hoping to come across as a well spoken, mild-mannered gentleman who can afford to pay the bill and won't lower the tone by farting or staying up talking all night. So, at this point, the daft helmet is a distinct embarrassment.

On the other hand, if I didn't wear a helmet I'd have to wear some sort of hat to protect myself from the sun. Also it keeps my head warm in the cold, and dry in the rain. I don't understand how it achieves all these apparently contradictory things but it does. Another important thing is that the top of your head is the very best place to attach your flashing light at night. You just pop it on your helmet with a simple Velcro pad. Finally of course the helmet is supposed to protect you if you crash. That hasn't happened to me yet, but my good friend Lee once fractured his skull while cycling. His helmet undoubtedly saved his life.

When all's said and done I'm not exactly in for the best-dressed cyclist competition, nor really trying to impress the girls. So I do wear the helmet.

And so does John.

At about a quarter-past one we come to Inch Beach. It's a magnificent sight; a huge expanse of clean sand curving out into the distance. The furthest visible figures playing about on it must be three miles away. The sun is out; nice and hot again. John toys with the idea of a swim but it's rather crowded so he decides against. Besides we'd better not dawdle because it's still quite a long way to our B&B where we were booked in by Kathleen O'Neill this morning.

Inch Beach

We pass a sign by the roadside which reads:

Inch Beach
Private and Semi-private Rooms

'Sounds fun,' says John, then after a pause, 'and semi-fun.' There's another pause, then he says: 'Or should that be the other way round?'

We pedal on into the afternoon till at five o'clock we come into Dingle town. I'm tired. It's been a long day and we'd like to stop. But our pre-booked B&B is out by Ballydavid head. That's six miles further on so we'd better not dawdle. If we're very late they might give the room away.

But first we'll have a refreshing pint. We go into a pub decorated with Irish flags, shamrocks, shillelaghs and green, white and yellow jesters' hats. There are blackboards with 'Come Inside' messages hand-written in coloured chalk. All sorts of entertainments are packaged and marketed: Traditional Irish music . . . Live bands . . . Gaelic coffee . . . Delicious pub food and boat trips out in the bay to see Foongie the dolphin. It's very staged. All the pub decoration and street writing seems to speak over your shoulder to someone up behind you. It's aimed at the American and Japanese faces peering down from huge coaches. These are far too big for the little streets of Dingle as they glide their hissing, stop-start way through the holiday traffic.

Inside the pub, mercifully, it's different. All is quiet and dark. A few locals are watching TV. It's the all-Ireland hurling semi-final. Clare are playing Kilkenny. It looks a terrific match but we don't know the rules. A large and portly gentleman kindly helps us out by explaining what's happened at crucial points.

Eventually Clare win. This is much to the delight of the Kerrymen in the bar; Clare being the next county up the coast. They'll meet either Wexford or Tipperary in the final which is in two weeks' time.

Portly gentleman watching
Clare v. Kilkenny on TV in Dingle

'You know' says John 'In the grand scheme of things we're just insignificant little creatures crawling about in cities.'

I chime in with: 'But don't we puff ourselves up outrageously.'

'Yes and make a poisonous mess of everything we touch.'

After a pause he goes on: 'We're just a creature that happens to be swarming all over the earth at this particular moment in time . . . time, which stretches back for aeons, and forward into cold eternity. We haven't been here very long and we'll probably be gone quite soon. In the words of the old English madrigal: "A man is like a rusty wheel upon a rusty cart. He sings his song as he rattles along and at night he falls apart." '

'What gets me,' I repeat, 'is how important we think we are. You just have to look at the Holy Bible; where it starts with all that crap about God made man in his own image.'

In fact the book of Genesis 1: 26–28 reads as follows:

And God said, Let us make man in our image, after our likeness: and let them have dominion over the fish of the sea, and over the fowl of the air, and over the cattle, and over all the earth, and over every creeping thing that creepeth upon the earth.

So God created man in his own image, in the image of God created he him; male and female created he them.

And God blessed them, and God said unto them, Be fruitful and multiply, and replenish the earth, and subdue it: and have dominion over the fish of the sea, and over the fowl of the air, and over every living thing that moveth upon the earth.

'That must be just about the most arrogant nonsense ever written,' I say, anger rising in my throat. 'The contrast between our heroic, noble self-image and reality is quite astounding.'

'How do you mean?' says John.

'Well, it's what you said a few days ago. We've done the most appalling things to ourselves, to other living creatures and to the ecosystems of the world. We've enslaved and even wiped out complete races of humans including American Indians both North, Central and South, and Australian aborigines. We've have repeatedly destroyed the great civilisations of history; Sumerian, Indus valley, Egyptian, Greek, Roman, Inca and Mayan. We've carried out mass cruelties and killings; in the Spanish inquisition, in Bosnia, Russia, Rwanda, in the persecution of witches, gypsies and Jews. We routinely go to war with-out justification, and we terrorise and enslave whole communities. We abuse children and we suppress and mutilate women. It's going on at this very moment all over the world. In cold blood we manufacture and lay down huge quantities of long lasting land-mines.'

The look in John's eye hints that we're in a pub and I should stop waving my hands about and keep my voice down. I try but it soon rises again, after all he is a little deaf.

'What's even worse is what we've done to other living things. We've driven many species to extinction, often just for fun – it's tremendous fun to shoot a tiger, club a Dodo or catch a salmon. We perform cruel and degrading animal experiments. We foul the air with smoke and poisonous fumes. We've destroyed most of the world's ancient forests, including those that once covered the British Isles. We pollute the waters of the earth sometimes so badly that rivers, in America for example, have actually caught fire. An animal that behaves like this can only be described as viciously dangerous, evil and destructive and yet we merrily ignore this appalling truth.'

I pause for breath. 'You mean' says John, 'that we always seem to turn a blind eye to these things?'

'Exactly. We label them "evil", and that helps us to parcel them up and hide them away, conveniently out of sight. And then if that doesn't work we've got all sorts of excuses. "It's not us, it's other people who are responsible, the Nazis, the IRA, the Ku-Klux-Clan, loggers in Brazil," a good one is, "We were only obeying orders." Or, "That was in the past, today we are modern, civilised and well behaved." Or again: "We know it's wrong but we are putting it right, we won't do it again." But we will, nothing has changed. As a species we seem incapable of behaving properly. It seems almost to be an evolutionary inevitability. Part of our nature.'

'Oh dear,' says John, 'you've really got it bad today.'

'Yes, I'm sorry, I think it's the mass tourism here in Dingle that's got me going.' Then, looking into my pint, I add: 'Well, you started it with all those questions about the destruction of salmon habitats and the ruthlessness of multi-national corporations. We named it the Awful Question, remember?'

But I haven't finished yet. 'At the bottom of it all, what really, truly, gets me is not actually the nastiness of mankind; it's that we all know perfectly well these things are wrong,' voice rising again, 'and I don't just mean people with university degrees. I'm talking about every modest little family in Botswanaland, New York and outer Mongolia. Little children learn right from wrong even before they can walk.'

I tell him the story of Selassie. A little white girl living in the middle of England comes back from school one day and tells her mother about a nice boy called Sally.

'That can't be right; it's a girl's name,' says her mother. 'Ask him tomorrow what his real name is.' 'Yes, all right,' says the little girl.

When she comes home next day the girl says the boy's name is Selassie.

'Hmm!' wonders her mother. 'Don't I remember . . . Yes, Emperor Haile Selassie of Ethiopia. He must be Ethiopian.' She thinks for a bit then she asks her daughter, 'Is he brown?' What she really means is black as your hat.

'I don't know,' says the little girl, 'I'll ask him.'

'That says it all doesn't it. The idyll of childhood is soon punctured. First at school there's bullying which seems to appear spontaneously from nowhere and which, we are told, exists in all races and societies. Then the child learns from parents and friends about strangers; children from other gangs, nasty men who mustn't be trusted.'

'From here it's a short step to suspicion and distrust of other groups: Catholic or Protestant, Jew or Muslim, big companies, politicians and bureaucrats, the government.'

'Why – this is what I really want to know – why is man such a nasty, destructive animal when every little child, all over the world, has learnt from its parents a clear knowledge of good and bad, right and wrong? How can it happen? What goes wrong between hearth and Hitler?'

'The distinction between good and bad behaviour is crystal clear to us all; to parents and children, to adults looking for mates and to people at work. So we should be able to define them for all times and all people. We should be able to prove them, like Newton's proof of the movements of celestial bodies. This would be a huge benefit to society and to the difficult business of making and enforcing laws. So why the hell can't we do it?'

'Dunno. I think you'll have to do the philosophy on this trip, I'll do the science,' says John.

'Well, for thousands of years people have focused multi-millions of

brain-hours trying to establish the principles of good behaviour. Zeno
and Socrates went at it hammer and tongs, so did Plato and Aristotle,
so did the great prophets, Buddha, Christ and Mohammed, and in
modern times we've had Hobbes, Hume, Kant, Bentham, Nietzsche
and Marx. They've all tried, but it's quite obvious that they've failed
because their followers are always arguing. The spine chilling fact
remains that for generation after generation and as far back into
history as we can go, humans have always indulged in killing,
destruction, deceit and theft, despite the fact that we've always known
it was wrong.'

At last I've talked myself out.

'Well,' says John, like a music-hall manager bringing the curtain
down rapidly lest I might start up again, 'there's your Awful Question
again; it sure is a depressing one, and a big one too.'

'Yes and there seems to be a taboo against even recognising it, let
alone talking about it.'

There is no more to say, at least not that we can think of. We agree
to parcel the Awful Question away for the moment in the hope that we
may be able to answer it later. After all, there's still a long way to go
before we get back to Cork, and questions you can't answer often turn
out to be trick questions or riddles.

19 Tourism blight. Getting lost. Restaurant manager's cycling father

Man shits in his own nest. It happens all over the world. You'll see it
in Florida, Benidorm, Accapulco, Tenerife, Kathmandu, Bangkok.
The list is endless. As Joni Mitchell sang: 'They paved paradise and
put up a parking lot.'

The selfish, greedy process of mass pleasure always fascinates me
and I'm caught gazing at it all like a rabbit mesmerised by a snake. But
John is quicker and more decisive. 'So this is Dingle,' he says as we
emerge from the pub. 'Let's get out of here quick.'

Anyway it's late and we'd better move it.

'Do we want to go out in a boat and see Foongie the dolphin
tomorrow?' I ask. John is the one who is fish mad so I leave it up to him.

'Oh no! I don't think so,' he says mildly. He has the instincts of the
trained ecologist and can smell modern man and his awful works at a
distance of five miles. He frequently swims with salmon and would

greatly enjoy swimming with a dolphin but not like this. His mild thumbs down conceals a shudder of disapproval.

On the way out to Ballydavid it starts to rain again and we get lost. Minor problems are always worse when you're tired. The road signs seem to have been muddled up for the precise purpose of confusing us. It's as though an instruction has been put out by the pucai. 'Look out! Here they come. Let's go and turn the signs around.'

During the second world war the road signs in the south of England were turned around to confuse the Germans in case they should invade. To this day people still joke about what a silly idea it was. They might think again if they tried cycling from Dingle to Ballydavid.

We frequently have to ask the way. This is especially irritating in the rain. You don't want to stop and get off, particularly if you are grinding rhythmically along with cold legs and wet underpants on an uphill stretch.

And somehow it's always uphill at the end of the day.

And whoever you ask is also huddled up against the rain so that answering your silly questions means they too get rain in their face and down their neck.

And if you fish the map out for clarification, it gets all wet and blows about in the wind.

And anyway they usually can't understand the map any more than you can.

We've noticed that when it really matters, our maps often don't make sense to the locals. That's not because they're stupid. Maps aren't written for locals, they're for motorists. I suppose the surveyors, the signpost office and the road map publishers sometimes find it difficult to get their act together at local level.

Our B&B is in Feoghanagh. Eventually at half-six we get to Moorestown. We then discover that Moorestown is apparently the same place as Feoghanagh. The place has two different names, one Irish, the other English. That would have fooled the Germans all right.

We do as we were told by the last kind person we meet: 'turn right between the school and the village hall, follow the B&B signs and you can't miss it.' At long last we're there. It's rather bleak in the drizzling rain. But we're expected and we get a kind welcome.

John is still alive but I'm completely washed out. We've done 45 miles today. For me it's been one of those bad days that happen one in

five. If you expect them to strike they're not too bad, you just have to
cycle on through them. The kind landlady brings us a cup of tea but
not even that does much good.

Then gradually a little life returns to the weary limbs.

The next question is where on earth will we get anything to eat
tonight. We are way out in the back of beyond. But amazingly there is
an excellent restaurant about a mile away.

'It's got a fierce reputation,' the landlady tells us, 'people come
from miles around.'

So when the rain eases off a bit we pedal round there and indeed it
turns out to be a real find. They're fully booked, but they fish out an
extra table for us. The place is packed with people from Dingle or
from holiday cottages along the coast. It's called O'Gorman's. The
food and wine are delicious. Just right for the tired, hungry cyclist.

People in O'Gorman's. Sunday evening August 10th

The manageress has heard from the waitress that we're aiming to cycle round the coast of Ireland, and when we've finished our meal, and the main rush of the restaurant has died down, she comes over for a chat.

'Isn't the weather disappointing?' We say it doesn't bother us all that much, which is true really, though a bit of sun would be nice.

'I'm only sorry for the holidaymakers,' she says. 'Cooped up in seaside cottages, B&Bs and caravans. They're all feeling a bit let down.'

We feel a distinct glow of pride and achievement when she says, 'And aren't ye great the pair of ye to be cycling all that way.' We demur with false modesty; hoping for more compliments, saying it's no big deal and we haven't got there yet.

But then she goes and spoils it all by telling us about her father. He died aged ninety only a few years ago. Once when he was seventy-two he cycled from Cork to Dingle in a day. The bastard! That's eighty miles and includes a mountain pass. We were going to give this lovely restaurant three Michelin stars, but this unfortunate conversation knocks them back to two. A young woman who has joined the conversation says, 'But sure, wasn't he a professional cyclist when he was younger?' The manageress admits he was. So that makes it better – well a bit.

On the way home to our B&B there's a warm fine rain. We cycle along enjoying the night. John breaks the silence. 'Of course he won't have been carrying heavy panniers loaded with clothes, books and stuff.' 'God yes, you're right!' I say. 'Hadn't thought of that.'

20   Billy Hutchinson. *The prime motivator is basic to all life forms*

There was theatrical thunder and lightning during the night and now it's slashing rain out of a grim sky.

Breakfast is in a dining room off the kitchen. It's unpretentious. The salt on the table is in the Saxa carton from the shop. I'd call the style honest but basic.

So far as I can tell we are the only B&B guests. John is still in bed. Except for the rain it's silent. There's one bare light bulb hanging from the exact middle of the ceiling. It isn't strong enough to light up the gloom. A couple of pucai flit about in the shadows while I'm doodling in my sketchbook. I pretend I can't see them, but they know I can.

The walls have paintings, prints and photos of men rowing in curragh races; there are singles, doubles and six-man crews. There are trophies, medals, cups and rosettes everywhere, all for curragh racing. Every available shelf, windowsill and display cabinet is crammed with them. It's not hard to guess that the man of the house is a curragh racing champion. His name is Eddie Hutchinson.

One of the nicest photos is of Eddie and his crew at a curragh racing regatta on the Thames at Putney. He must be in his mid-forties. You can see he's a huge, immensely strong man. Not fat but thick as a tree trunk; built like a brick shit-house. His wife, Hannah, tells us he builds curraghs as well as racing them but there isn't enough money in it so he has a lorry-driving job as well.

We would have dearly loved to have met this great man, but sadly he came in after we had gone to sleep last night, and this morning he had to go off with his lorry at the crack of dawn. So we missed him.

While doodle-thinking into my sketchbook about the Awful Question, I remember the half-formed idea that struck on the Healey pass during lunch, while John was going on about weed-killers. Might there be a connection between cooperation and morality, and might Darwin possibly show the way? It was a sideways leaping idea that the evolution of salmon and the destructiveness of man might be combined with the mechanisms of cooperation and morality into bigger blocks of understanding.

While I'm struggling to reconstruct the thought, John appears for breakfast.

'I've been thinking . . . '

'Yes. I suspected we hadn't finished,' says John.

'Well I think I'm going to need your help.'

'Oh dear, isn't this a bit early? I'm afraid I'm not much good on philosophy, especially first thing in the morning. I haven't got the brains.'

'Actually this isn't really philosophy. It's behaviour, and that in-cludes evolution, biology, and anthropology, with philosophy thrown in. Anyway we're all philosophers; it's just that the brilliant thinkers penetrate further than the rest of us, but eventually they all end up tangled in their own words like fish in a net.' I've thrown the fish in here to get his attention. 'The trouble is that ordinary mortals are seldom clever enough to question them. The way I see it: if the average person can't understand a great philosopher then the philosopher's probably wrong.'

'So where do you want to start?'

'Well that's the problem. I don't really know.'

'OK,' says John, 'the scholarly approach is to have a rough idea of what the problem is, and then to start with first principles. When a great idea collapses it usually turns out to have been based on faulty first principles. For instance, the majority of people don't understand how the moon works; they "know" that in the night it goes round the earth from east to west; clockwise like the sun. But then they can't explain the way it progresses the other way, anticlockwise, over a month from new in the west to old in the east. That's because their very first assumption is wrong; the moon actually circles the earth very slowly from west to east. It takes a whole month to get round. The earth meanwhile spins on its axis, in the opposite direction, within the orbit of the moon. Much of the rest follows simply from these first principles. So what I'm saying is that when you can't understand something very often it turns out to be based on false assumptions.'

I gaze out at the rain for a while thinking this over. 'Right-oh!' I say. 'Well the problem is the awful question about bad human behaviour, and the answer is somehow to be found in the evolution of cooperation and morality.'

'Good,' he says. 'Now let's establish some elementary principles. Humans are animals and Darwin rules OK?'

'Agreed . . . '

'And,' I go on, 'since we're talking about animal behaviour here's another first principle. It's simple but it needs to be tested.' I prattle on about what I call the selfish prime motivator: that no animal can survive if it is not motivated to eat and to avoid pain and discomfort. Nor, because all individuals eventually die, can they avoid extinction unless they are motivated to reproduce.

But why do they die and yet want to avoid extinction? It seems to be a perverse arrangement.

Anyway, leaving that aside for the moment, pain and pleasure are opposite sides of the same coin. Selfishness is evolutionarily ancient. It is very powerful. All animals, without exception from worms to humans, seek to obey it as their guiding principle. This selfish prime motivator, I say, 'is close to the very definition of life'.

'Right . . . good,' says John, 'we can build on that.'

But breakfast's not really the best time for philosophy.

He looks out of the window. The squalling rain hasn't quite

stopped but there's a promising strip of blue sky on the horizon. We pay up and set off.

21 Gallarus' Oratory, new tyre, Dingle Aquarium. *The slime mould is a primitive cooperator*

Quite soon the rolling boisterous thunder-clouds have swept inland and a lovely ceiling of blue has been laid out for us with bright sunshine and clear clean sea air. Fresh as fresh can be.

We set off towards Slea Head at the tip of the Dingle Peninsular.

After a while we come across a tourist-conscious little complex with tea-rooms and souvenir shop. What can it be? We go in. There's a space for parking coaches and bossy notices about 'National Heritage', and 'don't pick the wild flowers', 'respect nature' – that sort of thing. It's all a bit self-conscious and strange till at last we see the reason for it all. A little way off people are walking around an unusual building. It looks like a huge haystack, but it's made of stones.

There's a sign saying: 'Gallarus' Oratory, still dry after twelve hundred years'. Obviously it's something the cultured person already knows about and would travel miles to go and see.

We look at it across a small field. It is indeed a solid and well pro-portioned building, rather splendid in fact. The walls are made of rough stones, perfectly selected, and very well fitted; no cement, and the roof is beautifully tiled.

I'm sure you are expected to ask why is it called an oratory rather than a dormitory, or even a lavatory? And what did this Gallarus do in it, for heaven's sake? But it's seldom a rewarding strategy to give some smart-arsed knowledge-box a chance to show off, so we don't.

We don't go inside. We just wheel our bikes away feeling the guilt of schoolboy ignorance. The fear is that we might get caught by a fierce school mistress with huge bosoms, spectacles and hair done up in a bun. She'd smell of dried inkwells and chalk and she'd make us go and walk round it three times, and then write an essay of at least a thousand words on Gallarus and the great speeches he used to bellow out from his oratory. If that is actually what an oratory was for, which I suspect it wasn't.

As we set off again, I notice that my rear tyre seems to have a slash or hole in it. You can see where the rubber of the inner tube is bulging out slightly. Bad news.

A couple of Dutch hikers walk past while I'm wondering stupidly what to do about my tyre. They make jocular remarks in perfect English about how it's quicker on foot. So to get even I do a rapid sketch of them behind their backs. It's a bit like cocking a snook at a policeman when he's not looking, or jeering at a politician on TV, and it gives a similar minor pleasure.

Dutch walkers near Gallarus' Oratory

It's still about six or seven miles out to Slea Head at the end of the peninsular but my damaged tyre is a worry. So, much to John's disappointment, we change the plan and ride back to Dingle by the shortest route.

There's only one bike shop in town, and they have only one tyre left that fits my bike. So that's lucky.

Next thing of course is how to fit it. I'd like to ask the shop to do it, but that seems sort of feeble; cyclists are supposed to be able to do this kind of thing like peeling potatoes. And anyway they're busy.

Outside on the pavement, in the full view of passers-by and potential critics, I amaze myself by taking the old tyre off and getting the new one on without messing up the derailleur or breaking anything at all. Not only that but I manage it without any help or advice. And it only takes about ten minutes. Change a rear tyre? Piece of cake.

Then we go and visit the new aquarium in Dingle. We start with a coffee in the restaurant.

People having coffee next to us in the Dingle Aquarium restaurant

There are scores of small children flooding about like quicksilver. Teenage girls in green aquarium-staff uniform are trying to control them. 'Walk! Don't run!' They shout above the sound of running feet and children's excited voices.

One little girl is in tears. Her name is Dymphna and her friend has been nasty to her. One of the teenagers in green comforts her with the expert touch of an elder sister. The small boy who caused the tears is found and they make it up.

The aquarium is a splendid purpose-built complex which was first opened to the public last year. It sensibly concentrates on showing the fish and other marine life that live around Dingle. Moreover it's designed to show them in their natural habitat, which it does superbly.

We spend over an hour wandering about gazing at it all.

John points out all sorts of unusual fish and explains how evolution has shaped and coloured their bodies to suit their sometimes very exotic habits and lifestyles. His knowledge is professional and extensive.

I do drawings of some of the beautiful, elusive creatures.

The fact that these fish are already familiar to us makes it all the more fascinating to see them swimming in a good imitation of their natural habitat.

The glass of some tanks slopes upwards, away from the viewer at forty-five degrees. This eliminates reflections and lets you look down on the fish from above.

There is an absolutely huge cylindrical tank at the centre of the complex with mostly glass walls and lots of viewing stands. It must be fifteen feet deep and twenty feet across. You can look down into it from above, in from the side and, lovely touch, walk along the 'sea floor' through a glass tunnel. Flatfish regularly come and rest on the upper surface of this tunnel, so you can study their undersides.

The main body of the tank is full of big fish, including some five-foot sharks. Your vision is distorted as you look in. Straight ahead it's more or less OK, but sideways it's all aslant. You can see far into green, dimly lit depths where hundreds of fish are circling around. The shoals of bigger fish drift hypnotically; going round clockwise. Why clockwise? I wonder. They come past your viewpoint at regular intervals. The big ones are sharks, tunnyfish, cod and pollock. You can see common or garden mackerel, bass and mullet. And amongst all these are dogfish, conger eels and ray.

Denizens of Dingle Aquarium

Three glass pods protrude like caves into this big tank near the 'sea floor'. You can put your head and shoulders in and get a realistic impression of actually being right in the water with the fish swimming around you. Enchanting for biologically curious children.

On the bottom, flatfish, lobster, crabs, sea urchins, starfish, shrimps and prawns occupy the sand and rocks. The larger predators in this tank must be very carefully fed because if they felt hungry, it would surely be quite simple for them to gobble up the smaller occupants. A beautiful crayfish comes to rest looking out at us humans gazing into its world. It stays completely still so I start drawing it.

Crayfish posing for its portrait

The drawing must take two or three minutes, ending with the marks on its magnificent antennae. As soon as I have finished, the obliging creature moves on.

There's a fascinating display of how lobsters are reared in fish farms during the different stages of their juvenile lives. Apparently they are ferocious fighters so they have to be reared in separate little compartments otherwise they'd kill each other. 'Not unlike your typical Ulsterman,' says John.

One lobster is colossal, John estimates its weight at ten pounds.

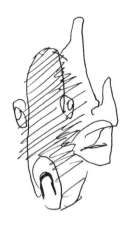

I watch a big octopus flashing spectacular changes of colour which pulse down its body in successive patches from deep rich brown to white with ochre spots and back again every three seconds.

Another display tank imitates a rocky seashore. It contains crabs, prawns and the small fish and things you find in rock pools. At regular intervals an artificial wave comes pounding in through a hole in the side while a tape-recording plays the evocative sound of crashing breakers and crying seagulls. You can see through the glass wall how the marine life skitters about very happily without being dashed on the rocks, as a human child would surely be, in the violent turmoil of foam and sand.

There are all sorts of posters and diagrams on the walls. One of them says: 'Today exports of fish from Ireland are worth more than 300 million Euros. In 1956 the value exceeded 1 million Euros for the first time.' John reminds me that a few days ago we were watching a trawler calmly hoovering up life on the seabed about two hundred yards offshore. It was flying a Spanish flag. 'You watch,' he mutters. 'The bureaucrats will quickly get that back down to a million Euros again.'

After an enjoyable hour we tear ourselves away. It's time for lunch so we queue up for a tray of sausages and chips in the cafeteria.

'Aren't some of those sea creatures marvellously exotic.'

'Yes,' says John. 'But there are lots of boring life-forms as well, like grass, seaweed, sardines and pine trees. Boring as sausage and chips. Think of sparrows, geese, deer, sheep, worms and civil servants.' He gives his food a sceptical prod.

'But I must admit.' He brightens up. 'There are some really amazing creatures as well. God has produced some wonderful triumphs, and it's fascinating to speculate how they can have evolved.'

'For instance?'

'I think my favourite is insect-eating plants. Insects can be a real pest and I can just imagine one trapping a fly and saying to itself, "Gottcha, you little bastard." It's a hilarious trick! God at his funniest!'

'What about stinging nettles,' I say, and it quickly becomes a 'most impressive life form' competition. We agree that bacteria, symbiotic eukaryotes and other microscopic creatures are excluded.

'Driver ants,' says John, 'because of their amazing, terrifying, ability to cooperate.'

'I do agree. Cooperation is certainly one of nature's triumphs.'

It's my turn. 'Coconut palms,' I say. 'As boring as pine trees at first sight. But actually they have several marvellous attributes. Their seed can float a thousand miles away and germinate months, even years later, in deep, sterile sand on tropical beaches. Their trunks grow tall enough to hold their heads out of the tops of twenty-foot sand dunes that are marched along in the wind several feet each year; and they are flexible enough to bend to typhoons and hurricanes without snapping. Their whippy leaves will also withstand high winds that can upturn cars and throw boats about. Their huge root ball ensures that even if a tree is bowled over in a typhoon it will right itself like a Russian doll. And they seem to have a sensor, which makes them lean out photogenically into the prevailing wind. This incidentally also helps to deposit their nuts towards the sea.'

John then plays. 'The slime mould. It consists of about a hundred thousand amoebae that mess about together, but as separate individuals, until they need to move on. When that happens they come together in a tight cooperative unit; a quasi-living organism, which can either move off almost like a little slug, or else turn itself into a breeding unit in which some individuals forgo reproduction to perform structural functions and others produce breeding spores which blow away in the wind to start up new colonies.'

I counter with hyenas. I don't get many points for them but they are so ugly and unloved and they are actually more effective hunters than lions.

'Octopus,' says John. 'They're lowly invertebrates, molluscs actually, in the same class as slugs and snails. But they have the most piercing, intelligent eyes and wonderfully muscular, flexible, extendible tentacles with suckers. They've invented jet propulsion and a "smokescreen-ink" defence system. For camouflage, they have spots which can change colour independently of their background body colour. This too can change colour, and if that's not enough these colour changes can pulse excitedly along their bodies and tentacles at three-second intervals or stay unchanged indefinitely. The octopus seems to me to be about as superior to other molluscs as humans are to other mammals.'

The octopus is John's ace and I concede the game.

Lunch was pretty basic. It's quickly finished and we're soon back on our bikes and out into the countryside.

22 Connor Pass, mountain climbing

This afternoon's ride takes us up over the Connor Pass through the spine of the Dingle Peninsular. These are the Slieve Mish mountains and they go up to 2,800 ft. It has to be admitted that this is only 850 metres. We prefer it in feet; they sound so much more heroic.

The pass is at 1,500 ft. It's a steady plodding grind which seems to go on for ever; painful and exhausting. But actually so long as you have low gears and take it steady, mountain climbs on a bike aren't all that difficult. Modern cars are not designed to expect steep gradients so modern roads never get too steep for a bike.

Cyclists have their own personal mountain-climbing strategy. Mine is to go extremely slowly; sometimes even down to walking pace. I make a conscious effort to breathe in rhythm with the pedals. And every now and again I like to stop for about two minutes to allow the heartbeats to calm down. But a stop exceeding five minutes is deadly. If you don't keep going you seize up, both mentally and physically.

As I grind and wind my way doggedly up a mountain, around the hairpin bends, hands on the lower handlebar position, brain down, staring at the tarmac, my head sometimes goes funny. I no longer have thoughts or get ideas. Instead a stupid phrase like, 'would you be able for it', or maybe my phone number, will come into my head and be repeated over and over again. Or else I'll start compulsively counting my foot revolutions. This will go on until my consciousness notices what's happening and tries to re-establish normal thought.

The most demoralising thing on a long uphill climb is a stretch of downhill. It's worse than irrelevant. It's a device of the Devil who laughs as he snatches away some of the precious height you have achieved.

Happily there are no downhills on the way up to the Connor Pass.

The weather is nice again. It's clear, Atlantic and fresh, and getting colder as we climb.

The sun comes out in occasional brilliant patches. The views are lovely.

The beauty of the scenery and the sense of achievement always outweigh the pain of a climb, which is immediately forgotten. That's the magic of the mountains. But you do have to have extra low gears and learn to be philosophical about the fact that when you think the top is round the next bend, it never actually is.

Or hardly ever.

Eventually we get there.

Up on the pass you can see the sea both to the north and to the south and the views are huge and majestic.

Looking north from the Connor Pass, 1,500 ft above sea level

There's a whistling cold wind up here that searches, like a vulture, for your liver and your heart. We rest for a short while in a car park with picnic area and panoramic view and chat to several other cyclists, French, Dutch and Irish. They are mostly in their twenties or early thirties and they treat us as normal people, almost as one of them. This is a nice contrast to being looked upon as an old age pensioner, which is our usual status down at sea level.

Of course, up here, we cyclists look down on the car passengers with withering disdain; we look right through them in fact.

We wrap up warm and head off down into the cold, biting mountain wind which is funnelling up the pass from the north. Being long and skinny I'm frightened of the cold. It quickly gets into me on a downhill run when I'm no longer pumping out energy, and then it takes me ages to warm up again.

But, to be honest, I have to admit it's not only that. The rattling pace of a full-tilt descent and the cold mountain wind make me keenly aware of my skeleton. It's all elbows and knees, and I imagine it flying over the handlebars and breaking apart like a bundle of sticks as it hits the tarmac. John in contrast is altogether more ruggedly built than me. He's quite fearless and doesn't seem to feel the cold at all. True to form he whizzes recklessly off downhill.

I descend more sedately, gripping the brakes, woollen mittens concealing my white knuckles. It's a very long and delightful freewheel ride round bends, under rock overhangs, beside fast running waterfalls, and out into twenty mile vistas. On the way up you are winding and grunting so desperately that you don't really notice the scenery much. But going down you sit back and drink it all in. You're like a soaring mountain bird; an eagle perhaps, or a raven.

We meet again at the bottom where I find John picking blackberries.

23 Solitary is the default condition. Evolution has no purpose. Cooperation is one of the pre-existing opportunities

That cold mountain air set me wondering about the evolution of morality. Why did it happen? What benefit did it bring? And is it evolved or taught? If it's taught does that mean that we have evolved a predisposition to teach it? These seem to be some of the basic assumptions John mentioned. So at the next opportunity I ask him.

'Tell me about behaviour and the great nature/nurture debate. What I need to understand is how can an animal evolve cooperation – how did it start?'

'Well, be careful; I think you may be skipping over an assumption here. Animals can be either solitaries or cooperators. I mean bears are solitaries, wolves are cooperators and sheep come in between; they herd but don't really cooperate to get things done. Between these two extremes there's a huge range of behaviours. Are you assuming that the most basic life forms are always solitary?'

'Yes, I suppose I'm assuming that solitary is the "default" condition. In other words, if a cooperating species finds that some environmental change means that cooperation is no longer a good idea then, in the same way that fish living in dark caves lose their eyesight, the species will abandon the ability to cooperate. Does that make sense biologically?'

'I think it does, yes,' he says. 'I see it like this. As you say, all animals have three imperatives. They must eat, shelter and reproduce, so each species evolves an inter-related set of features and behaviours to do these things. These features and behaviours are myriad. They include for example: teeth, legs, timidity, aggression, wings, sex organs, eyes, ears, cooperation, nocturnalism and hundreds more. Any of these that are not needed to do the three imperatives in the animal's chosen habitat are discarded.'

Then he goes on: 'People forget that evolution as we understand it, has absolutely no purpose; none whatever. People find that difficult to grasp. It may seem as though evolution invented fingers in our ape ancestors so that in due course humans would eventually be able to write. But evolution doesn't evolve with any direction or objective; it just floods forwards like rainwater falling on dry land. Water simply takes the best direction downhill that opportunity offers.

'The key here is opportunity. Life just exploits an environmental opportunity – an evolutionary niche as we biologists call it. You can think of light as the pre-existing opportunity which nature has exploited by evolving eyes. Or sound waves as the opportunity which allowed the evolution of hearing and speech. And the fact that the air is dense is the opportunity which allowed flight to evolve.'

'And features that are no longer needed to do the three survival tasks, they will de-evolve?'

'Right. An animal could evolve a smaller brain for example.'

'The same,' he explains, 'is true of cooperation. The pre-existing fact that the three survival tasks – foraging, sheltering and breeding – can often be performed more efficiently by teamwork than singly is the opportunity which engendered cooperation.'

'Yes, I understand.'

Well I think I do, but this is going to take a little time to sink in . . . And he hasn't even got on to the nature/nurture stuff yet. I tuck it all away for further thought while cycling along. It's still a chaos of inter stellar dust in which half a dozen excited pucai are orbiting like nascent planets, each one whispering, 'Look at me.'

'I don't quite see where this is getting us,' says John.

'I suppose I'm trying to close in on that idea I spotted on the Healey Pass about a possible connection between cooperation and morality. There definitely seems to be something there.' But it escapes me and my words, which just a few moments ago seemed all nicely joined up, now scatter like dried leaves in the wind.

We spend the night in a B&B to the north of the Connor Pass, and next morning we set off eastwards along the north shore of the Dingle Peninsular.

The geography and countryside are changing. Slieve Mish, at 2,800 ft, is still visible on our right. But you can feel from the way the surrounding hills and headlands are becoming less jagged on the map and less dramatic to the eye, and from the straightness of the shoreline, that we will soon be coming out of the mountainous part of Kerry.

The wild flowers all along the way are very lovely. As usual there's flaming montbretia and its contrasting partner, the acid-yellow ragweed. The big bulks of colour come from these two, assisted by trombone bursts from purple loosestrife, meadowsweet, and fuscia. But there's other humbler stuff as well, tinkling like harpsicord notes, delicately poised and flimsy. There's scabious, cornflower, bright blue vetch, and various dandelion and daisy type things. These all have evocative common names like samphire, pennywort, agrimony and five-faced bishop. It would be nice to be able to rattle them off, erudite and poetic, like a Gregorian chant.

It's mid-morning. John fancies a swim and I'd like to get my watercolours out, so at Castlegregory we turn off down to the sea to find a beach we've been told about. We cycle along a sunken lane half-filled with drifting sand, and there it is, a lovely stretch of sand, and there is nobody about.

We prop our bikes together on the coarse grass which covers the sand dunes.

I settle down to do a quick watercolour and, despite the fact that it's windy and not very warm at all, John puts on his bathing pants and canters off into the sea.

Then a car appears and an attractive young woman gets out. She's already in her swimming costume. Must have put it on before she drove down here. I give her a nod but you can see by her demeanour that according to her it's a pity we're here. This is her swimming spot and she likes to have it to herself. Body language can be very articulate. Nice figure though.

John carries on swimming vigorously. In the early 1950s he was a member of the TCD swimming team and he still swims like a seal;

fast, efficient and enjoying it. You can tell that in his previous incarnation he was a salmon.

The young woman walks past me down to the sea with self-conscious poise. She reminds me of a cat passing a dog: walking stiffly alert, tail in the air, all claws and radar and provocatively just within chasing range.

But I'm able for this: I play the artist's defence. It's like a sequence of chess moves. You adopt a pose halfway between superiority and privacy. It's a sort of prissy 'you can't get me I'm painting' attitude.

First of all, I'm not to be interrupted or spoken to because that would interfere with my inspiration.

Secondly, I'm superior to lesser beings because I'm an artist.

Thirdly, I can't really see you no matter how pretty you may be because I'm concentrating in a creative trance on my subject.

Fourthly, I know you'd love to come and have a peep at what I'm doing, to see if it's any good, but there is an invisible barrier around me which you're not allowed to cross.

And finally – anyway I got here before you did.

Bikes propped on Castlegregory Beach while John swims,
attractive young woman swimming here too

She too goes in for a swim.

Eventually she comes out – well she has to doesn't she.

So does John.

And I've finished my picture.

We all say Hello, and isn't it a lovely spot, the sea so lovely and clean and the marvellous scenery.

'Let's have a look,' she says. 'Oh that's lovely altogether, what you've done there.'

We chat for ten minutes and then go our separate ways refreshed; my silly self-consciousness overcome yet again and my frail faith in human nature restored.

In Tralee we have lunch, in the Kingdom Kitchen Restaurant, an honest down-market self-service place, serving good wholesome food. It's ideal for the long-distance cyclist.

As we pass through the streets we keep being reminded that poor old Tralee has been internationally immortalised in the sentimental song called 'The Rose of Tralee'. It must have been the Irish immigrants who started the nauseating American tradition of writing songs about their towns and cities.

There are half-torn posters and several out-of-date banners advertising the finals of the All-Ireland Rosebud Beauty Contest. It took place a month ago.

If she had been here at the right time the Lady with the Purple Arse would almost certainly have won first prize. John imagines the headline in the *Sunday Independent*: 'Purple Arsed Lady Wins All-Ireland Rosebud Final'. But sadly her timing was wrong.

We cycle on; out into the countryside north of Tralee.

25 *The prime motivator prevents cooperation. Why gene thinking and game theory are not the answer*

The countryside has changed now from mountains to gentle hills and farmland. We stop for a pee and blackberries by a nice little brook. It looks promising, so John gets out his rod and wanders off down the bank. I get out my sketchbook.

'Catch anything?' I ask when he gets back. But of course for John, fishing is not just catching them, it's the whole riverine experience.

'Just a few tiddlers. Actually I saw an otter.'

'Remember those first principles you mentioned?'

'Oh dear,' he says,' I knew I shouldn't have left you on your own.'

'And d'you remember the great chaotic swirl of interconnected ideas I was talking about, and the problem of finding a way of making sense of it all. You know, beating a path forward?'

'Go on.'

'Well, I've just realised that if the selfish prime motivator drives all life forms, as it must, then it has to be a massive obstacle against the evolution of cooperation.'

Pause . . . 'And is that it?'

'Well, yes.' He doesn't seem to get the point.

'The thing is, how's it done? Don't you think that could be a promising question? I mean the very essence of cooperation is unselfish behaviour, but selfishness, greed and fear will immediately destroy any cooperative venture.'

'So,' I say with a flourish like a magician pulling a rabbit out of a hat, 'cooperation requires the suppression of the selfish prime motivator.'

He doesn't seem terribly impressed, but I blunder on. 'Many different species in most types of animal have evolved various forms of cooperation. So how is it done? That's what I want to know.'

'OK, yes I see what you're getting at. There have to be major genetic developments to achieve this suppression.'

'That's right! Somehow I sense that if one could put one's finger on the answer, one might open up great vistas of understanding, especially about human bad behaviour and morality. Cooperation is such a terrifically powerful ploy. Look at the success of ants, rats and dolphins, and it's the very essence of human behaviour.'

'Yes I see,' says John, 'or I think I do.'

'Do you know about Dawkins's "selfish gene"?' he asks, 'and game theory – the prisoner's dilemma and all that?'

'Yes a little, but they don't seem right to me. Perhaps I don't know enough about them.'

'Well, they claim to solve what's referred to as the altruism paradox. This puts what you've just said the other way round; that since unselfish behaviour reduces an individual's chances of survival and reproduction, unselfish individuals are less likely to reproduce and pass on the behaviour, so altruism cannot evolve, and yet it plainly does. Gene thinking says that it's the gene which is selfish and not the individual; in other words, that natural selection takes place at gene level and that we are merely vehicles for their propagation. Game theory supports gene thinking. It shows by computer modelling that cooperation is evolutionarily stable in a social animal.'

'OK, yes I've read about that stuff, but I've always thought that gene thinking is a bit like what I call alphabet thinking. It's like saying that the evolution of a language is all about an imaginary competition for supremacy between letters. But that's not how it works. A language develops by the continual invention of new words and phrases and the weeding out of those which are less efficient, less fit, for communication and comprehension. The competition is between words, grammars, phrases and concepts. That is where the weeding takes place, not between letters and syllables. Similarly in bears say, or humans, the weeding, the natural selection, takes place between individuals, not their genes. This is very simple, there's no need to look for genetic complications.'

'And,' I go on, 'there's a similar problem with game theory. As you say it shows how cooperation is evolutionarily stable in a social animal but it doesn't explain how cooperation evolves in the first place. So it contains a monstrous circular argument.'

'How do you mean?'

'Well, you can't explain the origin of something simply by describing its mechanism. Neither the parts list of a jet plane nor even its flying instructions will explain how it was evolved or why it can fly. To put it more starkly, game theory is like saying flying animals fly; that may be true but it gets us nowhere. It proves nothing. Game theory merely says that the essence of society is cooperation. It demonstrates brilliantly how cooperation is naturally selected in a social animal, but it cannot explain or predict how solitary hyena ancestors evolved into cooperators. Game theory merely says that social animals will cooperate.'

'So where do we go from here, Holmes?'

'I'm not sure about that yet, Watson, but something tells me we could be on the right path. I don't know how it's done but the prime motivator has to be suppressed, and it must be done genetically, and gene thinking and game theory are not the answer. If we can solve this one we may be able to explain morality and find the answer to the Awful Question.'

'And one more thing,' says John. 'You do think the answer applies to all cooperating animals, not just people?'

'Oh yes absolutely. Anything in all this that falls foul of Darwin, like the uniqueness of mankind for example, immediately goes in the rubbish bin. Darwin is king.'

'It's a great pity salmon don't cooperate,' he says.

'Ah well, we can't have everything.'

Silence falls as we load up our bikes again. I'm already poised on my saddle, one toe on the ground. John's been studying the map.

'Yes,' he says pensively, 'but you know there's something worrying me. Solitaries must also be able to exercise self-restraint against the prime motivator.'

'How's that?'

'Put it this way; if the hungry frog can't restrain its urge to pounce on a juicy fat bluebottle, it may give itself away and be snapped up by the heron. And yet the frog is a solitary, not a cooperator.'

'Oh dear, you've got me there.' I dismount in dismay. 'Is this a torpedo amidships?'

'Well . . . Let's see . . . Not necessarily. Remember that evolution has no purpose, it just floods into an opportunity, as we said, like rain-water falling on dry land. So the fact that solitaries can exercise some degree of self-restraint doesn't mean that they will necessarily take the next step towards cooperation. If no survival advantage is gained by each incremental step towards cooperation, the species won't take those steps.'

'Yes, of course, I see. Oh well, thank goodness for that.'

But my thoughts shrivel with disappointment as the hope of an answer to the Awful Question diminishes. OK, a frog can suppress its prime motivator in order to survive, but how can an animal do it in order to cooperate? It just doesn't seem possible.

26   Ballybunion. Swim. John doesn't snore

The weather improves steadily and the sun comes out.

At half-five we arrive, exhausted as usual, at Ballybunion, Ireland's premier seaside resort with attractions and goings-on to rival Black-pool. It's B&B hunting time again.

We scout about following up friendly advice and hopeful leads. Several people tell us the town is full to busting and it'll be impossible to find a bed anywhere.

We nearly accept rooms in a soulless modern hotel, but the young lady at the reception desk clearly doesn't like the look of us, and the place is bristling with notices telling you all the things you can't do:

> Take hotel towels on to the beach.
> Walk sand into your room.
> Wash clothes in your room.
> Play music in your room.
> Come in after 11.30 p.m.

I'd much rather sleep in a police cell. But we eventually find a vacancy in Invergordon B&B.

We are made very welcome by Joan Daly. She brings us tea and cake in a big front room looking out over the sea. She stays for a chat. You can see she's curious to know more about us. She's a friendly, gregarious, sort of lady.

After settling in John goes down to the beach for a swim.

This is a real bucket and spade seaside resort. When I was a little boy back in the 1930s and 40s it was the legendary setting for holiday romances and pantomime jokes.

The summer holidays are in full swing and even at this late hour, the beach is packed with human activity. The sun is low in the western sky. It's shining slantwise, piercing the Atlantic breakers with sparkling shards of pale green. Children's shouts of, 'Mummy look at me,' and their laughter mingle with the crashing of the waves.

John has a bracing swim in this milling scene.

I do a quick drawing.

The beach at Ballybunion. Bright evening sun

Then, while he is still in the water, I try to hide his clothes in the pretence that they've been stolen. But he spots me. He may not be able to hear very well but he does have sharp eyes.

We have dinner in the Strand Restaurant. It's a big barn of a place. We've put on our smart clothes but they're clearly not smart enough because we're tucked away out of sight at a table beside the swing doors into the kitchen. Door-kicking waitresses stream in and out like bees at the entrance to their hive. I choose the curried chicken and John has the duck à l'Orange. The food is nice and there's lots of it.

We totter back to Invergordon B&B and collapse into bed.

It's been a good day. The weather improved gradually and eventually we had warm sunshine this evening.

We did 37 miles today. We've now accumulated 311 miles since Cork.

John has been sending masses of postcards. Must send a few myself. It's a modest art form in the same family as song writing and poetry but I've never mastered it. I always say too much.

John tells me that his two daughters and wife sometimes accuse him of snoring. I get accused of it too and I always think it's the most underhand accusation. When she says, 'And anyway you snore.' She knows full well you can't reply: 'No I don't.' You're unable to defend yourself because you were asleep while you were supposed to be doing it. You can't even plead that it wasn't very loud and that she's exaggerating as usual. And it seems copy-cat to say, 'Well so do you.' You just have to take it on the chin, and you might even come to believe yourself guilty, when in fact you might not be. It's very unfair and full of double hypotheticals.

Therefore I feel it's my duty to certify to whom it may concern that John does not snore. At least I never heard him, and we've shared a room every night so far.

I wake at about half-six. John is still asleep so I do a drawing of him.

Joan Daly has shown me how to make my own tea in the kitchen if I should get up early. So I go and do that.

Like I say, it's nice to get up early and do a bit of drawing, writing and thinking with my sketchbook. Most people have a wake-up ritual to remind themselves who they are, which way is up and that the sky is blue, and this is mine. Apart from sketchbook and pen, a cup of tea is the only other necessity for this innocent routine.

Every B&B lady so far has said yes, of course it's OK to wander into

John asleep in room 6, Invergordon B&B, Ballybunion.
This is to certify that he doesn't snore

the kitchen and make my own tea whenever I want. Very kind and hospitable. I can't imagine a hotel allowing that.

Invergordon B&B has a fine view looking out over the beach. So after drawing the sleeping John and writing a few notes, I do the view from the front window.

Yesterday evening, in our weariness, we decided that we need a rest day every now and again to revive the aching limbs. We thought Ballybunion would be a good place to laze about for a day. It's an unselfconscious, old-established seaside resort and it has a carefree, ice-cream, kite-flying and bingo-hall sort of charm. The people who

Ballybunion Beach from Invergordon B&B

come here have fun. Loud music thumps out of the slot machine
parlours. The shops sell beach balls, buckets and spades and those
traditional 'big-buxom-woman, small-worried-man' postcards, and
the pubs look well used. There are several ladies' hairdressers in the
main street. Most of the people are young. They walk sand everywhere. You can see where someone was sick on the pavement last
night. There is very little traffic.

The street advertising isn't stage-Irish, like in Dingle. There it was
all Shamrocks, Gaelic Coffee and traditional Irish Music. The dead
hand of mass-marketing has found no hold in Ballybunion.

Many of the young men have elaborate tattoos. Some of the girls too, and they often have rings in their belly buttons, noses and ears. John says they couldn't wear those in Canada or they'd get frostbite, quick as a flash.

Ballybunion is an honest to God, down to earth, popular playground. What you see is what you get.

But we realise this is a place for young families, not for a couple of old farts like us. And anyway the spirit of adventure says, 'Come on, let's go!'

Before setting off I ask Joan Daly which way is the coast road to the Tarbert Ferry; we don't want to take the direct road through Balylongford. Joan, who has lived here all her life mind you, isn't exactly sure. Her niece happens to be around helping with the bed-making, so Joan asks her. The niece isn't all that sure either. They eventually decide it's back up the main street. When we go that way we discover it's the wrong direction. The niece has also lived here all her life. They are obviously very content with where they are, and that's that.

We cycle over the hills and round the coast through Ardee to the Tarbert ferry. The weather is breezy and sunny. Our reserves have built up again during the night like petrol tanks and we're fit as fiddles again. As usual the morning ride is a delight. We bowl along feeling on top of the world; strong and carefree.

At ten to twelve we get to the ferry. It's a small vessel; basically a floating platform for about thirty cars. It's open at the bow and stern and has side walls with a bridge-house high up on one side. It takes you across the Shannon estuary, cutting out a sixty mile – two cycling days – detour back inland through Limerick.

There is a quarter-mile line of waiting coaches, cars and vans, but we just cycle past them all, right up to the head of the queue feeling slightly naughty. But people don't seriously expect cyclists to wait patiently behind the car ahead do they? Anyway we slip on board just as it's leaving. Cyclists' luck.

The ferry is called the *Shannon Willow* and the crossing is a two-and-a-half mile trip across a narrow part of the estuary.

Thus we cross the mighty River Shannon, the biggest river in the British Isles. And in doing so we cross the county boundary from Kerry into Clare.

27 Ferry and swallows. *African wild dog cooperation. Cooperators must solve the cooperate-or-split dilemma*

I'm watching the Kerry shore recede and absent-mindedly prospecting the scenery for a drawing when John notices some swallows dive-bombing a crow which is sitting on a rail beside the bridge-house. Then looking closer, he points out that several swallows have made their nests in the eaves under the bridge-house roof and they're telling the crow in swallow language to 'just piss off'. The swallows look fierce, but the crow pretends not to notice.

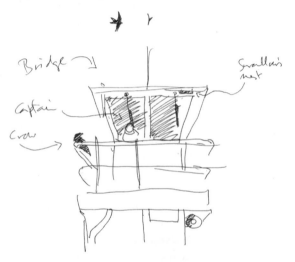

Swallows nesting in the roof of the bridge house on the Shannon Willow

But that's curious when you come to think about it. Imagine being a swallow. You've just come up from Africa, and you choose to build your nest in the eaves of a ferry. It would be confusing wouldn't it. The ferry goes two and a half miles north to Killimer, and then back again to Tarbert at half-hour intervals throughout the day. Your eggs hatch and you swoop off on the wind, like swallows do, collecting flies to feed your little hatchlings. But when you've collected enough to bring back, you find the damned ferry is not where you left it. Two and a half miles is quite a long way for a nest to move across the surface of the earth.

So how do they do it? We are told how migrating birds navigate by the stars, the sun and the earth's magnetism. But these wouldn't help you to find a moving ferry. Smell, they say, is another migrating guide that might help, but only if you were downwind. And next year when you come back to the same nest as swallows do, do you go to Tarbert or to Killimer? There'll be confused swallows over the Shannon saying to themselves, 'Now where is it? I'm sure it was here when I left for Africa.'

Who can tell us the answer? E. O. Wilson? David Attenborough? Answers on a postcard please. My theory is that the pucai must give the swallows a helping hand. The pucai and swallows are believed to have a close affinity.

After we've decided we can't solve the moving-nest problem, John says, 'Got anywhere yet?'

'What?'

'You know. With that cooperation and morality stuff about how the prime motivator can be suppressed.'

'I'm afraid not, no. I kept going round in circles. All I can think of is what an amazing evolutionary achievement cooperation actually is. It seems an even greater development than sight, hearing or flight. There's so much more to this than I thought. Actually I'm going off the whole idea, it's too difficult for my feeble brain.'

'But the selfish prime motivator as you call it is hard to deny, and yet many animals cooperate, so there has to be an answer.'

'Well I do agree . . . perhaps if we take it slowly . . . I've been obsessed by the damned thing all morning.'

'Why don't you go over it all for me,' says John. 'Telling someone else, I find, often helps to clarify my thoughts. They usually don't have to say a word; the answers somehow come in the telling.'

'No wait,' he says, 'I've got a better idea. Why don't I quote you something I was reading last night. It's about cooperation amongst African wild dogs. It might offer a new angle.'

'OK, good idea.'

So he fishes out his book.

'The African wild dog is called *Lycaon pictus*,' he reads.

'Wild dogs prey upon animals much larger than themselves, such as the brindled gnu or wildebeest (*Connochaetus taurinus*) and Burchell's zebra (*Equus burchelli*). They select a single quarry and run it down over a long distance. These communal hunts involve various forms of cooperation. There is a collective choice of prey. There may be exchange of leaders in a chase, enabling a pack to operate a relay system and so cover great distances. A trailing dog will often cut corners in an attempt to head off the prey. The larger prey are killed by the combined effort of the pack. The food is shared by members of the pack, and the adults often regurgitate food to the young. Sometimes a few adults remain behind with the vulnerable juveniles, and they are also fed when the others return. Cooperative behaviour of this type involves an element of sacrifice, because individuals do not act purely selfishly, but benefit others at some cost to themselves.'

That does the trick; it quickly re-ignites my enthusiasm and when he's finished I pick my words carefully while John listens.

'So the jobs cooperating animals do can include nursing, guarding, building, and hunting. Even termites do gardening. These jobs all require self-restraint by the members of the group. This means over-riding the selfish pain–pleasure motivator. It means not running away at the first sign of danger, trusting instead in the protection of the group. It means not diving in for the kill too soon when the hunting group, pelicans for example or dolphins, is rounding up prey. It means ignoring fear, exhaustion, greed or lust when this is necessary for the cooperating group to do its job.

'But the problem I hit yesterday, and this is what made me go off the whole idea, is that if a cooperating animal were simply to switch off its prime motivator, it would quickly become extinct from foolish overexposure to various dangers. And, on the other hand, if it never suppressed it the animal couldn't cooperate at all. Every individual in the working group therefore has to be able to judge at each stage of its task when to override and when to obey its prime motivator.'

'Yes, I see the problem,' says John, gazing across the estuary. 'You're saying that an animal's primary instincts are to avoid pain and dis-comfort, to eat and drink, and to have sex. If it then evolves a genetic obligation to suppress them but only in certain circumstances, then the poor animal is potentially in a very confusing situation indeed.'

'Exactly. When faced in the heat of the moment with danger, a juicy morsel to eat, or a nice mating opportunity, what does it do? Does it cooperate or does it split?'

'That's a big dilemma,' he says. 'So how do you think it's solved?'

Focusing on the animal's feelings, I point out that this cooperate-or-split dilemma is strictly an individual thing. It only exists in the animal's mind but it is very real. Thus I hover on the verge of psychology.

But John goes the other way. Always the scientist, he avoids the subjective, philosophical paths I've opened up; they can lead to questions like 'what is the nature of consciousness or of reality?' Instead, he summarises the dilemma in objective, biological terms by saying that to be able to benefit from the considerable advantages of cooperation, an animal species must evolve some method of selectively suppressing the prime motivator when appropriate.

Typical scientist; they always shy away from a nice philosophical problem. They don't like to speculate or use their intuition. They're always pinning things down, never widening them out. The scientist's war-cry, 'prove it', always kills further thought. I suppose that's the way they're trained, poor things. If I ruled the world I would insist that all university science exams would include a very difficult paper on poetry. It would carry twenty per cent of the overall marks.

We agree that either way, subjectively or objectively, it's not difficult to understand, but that this selectively appropriate suppression is a mighty impressive behavioural achievement. The prime motivator is deeply built into the genetics of animal design from worms to humans; therefore its suppression is surely not achieved by a simple or trivial evolutionary adjustment. By the flick of a gene or two, like a light switch.

'We're into a major design feature here. But we haven't got the answer; we still don't know how it's done,' says John.

'No, but the chaos is clarifying; we've defined the question and that's seldom easy.'

28 Killimer and hydroelectric schemes. Michael Gleeson & cycling technology

On the road to Kilrush we soon come under the shadow of an enormous concrete block. This is the deadly Killimer hydroelectric power station. This is what killed off the tribes of thirty pound salmon for which the River Shannon was once famous.

John looks away in disgust. He mutters imprecations and calls on God to throw all civil engineers into a stream tank teeming with piranha fish.

In an attempt to divert his attention from the foul works of the Evil

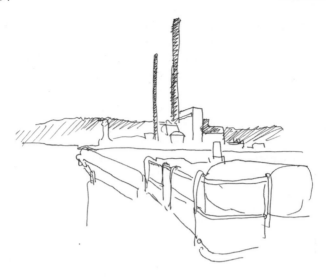

The Killimer hydroelectric station

One, I ask him what determines how big a salmon will become. He explains that it depends on how many years it stays at sea; the longer it stays the bigger it will get. But it is not yet properly known what decides how long the salmon will actually stay at sea. The current theory is that it depends on the harshness of its chosen river. He mentions things like strong currents, waterfalls, rapids, distance to travel to the spawning beds, and heavy gravel in the spawning beds. These conditions require a big strong fish. So it is believed that the tribe that opts for this sort of lifestyle will become genetically programmed to stay at sea longer and so become bigger than those who spawn in easier places.

But let's face it, I'm going to have to have the hydroelectric lecture sooner or later, and now in the shadow of this huge power station is as good a time as any.

'So how actually do hydroelectric schemes kill off the salmon?' I ask in an innocent little voice.

The broad answer says John is that they completely alter the whole ecosystem.

A deep lake is created above the dam. The juvenile salmon need fast water to live in. They don't cope very well in the lake and get eaten by pike and other predators.

Then huge numbers of smolt, the teenagers of the salmon family, travelling down to sea, go through the turbines and get shredded. Diversionary solutions to steer them past the turbines have been tried. They satisfy the politicians but are largely ineffective.

Below the dam, the natural riverbed gets washed away by the fierce gush of water. This becomes a barren environment with none of the invertebrate life which the juveniles feed on.

The salmon ladders, built to enable the returning adult fish to climb the dam, have been shown in repeated field trials to be ineffective.

And for various well-documented reasons, hatcheries don't work.

John says it's an established fact that hydroelectric schemes exterminate salmon. It happens every single time but politicians, architects and engineers choose to ignore it, or they pretend they now have new methods to solve the problem.

Here's what John said in a paper he published recently. It is entitled 'The Myth of Hydroelectricity as "Green Energy" '.

In Ireland stocks of salmon and sea trout have decreased alarmingly over the last few decades. This is not entirely due to dams, and more recently damage has been caused by dredging, and by pollution and enrichment of water courses from run-off of sediments, fertilisers, insecticides, herbicides and fungicides from agricultural activities, which interfere with habitat and the food chain (EPA 2000; Reynolds 1998). Unfortunately there is not specifically fish habitat protection as is enforced under the Fisheries Act in Canada, so that the many rearing streams are dredged to drain wetlands. Also riparian buffer strips of natural vegetation, which would do much to control harmful runoff, are not preserved, as they are in Canada. Nevertheless dams have in addition had significant negative effects on salmon stocks, despite mitigation with fishways and hatcheries. Hydroelectric generations presently produce six percent of the State's electric requirements. The Shannon, Erne, Lee and Liffey, which were among the principal salmon producing rivers at the turn of the century, were dammed for the generation of hydroelectric power between 1924 and 1957. There have been other dams in recent years, such as the headwaters of the Feale and the Crana in Donegal, with the consequent loss of habitat. The flagship of the hydropower development programme was the large dam built

between 1925 and 1929 at Ardnacrusha (Killimer), at the tidal head
of the Shannon. Migration problems, loss of habitat and predation
by pike on smolt reduced the salmon runs. The River Shannon was
renowned as a producer of large multi-sea-winter salmon to
commercial and recreational fisheries, but this component of the
stock has been lost (O'Farrel et al. 1996). The remaining salmon
fishery went into decline following the construction of the dam at
Parteen, which posed a considerable obstacle to the fish reaching
their spawning grounds (Twomey 1963). The impact of the Lee
hydroelectric scheme was immediate, the salmon stock collapsing
within five years of construction and related to impaired water
quality discharging to the lower river from newly impounded
reservoirs. Twomey (1991) attributed the collapse to de-oxygen-
ation of tailrace water due to large quantities of decomposing
vegetation in the reservoirs during filling in the latter half of 1957.
Predation of descending smolt initially by pike and subsequently by
brown trout was associated with the failure of descending smolt to
pass downstream and their consequent accumulation in reservoirs.
Before hydroelectric development salmon was abundant in the
Erne system, with 100 tons being taken by nets in a fishing season.
Stocks gradually declined after the construction of two generating
stations. Recent counts indicate that the annual run of salmon fell
from a peak of 10,000 in 1966 to an all time low of 300 in 1978. This
decline has been variously attributed to the combined effects of the
salmon disease, ulcerative dermal necrosis, high rates of marine
exploitation, pollution and drainage of nursery tributaries and the
impact of the hydroelectric development at Ballyshannon. Salmon
hatcheries were constructed on these rivers as a mitigation measure,
but have been unsuccessful.

When I first read that I thought, 'Why can't he put in some para-
graph breaks to help the poor reader?' But now I realise that's how he
talks when he gets going; in a relentless stream of rhetoric.

We cycle on silently out of the evil monster's shadow like Dante and
Virgil in the Inferno.

Eventually we stop at a woebegone place where the brackish estuary
water laps at a dismal, flat stony shore. There's dried seaweed, scum-
stained plastic debris and rough grass with occasional cowpats.

John spots the opportunity for a swim and I need to adjust my bike.

He puts his forefinger in the water and proclaims the temperature to be 'dix-huit degrés à la doigt' – pronounced 'dowit', in a French Canadian accent. He must be talking centigrade. John will swim in any old bit of water no matter how dreary or forbidding.

My gears have been giving trouble again, particularly at the front derailleur where the chain keeps coming off. I've decided it's time to master the whole question of how the derailleurs actually work. This time I intend to get right to the heart of the matter.

I crouch down with my tools and try to work it out. The problem seems to be in the rear derailleur settings. Shouldn't be too difficult.

I remember in the past being told it's a bit like trying to adjust the carburettor on a lawnmower or a chain saw. Unless you know what you're doing they said, it's unwise to fiddle with them. So I take it slowly and carefully. But these gear mechanisms only have a few variables to play with, so it ought to be possible to think it through if one stays calm.

There are two derailleurs which work together, one at the pedals and the other at the rear wheel. Each has its own separate gear lever.

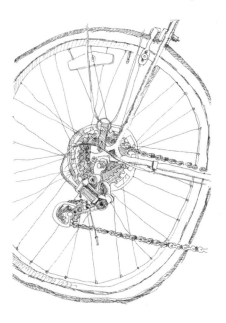

Rear derailleur mechanism on my bike

The derailleur is a beautiful mechanism; complex yet simple, delicate but strong. I love the idea of it. There's a metal arm that lifts and places the chain on to the required cog. With a simple pull or release of the cable this arm lifts the chain off the cog it's already engaged in, moves it a couple of millimetres to the side and lowers it on to the cog you've selected. In some ingenious way, which I can't quite work out, it uses the forward movement of the chain to help in the manoeuvre. You can only change gear when the pedals are going around, you can't do it while freewheeling. So the clever thing is that a simple pull or push of the gear lever moves the arm in three dimensions: up, sideways, forwards and down again. I always think it's a bit like the shell, muscle and sinew arrangement which operates a crab's claw.

Now then . . . Here we go . . . Those are the two screws that adjust the inner and outer limits of the arm. This adjustment seems to be the cause of the problem . . . But I can't quite see why . . . I fiddle about with the rear derailleur, turning the bike upside down to wind the pedals with one hand, using a twisting grip to stop the whole damned thing from falling over, and changing gear with the other hand. I watch as the arm moves the chain, and adjust the screws for more accurate chain placement. But every time I think I've done it, a trial ride shows I haven't.

What I really need is three hands. By now I have black bike-grease all over my hands and some on my glasses. I've had to have a pee during this investigation, so even my flies are embarrassingly smudged.

After more careful thought and a complete reappraisal of the problem, I notice that the whole set-up could be slightly wonky, just by a millimetre or two. So I loosen the metal strap which holds the derailleur mechanism tightly to the frame, and I move the whole thing up and round, very, very slightly.

That seems to do it.

I turn the bike upside down yet again and wind the pedals with one hand while changing gear with the other . . .

Yes! I've fixed it. Perfect.

John has finished his swim so off we go.

After about a hundred yards it becomes clear that I've made a complete mess of the rear derailleur and unbalanced the front one as well, even though I didn't touch it at all. Worse still, I'm quite unable to put it back the way it was before I started.

The result is that I can't change gear at all now and have to limp along stuck in one gear. And it's the one I normally only use on downhills.

The next town is Kilrush. Let's hope there's a bicycle shop with someone who knows how to fix it.

In Kilrush I'm directed to Gleeson's.

Michael Gleeson eventually appears from next door. He looks slowly at me and then at my bike with huge scepticism.

My heart sinks.

'I'll have a look at it when I can,' he says. 'Come back in thirty minutes.' I have the sickening impression that what I've gone and done certainly can't be fixed in this little town. And then what'll I do? I love my old bike.

We drift across the road and into the Haven Arms. Instead of Guinness we both have a cup of tea. We feel drowsy; half asleep in fact. As usual we were quite OK till we got off our bikes, but once we're off we feel totally knackered.

In the Haven Arms there's a large, strange-looking man sitting on a high stool at the bar. He's smoking a cigar, inhaling deeply. He's also sipping whiskey. His movements are ponderously slow. Smoking seems extremely difficult, or is it pleasurable? Perhaps it's some unspeakable hydroelectric drug he's on. Every few minutes he chuckles to himself. Finally he leaves; a mysterious figure.

Maybe he too has damaged his gears and the sight of John and me, a couple of bearded tramps, one with black smudges around his fly-buttons, obviously half-asleep and drinking tea for God's sake, in his local pub, has finally pushed him over the edge. Derailed him for ever.

We finish our tea and wander back over the road to see what Michael Gleeson has been able to do.

Well, huge relief, it turns out he's one of those quiet, modest men you occasionally meet who

Strange looking man in the Haven Arms in Kilrush

are complete masters of their trade. He has fixed it. He's balanced up and reset both front and rear derailleurs for me. He refers to them as 'the mech'; the front mech. and the rear mech.

When we say how impressed we are, Michael Gleeson admits he was once a professional racing cyclist.

He gives me a severe but kind talking-to about how to change gear with derailleurs. This has been explained to me before but of course I'd forgotten it.

The thing is to avoid being linked from a cog on one side of the mech. at the front with one on the other side at the rear. The extreme diagonal pull this creates, says Michael, is what causes all the trouble. In other words, never get caught in the fastest gear in front and the slowest at the rear, or vice versa. It's not difficult to understand, but it's very easy to get caught out particularly when you're tired at the end of the day. It happens when you need to change up in a hurry, or when you're setting off again at traffic lights if you didn't change up before stopping.

We linger a while talking to Michael Gleeson about cycling, he's raced all over Ireland in his day, and abroad. We'd love to hear more about his professional career, but you have to drag it out of him. He's too modest to tell us much.

We ask him about modern bikes and he shows us the latest models he has in the shop.

I ask if my gears might be a little old fashioned. John's are indexed which means you change gear with a satisfactory locating click. Mine aren't; I have to fish around for the position I want, like a trombone player finding the right note, and quite often the mech. jumps cogs.

Michael says, with a kindly smile, that my gears aren't just old fashioned: 'They're stone age.'

John's bike is secondhand, and it's what they call a hybrid. That's halfway between a road racer and a mountain bike. It has straight handlebars. Mine is secondhand too, but it's a thoroughbred, a Puch, made in Austria. I bought it over twenty years ago from a dubious character at the open-air market in Petticoat Lane in London. I've been telling John that my bike is a real greyhound of the road with proper drop handlebars, whereas his, in comparison is a sort of mongrel bike.

That's been my claim. So when he hears about my stone-age gears, John follows up smartly with questions to Michael Gleeson about how generally obsolete and worthless my beautiful bicycle actually is. Like the attorney for the prosecution in those American TV courtroom dramas, he asks a quickfire series of questions about my brakes, frame, spokes and wheels. When he's finished my case is completely demolished. He turns away, triumphantly implying, 'No further questions your honour.'

Michael Gleeson, kind chap that he is, comes to my rescue saying, 'Ah sure those gears are good and sturdy. They've got a few years in them yet, if you treat them properly.' Then, taking in my advanced years and deteriorating physique, he adds, 'They should see you out anyway.'

I make a mental note never to criticise John's bike again.

Repaired and admonished, I'm ready for the road.

29   Rover, young French family

We pedal on up the middle of Co. Clare through Cooraclare, Creegh, and Kilmurry.

Late in the afternoon the road brings us back down to the sea.

The landscape has changed. Kerry was lush and mountainous, washed by the warm waters of the Gulf Stream. Clare is flatter. The trees are smaller. The views are calmer with broad sweeps of horizon and sky.

We come to Quilty and the very first B&B we try has a room for us. It's called St Anthony's.

Grassy fields slope down to the sea half a mile away. You can see Mutton Island from the dining-room window.

View towards Mutton Island from St Anthony's B&B

We get a warm welcome from a busy little dog; a Jack Russell variant. He trots around with us wagging his tall and barking.

'Do be quiet Rover,' says the landlady gently. Her name is Marianne Murnane. She is as modest and retiring as Rover is voluble and bumptious. He probably thinks he has to compensate for her shyness.

When we've settled in, with Rover's assistance, we're told there's a pub, Cooney's, down in the village, where we'll get a decent meal. So down we go.

Quilty is little more than a pub, post office, a few buildings and a tiny harbour built of well-cut granite blocks that looks as though it will last for ever.

We sit outside Cooney's bar and start with a pint. It's a beautiful evening. We are right on the sea watching the evening sun. The next land, looking down the western sky, is John's beloved Newfoundland.

Two herons are chasing each other around the rocks. They unfold surprisingly big wings and flap about squawking, swooping and gliding, and landing awkwardly on long dangling legs. They look like prehistoric gladiators.

'Probably a parent chasing away one of its children,' says John. 'Not a bad idea really; good example to humans. The youngster has to go off and learn to fend for itself.'

Our food arrives; the first course is mussels in garlic with chips and a bottle of red wine. Next comes a wholesome stew followed by bread and butter pudding.

We finish our meal with a glass of whiskey and at last the sun touches the horizon. It takes almost exactly five minutes to travel its own diameter and finally sink into the sea.

Next morning, I'm having my breakfast when along comes a young French couple. They are both tall, handsome and well mannered: 'bien élevé' as the French say. They have a two-year-old baby girl.

They look clean and healthy in the style of well-brought-up young French people; haircuts neat and tidy, dressed in understated harmonious colours and simple but expensive fabrics. And there is a hint of the healthy outdoors; it could be walking or that pat-ball game the French play on the beach with a high net.

In other words, these two look typically French. They are about as far removed from the 'look at me' middle-American equivalent: the Coca-Cola, very new trainers, teeth and tits on show, bouncy hair, Walt Disney culture, as you can possibly get.

People silhouetted against the setting sun outside Cooney's in Quilty

I've said good-morning to them when they first came down to breakfast, but they've quickly let a brittle silence resettle.

When they talk to each other it's in a polite semi-audible whisper.

The only problem is that their lively little girl hasn't got the message yet. She whoops and laughs delightedly much to the embarrassment of her young parents. They don't smile indulgently. That might invite me to share their experience of the little child's joyful antics.

They don't actually tell her that it's wrong to be so uninhibitedly extrovert at the dining table, or that this is one of the sacred shrines of French culture. Instead it's done by example. Each joyous outburst is answered with quiet restrained whispers as though we were all in church. She'll learn how to be French in due course, and thus how to teach her own children in turn. So it is that national character is confirmed and passed on down the generations.

In Ireland, of course, it's quite the opposite. You are taught from the same early age that a silence in the conversation is a social embarrassment, a small disaster. Your parents teach you that it is your duty to entertain, and at school you have to learn poems, songs and stories or to play an instrument for this very purpose. I can still recite two very long poems and sing several dubious songs to prove it.

After breakfast we fish our bikes out of the garage where they were locked away for the night.

Rover trots around with us.

He watches, barking occasionally while we carry out our panniers and get ready to load up and leave.

He shoots off to chase a tractor which is trundling down the road.

When he's dealt with that he comes back proudly wagging his tail; trots around with us, prods us with his nose and sits down for a scratch.

Then, oh dear, he disgraces himself by lifting his leg and piddling all over an already packed bin-liner which John is about to stuff into his pannier.

Rover

Poor Rover, and he was doing so well up to that point. Obviously an Irish dog; brought up to entertain. Nothing whisperingly French in his upbringing; he just needs to rehearse his act a little. I have no doubt he will.

It's a lovely morning. And as we spin along on the road to Lahinch one of those rambling daydreams emerges from the semi-conscious. Cycling can do that. Normally your daydreams evaporate before you can catch them, but occasionally some passing incident jolts you wide awake and brings the thought to the surface. In this flip between the subconscious and the alert, ideas which would normally escape, sometimes get captured and inspected.

'Propensity,' I think to myself. 'Propensity, propensity.' It's been building up in the clear morning air, and now it surfaces, amongst these panoramic views. Modestly it appears like a frog coming up to breathe when it thinks nobody's looking. But being in that cyclist's semi-conscious dream-mode I catch it.

Excitement mounts. I catch John up. 'Propensity,' I shout, 'that could be it. That could be how it's done.'

'What's that?'

'It could be propensity, you know – predisposition.'

'Position? What position?'

'Tell you when we stop.'

These fleeting ideas can evaporate as quickly as they arrive. I've already lost several on the journey so far. In an effort to keep hold of it I say 'propensity' to myself with each turn of the pedals. 'Propensity, propensity, propensity.' Soon it loses all its meaning and its promise of revelation, so I try to banish it.

We dismount for another piddle and blackberries.

'What I was trying to say was, I've got an idea about how the selfish prime motivator can either be suppressed or obeyed in the interests of cooperation. You know? How the cooperate-or-split decision is taken in the best interests of the team.'

'That's the question all right. Got the answer?'

'Well, try this. I was daydreaming about the alphabet fallacy in Dawkins's selfish gene and about language generally, when I realised that there may be an analogy between language learning and the cooperate-or-split decision.'

'I'm always suspicious of analogies and metaphors.'

'But you do like paradigms.'

'Oh all right then.'

'Well anyway try this one: You know how we are not born with a language, ready-made like fingers and toes. Instead we are born with a genetically evolved propensity to learn, speak and teach any language. Any human baby can equally well learn Chinese or Italian.'

'OK, yes. Actually there's some well-known research, by Mazukazu Konishi I think it is, on the American white-crowned sparrow which demonstrates that genetic predisposition or propensity enables them to learn specific languages.'

'There you go: propensity. Excellent. So perhaps all animals that cooperate have achieved this miracle of selective self-restraint by evolving a similar propensity for rules of social behaviour.'

Silence, followed by: 'And that solves your cooperate-or-split dilemma?'

'Well it could. First of all let's remember we're talking about all cooperating animals, not just humans. I'm suggesting that youngsters of a cooperating species are born with a propensity for rules of behaviour, and that as they mature they are taught "good" behaviour by their parents, this is then modified in play and social experiment. In this way they each build up their own personal instant reference library of rules for social behaviour. This then enables the cooperate-or-split dilemma to be resolved intuitively and pragmatically. It's just like learning to speak'

'I'd have to think about that, but it sounds possible.'

'So, ignoring humans for the moment, this dilemma is really no problem at all to cooperating animals, and the decision can be made in an intuitive split-second. Individuals will sometimes get it wrong, but genetic propensity and education ensure that the working team functions adequately. This is because its members can selectively over-ride their individual prime motivators in willing harmony so that the job done gets done. In this way they are able to judge, for example, when it's best either to cooperate by supporting the team at the risk of injury, or to split and avoid injury at the risk of team breakdown.'

'Not bad,' says John. 'You've thought up a nature plus nurture bit of genetic wiring which could enable cooperation by the development of social rules for self-restraint; rules which allow the selective sup-pression of the all powerful selfish prime motivator. You're saying that what the species has evolved is not the rules themselves but the predisposition for rules.'

'Yes exactly.'

'And that the example of language shows that such an evolutionary development is entirely possible.'

'Yes!'

I'm swelling with pride, but then he goes on: 'Ah but what about the social insects? I wonder if ants, bees and wasps use this propensity technique. I rather doubt it, and yet they are terrific cooperators, especially termites.'

There's another silence while I savour the bitter taste of impending failure, then he goes on. 'There are three possibilities. It's been thought of before, it's wrong or it's a new idea, and I'm afraid the chances of that are minimal.'

'Well, I guess you'll be right, but I'm not giving up just yet because the chaos of interstellar dust still seems to be clarifying. For instance, I do still think one of the forming planets could turn out to be the evolutionary origin of morality.'

'And,' I add after a pause, 'if propensity does fail to explain the social insects, does that mean it can't explain vertebrate cooperation either?'

'I'll have to think about that,' says John.

Bloody scientists! Why do they have to be so damned methodical, why can't they just leap ahead like the rest of us?

But my hope of finding a link between cooperation and morality seems so close to failure that I'd rather not pursue that question lest it bring the whole edifice crashing down.

31 The Burren and the Cliffs of Mohr. The pucai plant the obsession

It's not long before we come to the Burren. This is a series of smoothly domed four-hundred-foot limestone hills. They could be crossed in one stride by a giant in his seven-league boots.

John and I are just cycling round the coast of this mysterious landscape and it certainly won't reveal its magic to such superficial visitors. Nevertheless, even to us, it feels strange and different.

There are puffins and whales, and caves with prehistoric human and animal remains and early Christian bones and artefacts. There are pine martens, foxes, badgers and ravens. The list goes on and on. There are lots of little wild flowers all over the place. Keen gardeners tell about one or two plants here which exist nowhere else in the world. The Burren also happens to be a great place for Irish music and folklore.

But sadly we are just pedalling through and past it all.

Soon we come to the Cliffs of Mohr. The place is crawling with tourists. There is a three-acre car park and a separate two-acre coach park. There are about ten, maybe fifteen coaches, parked here. Most have their engines throbbing in neutral to keep their air-conditioning and fridges going.

There are gypsies, buskers and dubious-looking characters about, so we prop our bikes against a low wall, very carefully locked together.

You don't see the actual cliffs or even the sea until the last minute because you come up on them from behind. Sometimes sea cliffs occur on the down side of a mountain after it has reached its highest point and the ground is sloping down again towards the sea, but not in this case. Here the land is still rising, and seems to end in the sky. You go up a paved pathway past people walking back down, and suddenly the land ends right below your feet.

The magnificent cliffs of Mohr are black, perpendicular and very high. They drop straight into the sea far – echoingly far – below. The viewing place is close to the cliff edge and the immense vertical drop is terrifying. Sea birds are wheeling around down there. Occasionally one lands on the cliff wall. There's a strong wind.

John, of course, goes right up to the edge and peers over. I stay well back; tingling with fear at the thought of a human body, mine even, falling out into the winds of space like a rag doll. The fear starts in my legs and spreads upward into my bowels.

I do wish he'd come back from there.

People are taking cliff-view photos all around us. An Italian couple asks John would he take a shot of them with their camera. He poses them on the edge, in the wind, makes the 'back a little further' joke, and then snaps them.

Though I know I should, I don't attempt a drawing. I don't seem to have the mental energy to assimilate the potent visual combination of mass tourism with natural grandeur. Feeling feeble-gutted I shirk it. Or maybe it's the feeling that if you try to capture magic it will evaporate.

We queue for a cup of tea and a sticky-cake in the Cliffs of Mohr Tea Rooms.

'Don't those cliffs put us in our place,' says John.

'Don't thy just!'

This demonstration that man's comic arrogance on his rusty cart is overshadowed by nature's glory reminds me that my chances of linking morality to cooperation seem to have collapsed.

We pay the bill and pedal along the north shore of the Burren. We're heading east now.

At half-ten we stop for a pee where the hills consist of flat limestone slabs with deep cracks between them. These narrow crevices are two or three feet deep, sometimes more, and they go at crazy angles in fifty-foot-long, crisis-cross lines. It's as though the dome shaped hills are covered with a stone casing and the local giant has come along and slashed it with a Stanley knife in a furious fit of vandalism. The limestone is a pale bluish grey. Down at the bottom of the crevices you can see bright little flowers. These are said to include a unique gentian and several rare species of orchid.

Burren landscape: limestone with deep crevices

Black Head lighthouse comes next. It's a modest little unmanned building on the shore to our left just below the road. The rocks down there are all over the place. They are the same limestone slabs except that they've obviously been broken up and hurled about in the violent storms that occasionally batter this Atlantic shore.

I'm not surprised when in this hallucinatory landscape three pucai appear. They are playing along the shore, floating above the rocks, tumbling about in the pearly light.

They feel like an idea or an obsession infiltrating my semi-conscious.

Eventually they fade away into the air and it's not till I regain my focus on the real world, that I realise I've been daydreaming about propensity again.

It can be difficult at times to distinguish between a puca and an idea. Sometimes it's almost impossible to tell them apart. Sometimes what you think is a puca turns out to be a good idea. More often it's the other way round.

*Pucai looking for mischief on the north Burren shore
near the Black Head lighthouse*

I don't realise it yet but this idea about propensity is going to obsess my thoughts for the rest of our journey back to Cork. It's going to combine cooperation and morality, and with John's help, it's going to answer the Awful Question and provide explanations and solutions for much of man's social behaviour. These are going to include such diverse questions as bullying, terrorism, the vital importance of the gutter press, the basis of law and even the meaning of life.

32   John uses the driver ant to rediscover the trail. Caught by the tide. The pucai use my sketchbook for a message. *Cooperation among driver ants and robots. Extreme cooperation. The cooperate-or-split dilemma is no dilemma to other animals*

We cross the county border from Clare into Galway. In fact it's also the border between Munster and Connacht. These milestones are nice little marks of progress and achievement. They move you up the map. Could you see the difference between Munster and Connacht if you were standing on the moon? . . . With binoculars? . . . We may be insignificant little specs in the scheme of things, but we're inching along.

At about half-one we come to Aughinish Bay. It's a nondescript estuary full of that dirty reddish-brown seaweed and pungently stinking of it too; the way only exposed seaweed can. The tide is out and it's trying to rain.

John thinks this might be a good place for a swim. The very idea makes me shiver. As swims go this one will be more to do with wild life than the usual idea of sun-drenched Mediterranean beaches: more a case of scum, seaweed and shrimps than sun, sea and sex. We pedal down a dirt track to the shore.

There's a small mound. It's a piece of raised ground with a bit of streaky-grey, methane-fluffy sand and some rocks partially covered with the smelly seaweed.

Looks the best place for lunch. It'll be covered when the tide comes in but that won't be for hours.

We push our bikes over there.

I can remember as a little boy, being impressed by Merrion Strand in Dublin Bay. How strange it was that some days it was all sand for miles, and on other days it was obviously deep water. My mother explained about the tides. She told me about the tide coming in over the sand at a place called Morecombe Bay in England, and about how it comes roaring in 'at the speed of a galloping horse'. I visualised a huge wave; a wall of water ten-feet high, which came crashing and foaming in every day, and I longed to see this spectacular event. She said that people regularly got drowned there. They went out collecting cockles and got cut off by the tide. Later in life I learnt with a twinge of sadness that what actually happens is rather less dramatic. People do occasionally get cut off, it's true, and if there's a fog they can become disoriented and be drowned. And the tide does indeed race across the sand; it comes in little surges rather than at an even pace. But sadly it isn't a ten-foot wall of crashing, foaming water.

Never mind. The tide coming in at the speed of a galloping horse is still one of my favourite images. The horse's tail is flailing in the wind and you can hear the drumming of its hoofs and see the sand fly. Its got its head high in the air and is rolling its eyes. You can see right up its huge nostrils as it gallops ahead of the crashing wave. I describe it to John pointing out that we'd better be careful not to get cut off.

It's overcast, windy and not at all warm but John gets into his bathing pants and picks his way through the rocks and seaweed into the grey water of the estuary. He plunges in without hesitation and swims vigorously about.

As I've already noticed, John, the true marine biologist, will muck about in any old bit of water. In fact the seaweed-smelly shore has far more fertility and abundance of wildlife for him than a nice clean beach. He considers a beach to be sterile. According to him a beach is one of nature's rubbish dumps where dead things: driftwood, broken shells, crab claws, plastic bottles and bits of expanded polystyrene, and, of course, sand, are deposited by the sea.

Ignoring the seaweed's brackish smell and its cold clammy slap, he'll turn it over and find all sorts of muscular and lively little creatures: sandhoppers, crabs, worms, shrimps and stubby little spiky fish. This is nature in abundance, and animal life higher up the food chain; larger fish, otters, herons and seals will feed on it.

Living things eat all day long and other life forms is what they eat. For centuries physicists have been searching for the secret of perpetual motion, and yet here it is under their very eyes. Come to think of it, the fact that life is eating itself all day long is almost a definition of life.

To John even the seaweed isn't just seaweed; there are many different sorts. They have names like kelp, porphyra, oar weed and bladder wrack. He tells me about the giant Kelp, *Macrocystis*; it grows to over three hundred feet long and being just one stage above bacteria is one of the most primitive life forms on earth.

I try to get on with a watercolour but it's too windy and there are occasional drops of rain.

Eventually John comes out looking blue with cold. He gets dressed and we settle down to an excellent lunch of mix 'n' squash. The main ingredients are a tin of sardines, bread, some of that lovely bright orange Irish Cheddar, a raw onion, whiskey cake, an apple and some black chocolate. Doesn't sound gastronomic, I know, but as usual it's consistently good.

'Had any more ideas?' says John.

But I'm feeling a bit withdrawn. 'You know,' he says, 'about propensity and all that. It seemed to have great potential.'

'Not really, no. I did think it was exciting at the time, and I had intended to work it through properly; you know, write it out in my sketchbook or something. But, as you pointed out, the social insects are terrific cooperators and it seems highly improbable that they can use a language-like propensity. Well that sort of did it. I went off the whole idea.'

'Oh that's too bad. I've been looking forward to sorting it all out. I don't think you should give up yet. Biologists have done very little on cooperation; they're still only scratching the surface. And they certainly haven't considered morality to be in their competence.'

His reluctance to abandon the subject fuels his rhetoric. 'And yet cooperation as a behaviour can be immensely powerful. It must be about the most effective ploy that nature has ever invented. In a competition for survival, even if carried out over decades, I would be much more frightened of a cooperator than a solitary.

'Ants, for example are amazing cooperators; astonishingly effective and fearsome for such a small creature.'

He happens to be reading E. O. Wilson's *The Diversity of Life*. He fishes it out. 'Yes here we are; this is what he says about driver ants.'

He reads it to me: 'For millions of years the great herbivores of sub-Saharan Africa ranged freely over the vast parklands, creating a mosaic of habitats, a swathe of grassland here, an acacia copse or remnant of riverine forest there, reed lined pools grown from mud wallows scattered widely about. The total effect was a huge enrichment of biological diversity.

'Focusing now from the kilometre reach of elephants to grass root level, we find a wholly different class of keystone species. Where big mammals control the vegetation structure, a colony of driver ants at their feet captures millions of victims each day and alters the nature of the community of small animals. Viewed a few meters away, a driver ant raiding column seems a living thing, a giant pseudopodium reaching out to engulf its prey. The victims are snared with hook-shaped jaws, stung to death, and carried to the bivouac, a labyrinth of underground tunnels and chambers housing the queen and immature forms. Each expeditionary force comprises several million workers who flow out of this retreat. The hungry legions emerging from the bivouac are like an expanding sheet that lengthens into a tree like formation. The trunk grows from the nest, the crown expands as an advancing front, and the numerous branches pour back and forth between the two. The swarm is shaped but leaderless. Excited workers rush back and forth throughout its length at an average speed of a centimetre per second. Those in the van press forward for a short distance and then fall back to yield their front position to other runners. The feeder columns resemble thick black ropes laid along the ground, slowly writhing from side to side. The front, advancing at twenty meters an hour, blankets all the ground and low vegetation in its path. The columns expand into it like a river entering a delta, where workers race back and forth in a feeding frenzy, consuming most of the insects, spiders and other invertebrates in their path, attacking snakes and other large animals unable to move away. Day after day the driver ants scythe through the animal life around their bivouac. They reduce its biomass and change the proportions of species. The most active flying insects escape. So do invertebrate animals too small to be noticed by the ants, particularly roundworms, mites and springtails. Other invertebrates and insects are hit hard. One driver-ant colony, comprising as many as twenty million workers – all daughters of a single mother queen – is a heavy burden for the ecosystem to bear. Even the insectivorous birds must fly to a different spot to find enough food.'

'Bleedin' Ada! That is impressive.'

'Isn't it just! Can you imagine what behavioural marvels these tiny primitive animals must be capable of? I mean when relating to each other.'

'Yes, I've always been fascinated by ants.'

He's into his stride now. 'Think of robots. They're used for difficult or dangerous jobs like recovering equipment lost down oil wells, guiding miniature cameras inside human bodies and dealing with breakdowns in space craft. So cooperating robots are theoretically possible too, and one can think of the design features required in each individual member of a team of robots to enable them to work together to get a job done.'

'OK go on.'

'Well, individual robots would have to be able to recognise each other and to communicate together. They would be programmed to work under a leader. They would have to be able to replace an injured leader. They would have to make wise and fast judgements as to whether to act or hold back: cooperate or split as you put it. The computer programming required would be complex beyond comprehension. This demonstrates what a behavioural miracle co-operating animals routinely perform, including the honeybee, the termite and the tiniest ant.'

'But didn't we agree that the social insects probably don't use social codes of self-restraint to enable them to cooperate?'

'We did, yes,' says John patiently. 'But that's not the point; as we said the African wild dogs probably do, and they are vertebrates, so the illustration still applies.'

He's right!

'Don't you see,' he says, 'that it's actually cooperation which has enabled us to achieve our amazing ecological dominance. Space exploration and the cloning of living creatures would have been completely impossible without cooperation. A race of hermits no matter how intelligent or articulate, could never have achieved these things. People think that superior intelligence, culture and language are the gifts which set us apart from other animals. But that's wrong; it's not intelligence which is our "crowning glory"; it's our ability to cooperate.'

'Yes I suppose you're right. What really sets us apart could be called extreme cooperation. In the same way that swifts and arctic terns have evolved extreme flying, and giraffes have evolved extreme necks what really distinguishes humans is extreme cooperation. And by the way, the Awful Question we were deploring earlier demonstrates very clearly that we certainly haven't perfected it yet.'

But John's following a different line of thought. 'Yes OK, but you were definitely on to something,' he says, 'with all that stuff about propensity. What was it you said? Something about how the selfish prime motivator can be selectively suppressed by an evolved propensity; a propensity which is very similar to our evolved propensity for language. Was that it?'

'Yes that's about it.'

'Well, You mustn't let it all drop.'

'No. Right oh.'

Then I remember: 'Well actually, before your question about the social insects floored me, I was going to speculate about the philosophical angle. What must the self-restraining mechanism actually feel like to animals. I was going to go into the subjective side of it all, where you scientists fear to tread. And, of course, that question can be asked of vertebrates, the social insects can indeed be left out of it.'

'How do you mean?'

'I was talking about team members using genetic propensity plus education. So even though individuals will sometimes get it wrong, the team itself works well, with members selectively over-riding their prime motivators in harmony to get the job done.'

'OK. Yes.'

'Well what does it feel like and what goes on amongst cooperating animals when they work together?'

'Search me.'

'I had an imaginary conversation with an African wild dog. You remember – *Lycaon pictus*.'

'They can lock you up for that sort of thing, you know.'

' "*Lycaon* old chap," I say, conjuring up a wild dog to talk to us, "tell me this; how come in a fast-moving skirmish you are able to solve these immensely complicated cooperate-or-split problems in the twinkling of an eye?"'

' "You what?" says *Lycaon*.

' "How do you decide if it's best to hold back for fear of injury, or take a brave risk for the good of the team? An important personal decision might affect your whole tribe; get it wrong either way and you could all suffer badly. It's like a chess move whose consequences can be complicated and far-reaching. How do you do it?"'

' "Oh, I see what you mean," says *Lycaon*. "I've never really thought about it. It's no problem at all; comes with experience; second nature really. If we stopped to think about it we'd almost certainly mess it up."'

' "Think of those crazy cricket or baseball games you humans play."
he says. "The batsman facing a fast bowler doesn't analyse the flight of
the fizzing ball like a chess player. Intuition takes over, and that's a
totally different mental process. It's a learned skill in which genetic
predisposition is combined with coaching, practice and experience to
tell him whether to swipe or duck; cooperate or split." '

'And *Lycaon* is absolutely right,' I say. 'The soldier receiving his VC
invariably tells the admiring world press afterwards that he really
didn't think about bravery at the time; it just seemed the right thing to
do. The cooperate-or-split question is not like a chess move at all. It
only resembles one when you subject the process to cold cerebral
analysis.'

'And where does that get us?' says John.

I'm surprised at his scepticism. Then I realise that, for him, I've
strayed too far from biology into philosophy, and in a perverse way
that gives me encouragement.

'I'm not sure, but even though the social insects might have
escaped, perhaps we may still be able to pin down the elusive idea of
morality, at least in vertebrates. And that would be a very big deal.'

'Hmm . . . '

Needing time for thought we both go silent and take in our
surroundings.

'Crikey!' says John suddenly. 'The tide's come in.'

And so it has. It's come in fast. If not at the speed of a galloping
horse, then at least as fast as a strolling donkey. We're now sitting on
a little island surrounded by surprisingly deep water.

Disaster . . . Talking too much, as usual.

The fluffy grey sand is bubbling gently as the water rises. There's
no time to lose. At the nearest point to the shore it's already up to our
knees.

John unhooks his panniers and lifts his bike across. But there are
rocks under the water now and I'm afraid that if I try to carry my bike,
I might fall over them, so I decide to leave my panniers on, and wheel
my bike through the water.

Big mistake. It's deeper than I thought.

In mid-channel my sketchbook falls into the water and starts to
float away. My panniers also get half submerged.

In a dripping muddle I scramble everything across to dry land and
try to minimise the damage.

First I prop up my sketchbook against a wall to drain off. Next I pick the seaweed out of my spokes and derailleur 'mechs'. It's lucky Michael Gleeson isn't here to see this. Then I anxiously look to see what damage I've done to my sketchbook.

The line drawings are OK, thank goodness, but the watercolours and the binding have suffered.

In a panic I check the most successful watercolours; the ones I like best, for example the two bikes propped together at Castlegregory, the view of Mutton Island at Quilty and the view from Lakerise B&B in Waterville. Mercifully, and indeed rather strangely, all the best ones seem to be OK. It's only the bad watercolours, the failures, which have been smudged by running paint.

It's rather amazing really. Have the pucai have been at work here? It seems that first they cast a spell that made us ignore the incoming tide, even though we had joked about the risk. Then they made me stumble as I waded back so that my sketchbook fell in. And then they arranged, like editors, for the sea to damage the bad watercolours while leaving the better ones unaffected.

My sketchbook is the medium through which the pucai appear. If I didn't doodle absent-mindedly in it I don't suppose I'd notice them at all. So I wonder is this a message from them? A warning that though it's OK to acknowledge their presence, and even to draw them, it's definitely not on to mock or annoy them in any way.

And . . . I wonder . . . Might it even be a hint that, if I'm respectful, they might help me with the awful question of man's appalling behaviour? You never know with the pucai.

John waits without a hint of impatience for at least half an hour while I try to minimise the damage to my sketchbook.

33 *Natural selection occurs between rules of behaviour. Humans wrongly rationalise morality as an absolute; morality is the language of cooperation*

We stop for an afternoon pint at a nice little pub by a river.

Sitting at an outside table, I lay my sodden sketchbook out to dry while we wait for our pints to appear.

Now I slowly begin to recognise what's been staring me in the face for the past twenty-four hours. It never ceases to amaze me how ideas can be so near and yet remain unnoticed.

'What?' says John. 'More philosophy?' He must have seen me lighting up.

'I think I've got it. It's an evolutionary theory of morality, and it links philosophy to science.'

'OK, so scientifically speaking what is morality?'

'Yes, that is the big question . . . Well try this,' I say, taking a deep breath. 'I suggest it's not an eternal principle like $2 + 2 = 4$; it's an animal cooperator procedure. So it can't be a uniquely human absolute as most philosophers claim.'

'Does that mean it's not fixed for all people at all times, and animals can have it too?'

'Right. I'm saying that morality – you know, the whole question of good and evil, right and wrong – is like language in that flexible, selective rules of social behaviour are adopted, taught and learnt by a particular tribe solely for its own use. Different tribes can, and do adopt different rules, and the tribe which adopts the most appropriate rules for its particular situation will have a prosperity-and-survival advantage over neighbours with less appropriate rules. That's how ancient Athens eventually got the better of Sparta despite losing the Peloponnesian war. You could call this the natural selection of codes of behaviour or social rules.'

'How do you mean exactly?'

'Well the tribe which tolerates stealing, lying and cruelty will risk takeover by any neighbouring tribes whose rules are more conducive to cooperation. If that happens the rules that tolerate stealing, lying and cruelty will die out; they'll be replaced by the rules of the surviving tribe. Like I say that's the natural selection of rules.'

'Phew!' says John.

Our pints have arrived but I've only just started. 'As I see it there are two aspects to these rules: flexibility and selectivity. First of all the flexibility of rules is illustrated by the differences in acceptable clothes worn in a Saudi Arabian bazaar and on a Mediterranean beach. And secondly, as we've said, the selective application of social rules becomes obvious when you recognise the cooperate-or-split dilemma. To put it another way; when a politician tells a lie it's normal, but if a doctor does she risks being taken to court.

'So the principles of good behaviour are too elusive to be written down for all time. They shade from forbidding murder to spitting in the street. We want to prove them like a Euclidian proof in geometry.

But we can't. There are rules some people seem able to violate with impunity while others are punished. Big corporations seem able to ignore most rules.

'And these rules have an incredibly persuasive small still voice attached. What is this conscience thing which says, "Nobody's looking but I mustn't just slip that little digital camera into my pocket," or, "Nobody would find out, and it would be the simplest thing in the world, but I can't have sex with that gorgeous man."? Where does this voice come from? How does it work? And why can't we define it?'

'OK, OK.'

'No but here's what I'm getting at. What I've just realised is that we can now disentangle the crazy muddles philosophers usually get into when they discuss ethics. I'm saying that though all cooperating vertebrates inherit the propensity for self-restraint, only humans try to reason it through verbally. Only humans can speak and write. But we've led ourselves up the garden path with faulty reasoning. We've mistakenly believed that we should be able to pin up our own particular tribal codes on the noticeboard for use by all mankind. We believe them to be universal and absolute, and that they should be written into international law on tablets of stone. But sadly that's impossible because codes of behaviour have to be both flexibly adaptable and selectively applied.'

'Go on, that seems to be quite important.'

'I've said it really. The rules have to be both flexible and selective, so the huge and rigid edifices we've built for ourselves, for example in Christian and Islamic ethics, democracy and communism, are much too brittle to withstand international analysis. They can't apply across cultural boundaries or endure for millennia, and they certainly can't apply rigidly in everyday life because individuals must be free to cooperate or split; swipe or duck as Lycaon put it.'

'So you're saying morality, the whole huge question of what's right and what's wrong, is simply the language of cooperation.'

Brilliant! He's pinned the idea perfectly with a single phrase, but before I can express my delight he goes on: 'Does that mean that Christ and Mohammed were barking up the wrong tree then?'

'Well yes I suppose it does, and so were Socrates, Plato, Hume, Kant, Bentham and Marx to name but a few. Some were on the right track though, especially Zeno, Aristotle and Machiavelli. As I've already said it's obvious that philosophers have failed to explain morality because Islam disagrees with Christianity, and the followers of Plato disagree with those of Aristotle.'

'Ah! so science rules OK then?'

'I didn't say that. All you lot have been able to come up with so far is the alphabet soup of gene thinking and the circular arguments of game theory.'

Now I'm the one who's sounding like a barrister summing up in court: 'Morality tantalises us for two reasons. First we still don't understand its origin. And second we believe morality, when we do eventually pin it down, will reveal an absolute and God-like principle, like $2 + 2 = 4$, which will be the basis for universal fixed codes of behaviour, and law, for all peoples at all times. But these beliefs, unfortunately, turn out to be untrue. They're wishful thinking.

'It's a bit shocking – almost blasphemous – to say that virtue is not intrinsically virtuous at all. But that's the truth of it. Good behaviour is simply a biological necessity; without it we couldn't cooperate, and if we didn't cooperate we would immediately become extinct.'

'So,' says John, 'when the big bang is finally linked up with quantum physics we still won't have a universal moral code.'

'That's right. What was it you just said? Morality is the language of cooperation; that puts it perfectly; it's a language not a pre-existing principle.'

My words have been tumbling out in a gush. The people at the next table glance at us. John clears his throat theatrically and looks into the middle distance with that 'he's not with me' look in his eye. My raised voice and wild eyes must be making me look a little dotty. But I'm relieved to have spewed it all out.

John pretending he's not with me

In an effort to calm down I carefully separate some of the sodden pages in my sketchbook, to help it to dry in the breeze.

34   Clarinbridge, oyster festival

We've left the Burren behind. The countryside gets flatter and flatter like the sea calming down after a storm.

Eventually at half-four we come to Clarinbridge and find a room at the Claringrove B&B.

When at first she opens the door the landlady looks us over very carefully. You can almost hear her thinking 'Is this the IRA? Should I call the Garda?' As for us, we are tired, salt-water damp and dirty and anxious as to whether she'll let us in.

It's no good trying the 'my good woman' approach; putting on upper class English accents. The thing is we are just not made that way and would probably get the giggles. Then we'd certainly be turned away. We might have carried it off fifty years ago but now we just stand there smiling sweetly through our beards and mentally wringing our hands. In fact we're trying to look pathetic, which isn't difficult. Luckily we've taken our stupid-looking helmets off. After a pause she relents and lets us in. She's seen loonies in her day and these two look harmless enough.

It's a lovely big comfortable B&B. She gives us a cup of tea and has a chat. Yes of course we can use her washing machine to clean our sweaty, mud-splattered clothes but we'll have to operate it ourselves because she's going out.

We settle in, unpack and shower.

The Clarin River flows right past the house and John fancies a quick flip of the rod before we go out to eat, so off he goes with his rod to try the evening rise.

I stay to dry my sketchbook and to oversee our laundry.

I lay the sketchbook out on a radiator to dry, turning the pages over at regular five-minute intervals. And I try to hold the binding in the correct shape while the glue and stitching dry off.

Eventually John gets back. He didn't do any fishing because the river has been straightened and enclosed between stone walls for about a mile. It was done years ago and the river would be quite hopeless for fishing. He didn't even try. There's expert knowledge for you.

The landlady mentions Paddy Burke's, just down the road in

Clarinbridge. But she says it's running its annual oyster festival this very week, so we might have difficulty getting a table.

We get smartened up and cycle down there to try our luck.

The restaurant is absolutely packed, but they manage to squeeze us in. This is done in a manner that mixes kindness with a hint that they don't normally let people in if they aren't either film stars or criminals. I have the clear impression that if we were respectably dressed and properly shaved we would certainly have been turned away.

Paddy Burke's is very proud of itself. On the walls it has oyster festival memorabilia. There are photographs and cartoons of famous people from scallywags to pop idols all eating oysters. There are cuttings of newspaper articles saying what a great place it is, and posters advertising previous years' festivals.

We have a terrific meal based on oysters and Guinness.

35   Galway, Gaeltacht, rain and grim ride. *A cooperating group is a quasi-living organism. Slime-mould behaviour. Group selection rules OK. Groups must be amoral. Ockham's Razor applies*

There's nobody about when I get up next morning, so I tiptoe into the kitchen to make myself a cup of tea.

The weather looks OK: it's quiet and promising. My sketchbook has more or less dried, so I do a bit of drawing and recording in it. I tell it that we did 31 miles yesterday, it was our fifteenth day, and we've done about 400 miles so far – that sort of thing.

People we meet say holiday bookings are down this year. But then if you ask them people will tell you anything. They seldom know or understand the trend in their lives, and they are somehow compelled to tell you what they think you want to hear. It's the same the world over. The only people you always get the truth from are children, even if it's only to tell you that they don't know, in which case that is indeed the truth.

There is just one exception to this 'tell them what you think they want to hear' rule and it is of course the French. They get their kicks by telling you what you don't want to hear.

I make a note in my sketchbook to stop being rude about the French. I love them; they have terrific character and style and they do play great rugby.

John surfaces. We collect our laundry, and soon it's time for us to pay and leave.

We reach the main road from Dublin to Galway. Fast cars and powerful lorries thunder past. We feel flimsy and vulnerable.

Wet clouds have chased away the promising start to the day. It begins to rain again, fine at first but soon it gets heavier and heavier. The cars and lorries all have their windscreen wipers fully on. There's a nasty wet headwind.

I want to shelter but John prefers to push on and get off this splashing, noisy, dirty main road. He's right, so we do.

Then I get a slow puncture in my front tyre. Every mile I have to get off and pump in more air. And every time I do so the wet wind, the thundering lorry spray and surface grit swirls around my skinny legs and up inside my shorts.

We limp into Galway dripping wet.

We stop at a supermarket on the outskirts of town to buy picnic supplies and I put a new inner tube in my front tyre. That fixes it.

Mercifully the rain eases off to a drizzle.

The first thing we do in Galway is make a beeline for the Salmon Bridge over the Corrib River. At the right time of year you can look over the parapet and see several hundred salmon waiting to move on upstream to their spawning beds. But unfortunately there are none to be seen today. With his X-ray eyes John finally spots one. Two more then give themselves away by flashing their silvery sides as they investigate the riverbed, but that's it, we don't see any more.

'Grilse,' says John in an offhand sort of way.

'What exactly is a grilse,' I ask.

'It's a salmon that has only stayed one year at sea. You can tell they are grilse by their size. Look: see, they're small twenty-inch fish. They'll go up and spawn. Then most of them will die, but not all.'

View from the Salmon Bridge in Galway

Wet street scene in Galway

The rain gets even worse. Then it develops into a cloudburst. Galway is full of people. The pavements are packed with shoppers and holidaymakers in light summer clothes. They get soaked and take cover. Occasionally people dash from one doorway to the next. The gutters quickly fill up with rivulets of water. Umbrellas are opened. Cars splash slowly along in the wet.

We quickly dismount, lock our bikes and nip into a flashy café to shelter. It's a fast food joint. We sit in a big window and have coffee and buns while we look out at the people dodging about in the down-pour outside.

Eventually it eases off slightly and there is a patch of brighter sky coming in off the Atlantic, so on we go.

We cycle out along the south shore of Galway Bay. Dismal straggling suburbs stretch on for several miles.

Punching into a half-gale we pass through Salthill. This is Galway's seaside playground. But its summer-holiday smile is stained by the rain, and its flags and municipal shrubs are thrashing about in the wind.

After about six miles we come to Barna.

We stop at Donnelly's Bar. Drenched – we are like drowned rats. The place is full of people who would clearly rather be out on the beach, but there is a cheerful, if somewhat wet and steamy, atmosphere and there is a healthy smell of Guinness. We ask is it OK to eat our mix 'n' squash in the bar. 'Sure of course it is,' says the lad pulling the pints and all's well.

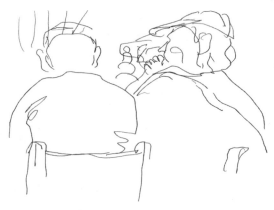

People at the bar in Donnelly's, Barna

We chat to various people including some pretty girls who are giggling and going on at the table next to us. They are doing summer-holiday jobs as chambermaids in the local boarding houses and have hilarious humanity-on-holiday stories to swap.

Like corks in a millrace, more thoughts about cooperation being the language of morality bob to the surface through this chatter.

'I expect the little green men in the Martian space ship are actually sterile females.'

'You what?' John braces himself for action. 'I'm not with you.'

'You know, like those driver ants, the bit you read out yesterday – was it yesterday?'

'Possibly,' he says; the cautious scientist once more.

'I was imagining a Martian watching us from her space ship. She would notice that a cooperating group of humans behaves just like a single living organism, with a quasi-mind of its own. I thought of a football team. Like an amoeba it has a nucleus and nervous system in its captain and manager. It also has a skin or boundary in its finite membership. And it acts with a purpose to do things: to move forward and score goals. A football team has a corporate will; it is self-aware, it even has corporate moods; such as confidence and despair, which are actually vitally important. The corporate will is ultimately independent of the will of its captain and manager. The thing is, you can say exactly the same of any manufacturing company.'

'Yes. I get it. I think you're right,' says John. 'That bit about driver ants did actually regard the colony as a single quasi-living organism. The slime mould is another good example. The same can be said of hyenas and humans.'

'Tell me again about the slime mould, it sounded quite amazing.'

It's in one of the books he's brought along, so he goes and fishes it out of his pannier. 'The slime mould is all the rage in popular science at the moment,' he says.

'Let's see . . . Yes here it is. Latin name *Physarum polycephalum*. I won't read it all out but basically this is what it says.

'It consists of about a hundred thousand amoebae that mess about together, but as separate individuals, until they need to move on. When that happens they come together in a tight cooperative unit, which can either move off almost like a tiny slug, or else turn itself into a breeding unit in which some individuals forgo reproduction to perform structural functions and others produce breeding spores which blow away in the wind to start up new colonies.'

'Incredible! Such tiny things. Makes you realise how arrogant humans are in thinking they are superior to animals.'

'Yes and slime moulds aren't even animals; they're almost a fungus. 'But,' he continues, 'what gets me is how do they communicate?'

'Communicate?'

'Well these hundred thousand individuals must decide whether it's best to move on or to reproduce. Once the decision is taken, and that's a marvel in its own right, how is the message put out to all the others?'

'Could it be,' he goes on, 'that somehow the prime motivator we've been talking about is, amongst them, a shared rather than an individual thing? Is the pain and pleasure shared, through a communication system, in common among all the different individuals in the cooperative? Something like that must happen. These individuals, remember, do specialised jobs, but only sometimes. The jobs have to be prioritised and coordinated in order for the cooperative to work. What I mean is that for the cooperative to find food, avoid pain and destruction, to attack, defend, and to reproduce, the individual amoebae must decide exactly when to drop what they are doing and, recognising other members of their own species, get together with them to move on or reproduce. There can be no other way to describe it. They must have some system of intercommunication.

'And,' he goes on, 'we're saying this applies in varying degrees to all cooperating animals; when cooperating they all behave like single, discrete organisms. They share a communal prime motivator and they intercommunicate to do so.'

'That's exactly what I mean! A human cooperating group also has a quasi-mind of its own! Not a true mind but shared or corporate moods and ambitions.'

'Yes,' says John, 'but does that get us anywhere? I'm sorry but I don't think this sort of assertion can be proved biologically. It's just a metaphor; it's potentially useful for organising one's thoughts, but it is not a scientific fact.'

Sensing my disappointment he continues. 'Well maybe it's enough to say that if cooperating groups invariably act like single discrete organisms when doing their work; hunting, running a business, raising a family, building a lair, then the metaphor is sound. As they say, if it looks like a duck, walks like a duck and quacks like a duck, then it is a duck. So I suppose it could be a step in the right direction.'

He's brought me back down to earth.

There's nothing particularly new in this quasi-mind idea, I realise. It has been plainly obvious since cooperation began millions of years ago, but maybe the quasi-mind of the tribe should be taken more seriously, at least in the study of human behaviour.

'It might be worth developing,' I say in a hopeful little voice, 'and the idea of having to suppress the prime motivator in order to cooperate, supports the metaphor of the group as an organism. I mean; when rules of self-restraint are adopted by the group and then taught by it, this adoption and teaching process imparts a feeling of shared identity. I see it as a self-perpetuating loop in which the exercising of an inherited predisposition helps to weld the tribe into a functioning unit. And, certainly in humans, the members of the tribe are proud of its traditions and symbols and of their membership. They seek out a tribal mind, and when it's established they cherish it.'

'That reminds me of those music-hall jokes about foreigners,' says

John. 'You know; making the Belgians so very Belgian, or the Turks so Turkish. What makes them funny is that though they're insulting, they are absolutely true. Nationalities are amazingly different. The English are opportunist, hypocritical hooligans, and have been for centuries. The Americans are naïve, boastful, friendly. Your average Johnny Frenchman is logical, eccentric, insular. And the Germans! They have the most distinct characteristics of all. The real thing about the Germans is that they're so obedient. That's what German jokes are all about. I mean the way they cooperate so enthusiastically among themselves – not with outsiders of course. Groups don't do that. Then you have the Italians who are quite the opposite. Obedience in Italy is paper thin, it's every man for himself, lying is natural and devil take the hindmost.'

Hold on, I think to myself. What was that he said about the Germans? I thought he was about to talk about them going around in comical groups singing 'Umpah! Umpah!' songs, but he didn't; he said that groups don't cooperate with outsiders. Is there a clue in there somewhere?

Then suddenly I get it. 'You're absolutely right, you're spot-on with what you said about the Germans. The Martian would immediately notice that all cooperators, humans included, have two distinct modes of behaviour: one as individuals working together and the other as the tribes – the teams – themselves.'

John's big eyes and shaggy beard radiate the calm scepticism of the scientist lying in wait to puncture the philosopher's balloon.

'This could be the big one!' I say while I'm searching desperately for where to start. 'We've already said that teams can be regarded biologically as discrete units with quasi-minds of their own. This is reinforced by the claim that the true unit of Darwinian selection is the tribe, not the individual. In fact it's a huge flaw in gene thinking and game theory that they resist this.'

'Just explain that again.'

'Well, they dislike the idea that in a cooperating animal the chances of survival and prosperity can be better for an average member of the fittest tribe than they are for the fittest member of an average tribe. When things get tough it's the tribe that survives or goes under; carrying the individual along with it. The slime mould is an extreme example.

'So where was I? Yes! The distinction between these two modes of behaviour; as individuals and as teams is, so far as I know, never properly made in our daily lives or in our analysis of human affairs. The result is that we expect the working teams that make up society to recognise and willingly obey our codes of moral behaviour. But this could be a colossal mistake. OK, the propensity-for-morality-thing regulates individual behaviour – but group behaviour? No!'

The rain is still lashing down outside. I've noticed that one of the giggling girls glances at me occasionally, but I ignore this because I'm tremendously impressed with the speech I've just made. And anyway if you can't hold forth in a public bar, what's the world coming to? And I'm not the only one; there's animated talk going on all around us.

However I am a bit disappointed when I realise that John is less than overwhelmed. He's used to my enthusiasms which often turn out to be froth.

At this point most people would say: 'psychobabble', 'claptrap' or 'give me a break', but John is much too courteous. He just says, 'Hmm!'

'Why not – what's wrong with that?'

'Well it seems much too simple; I don't see how it can solve anything. I mean will it answer the Awful Question?'

I've clearly got to defend myself here. 'It may not give the answer we were hoping for, but that doesn't mean it's wrong.'

That isn't much of a defence, but then I find a biological one. 'I'm saying that though the individual responds to tribal rules of self-restraint because of her genetically inherited propensity, the tribe itself inherits nothing at all. That's because it's just a confederation. It's not a living organism, so it cannot feel any predisposition for self-restraint. And, lo and behold! When the chips are down, it never does exercise self-restraint. In fact doing so would hamper its chances in competition with other, more "ruthless" tribes. As you biologists would say to the extent that the tribe is the unit of selection, altruistic self-restraint cannot apply, so the prime motivator motivates the tribe without hinderance.'

I feel a surge of affection for John when I realise from his occasional interjections that unlike most people I know, he's still listening intently. 'I think I've got it; you're saying the raw evolutionary drive of the prime motivator still applies without hindrance in cooperating vertebrates, but that it operates at tribe rather than individual level. I like it; morality operates at team member level only, and the prime motivator takes over at group level.'

'Yes!'

He goes on. 'Actually, remember E. O. Wilson's elephants trampling all over sub-Saharan Africa? Well. It's perfectly reasonable to think of them as having two distinct modes of behaviour. The first is behaving considerately to one another and according to the rules of the family hierarchy. The second is as a trampling herd which has no consideration for the outside world, no rules of behaviour; it's just a herd. That implies that, as cooperators, humans have a dual nature; on the one hand we behave as individual members of groups, teams or tribes, and on the other as the teams themselves. As individuals we behave with selective self-restraint, our propensity to obey the small still voice of conscience is what enables teamwork. But our teams themselves recognise no such restraint, and in fact natural selection requires them to be totally amoral.'

'Yes, yes!'

After a pause he continues: 'Well, Holmes, you seem to have unearthed a complete theory of human behaviour in two parts; as individuals and as teams, moreover it applies to all cooperating vertebrates. That's what you're saying, isn't it?'

'Yes, Watson, I suppose that is what I'm saying.'

There's another pause, then he says: 'You could call it dual-nature theory.'

But it seems a bit too soon to give it a name.

'I know it's simple,' I say, 'almost ridiculously so. But the simplicity is only a shock when it's compared with the crazy tangles theologians and philosophers have got us into. The conventional belief is that morality is an absolute, and that it applies to group behaviour just as it does to individuals, but what we're now saying is that this is disastrously wrong. We're saying that for the past two and a half thousand years we've been up the garden path, led there by people like Socrates, Plato, Christ, Mohammed and Kant, and even by Aaron and Moses who were there before Socrates. Along this garden path we've built ourselves these monstrous biologically illogical edifices of Judaism, Christianity and Islam, all incidentally, in competition with each other.'

As I pause for breath John interjects: 'And you're saying that in comparison with these crazy constructions the biological truth is stunningly simple?'

'Exactly! Have you heard of Ockham's Razor?'

'Yes, vaguely, but I don't remember what it is.'

'Well, William of Ockham,' I tell him, 'was a medieval thinker who said that if you have to choose between two competing theories you should always favour the simpler one. This became known as the principle of Ockham's Razor. It says that if our very much simpler biological explanation of morality works, then it's up to the traditional edifices to defend themselves and not the other way round. The question of course is; does our theory really work? Because if it does it blows any more complicated solutions out of the water.'

I sense excitedly that if it works, explanations for several paradoxes of human behaviour may fall into place like the levers of a giant combination lock. But once again I'm racing ahead too fast.

John brings me back down to earth: 'OK then, so can we have a go at answering the Awful Question of man's bad behaviour? Particularly as we're now getting closer to Ulster where there's a lot of it going on.'

'Hmm,' I go, playing for time. 'Have to think about that, maybe it'll turn out to be a non-question, you know; a question that has to be turned on its head.'

But there isn't time for that now because the weather seems to be clearing slightly. It's half-past three and we don't fancy staying the night on this flat windswept shore with its holiday ribbon development. One or two people have already left the pub. We'd better get going.

Besides I need to sort these ideas out more carefully, and the very best place for that is breezing along on a bicycle, even into a head-wind in the rain.

36   Rain in the Gaeltacht. Connemara

We didn't exactly dry off in the steaming press of people in Donnelly's Bar. It was more a case of the damp spreading itself more evenly and warmly throughout our limbs and cycling clothes. So when we're back on the road again we soak up the wet like blotting paper.

Soon the rain gathers strength as another squall comes blustering in off the sea. The most persistent damp spots are always your bottom and the insides of your legs where road grit comes splashing up from your front tyre. That problem will have to wait till a change of under-pants this evening.

On and on we go, heads down staring at the tarmac. On and on, past holiday homes, B&Bs, front gardens and trimmed hedges dripping in the rain. We wonder are we quite mad and why did we ever set out in the first place?

We were a team, but now we're a couple of forlorn, bedraggled solitaries. We plod on in silence. I'm going very slightly faster than John and soon there is about a half-mile gap between us.

We come to a sodden landscape where all the traffic signs are in Gaelic and there is Gaelic writing on the road surface.

The shrill incomprehensibility of these messages and their defiance against the usual protocols of road-sign language combine with the headwind and the rain to bring on an irritated 'ah, shut up' feeling.

All right. I know, I know. We're in the Gaeltacht. And I do agree with the effort to preserve our ancient culture, and that language is key to that. If you want to preserve salmon tribes against the march of modern man then the same goes for the vanishing traces of yesteryear.

But do we really have to do it with bare legs and a cold, wet arse, head down into a squalling wind? The answer I suppose is yes, right now we do.

After three hours of grim pedalling we come to a little place called Rossaveel. It's the usual pub, shop and post office. There's a modest B&B which has room for us. It's a nice little house called Cois Cuain. We are put in an attic room.

What a relief it is to have a hot shower and to change into clean, dry underpants.

We go to the pub; a neglected, run-down sort of place. We are the only customers. It's so gloomy and the service is so hit and miss that we come to the conclusion that it's either gone bankrupt or is changing ownership. The only person in the pub is a timid schoolgirl serving behind the bar. She's aged about thirteen. The only beer is out of a can, and the only food is a microwaved pizza out of a packet. She puts the TV on while we eat. It's a programme about the life of Mickey Rooney. We watch it in stunned silence, simply because we don't have the energy to talk or even look away.

Next morning I wake up feeling tired. Then I remember yesterday's miserable slog into all that wind and rain. Maybe my weariness is more in the mind than the limbs. Hope so anyway.

Today and tomorrow we'll be in Connemara, aiming for Leenane by tomorrow night.

Rather like the French Camargue or the Everglades in Florida, Connemara is an area without official boundaries; it has no recognition on the map. These are such special places that they have had a name since the beginning of storytelling but nobody knows precisely where they begin or end. And indeed it's a minor pleasure when you realise that nobody needs to know. The Burren's the same; an enchanted place. When you are there you know you are there, and that's enough.

Connemara is basically low-lying turf bog with dramatic mountains dotted around. The mountains are only 2,300 ft high, but what makes them majestic is the way they come straight up from sea level and are more or less bare of trees. No trees can grow because the mountain sheep eat everything that sprouts, so it's just green with tough grasses and sphagnum moss. The central range is the Twelve Pins; a grand and shapely set of granite peaks sweeping up out of the bog.

Some say that if you can see the Twelve Pins from where you are standing then you are in Connemara and I have a mental picture of an old man with a tub of that whitewash they use for marking football pitches. It's a magic tub which never empties no matter how much he paints. He has a big floppy brush and his job is to start on the southern shore at the mouth of Killary harbour. He has to go anti-clockwise and, by keeping to the edge of the visual limit of the Twelve Pins, he has to paint the boundary line of Connemara. Of course the line is extremely wiggly. He's got to Recess, and will eventually end up back at the mouth of the Killary. He takes it slow and steady. He's been doing this job all his life and when he eventually finishes he will lie down on the shore exactly where he started. And he'll die there, a contented man who has completed his life's task.

John and I are still far from completing our task, so we rouse ourselves, say farewell to Rossaveel and set off down the road.

The weather has improved and the wind has changed direction so it's a nice ride. Our legs respond effortlessly to the spin of the wheels. We are healthy and alive once more; yesterday's exhaustion a fading memory.

The road crosses occasional small bridges. The little rivers are in flood from yesterday's rain. They tumble energetically down from the hills inland on our right. Our road continues west along the north shore of Galway Bay.

At half-past ten in Screeb we get our first sight of the Twelve Pins.

Screeb. First view of the Twelve Pins. We are in Connemara

Great joy. We have crossed the old man's whitewashed line into Connemara.

Then I get yet another goddam slow puncture. We limp along looking for a good place to stop.

At half-past twelve we come to an extremely solid and ugly concrete block of a bridge. Who can have designed such a monstrosity in this beautiful setting? Some pre-republican English civil servant I suppose. It's over a nice little river galloping merrily down to the sea, which is half a mile away. We're near Derryrush.

I find my puncture-repair kit and John gets out his fishing rod. He catches one little brown trout while I give my tyres and inner tubes a thorough going over. I remove a sharp little bit of wire from the inside wall of the rear tyre.

John's lucky not to have had any punctures at all so far. They really are a damned nuisance. But I'm getting quite slick at repairing them. In fact I'm now ready to enter a 'quickest rear tyre puncture-repair' contest.

Yet again my fingers get all covered in that dirty black bike gunk; the sticky emulsion of chain oil and road muck. Yet again it starts to spread like a contagious disease. If I don't wipe my fingers frequently with grass it'll spread from one touching point to the next: from fingers to

Fishing, puncture repair and lunch stop beside
ugly little pre-stressed concrete bridge near Derryrush

hands, and then in quick succession to my handlebars, to the pockets of
my shorts, to my eyebrows. Then smears will get on my glasses and
around my fly buttons until finally, and this is what the nasty stuff has
been aiming for all along like gangrene targeting the brain, it makes
smudges on my sketchbook.

Punctures and chain-offs are a right pain in the arse.

Finally I pump up my tyres as hard as I possibly can. That's what
you're supposed to do. You'd think hard tyres would give an extra
bumpy ride and make punctures more likely, but the reason has been
explained to me several times. It has to do with giving more efficient
propulsion, it being easier to push a hard tyre along the road than a

soft one. I suppose that does make sense, but why not have solid tyres then? Perhaps they would be too heavy? But foam would be light. It just goes to prove that there are always more questions than answers.

Cycling is full of expertise like this. If you let them, experienced cyclists will go on at length about best saddle and handlebar height, toe clips – for and against, spoke adjustment, chain maintenance, types and best size of frame. There's half an hour's worth of preferences and anecdotes just on saddles alone, and another on brakes and how to combine front and rear brakes in an emergency stop. And of course, as we learnt from Michael Gleeson, the biggest topic of all is gears and gear changing. This usually includes a debate on 'cadence', which is the right speed at which to turn the pedals in various road conditions.

When my repair is done and John has finished fishing we have a modest mix 'n' squash lunch from yesterday's leftovers.

We slowly emerge from the Gaeltacht, or at least from the landscape where the road signs are all in Gaelic. You somehow can't help feeling that if you don't speak Irish you really have no right to be there. This is unfortunate because, even though they might enjoy reminding the English about past injustice, I'm quite sure that's not at all the impression they want to give the European tourist.

The shore becomes rocky with inlets and tiny islands. It's low tide again and the rocks are fringed in that yellowing seaweed and mucky sand. If you can see it you can smell it.

The Twelve Pins are clearly visible in all their grandeur now. It's a lovely, clear sunny evening. The heart sings. The sky and sea are deep blue. It's truly beautiful.

At half-four we arrive in Roundstone.

Just before the village we get a room in Heatherglen B&B. It's really a small impersonal hotel, nothing nasty you can say about it, nothing nice either.

After a cup of tea, shower and change, we go down to O'Dowd's where tourists, locals and people just in off the sea look down over the little harbour and talk to each other in various languages and accents. It's a place for gossip, stories and memories. This unpretentious little pub is perfectly positioned. Roundstone attracts people from all over the world and sooner or later most of them drift into O'Dowd's.

There is usually something happening in Roundstone; it's that sort of place. This evening it's a small seaplane which lands just outside the harbour while we are chatting to a Dutchman at the bar.

Gossip, stories and memories in O'Dowd's

Nobody pays much attention. It's as though seaplanes are landing here all the time. In fact I personally haven't seen one anywhere for at least five years.

If I hadn't drawn it I would soon begin to doubt that it had ever happened.

Later somebody tells us; don't look now but that man leaning on the harbour wall outside the pub, in the evening sun, looks very like Rory Quinn.

'Wasn't he finance minister under John Bruton?'

'Sure that's him all right,' says someone else. So, being in the mood I draw him too.

He must have arrived on the seaplane. What a stylish way to go pub-crawling.

Seaplane outside Roundstone harbour

We have an excellent meal in O'Dowd's:
oysters and fish pie and more Guinness.
As the noise level rises John falls silent,
he's finding that his deafness makes the
sounds and voices hard to distinguish.
So we go out and join the people leaning
on the harbour wall. It's warm and
completely still. It's more like a theatre
setting than a landscape.

The weather improved gradually all
day and blossomed into an idyllic
evening. Let's hope it's nice tomorrow.

Side view of Rory Quinn;
not very much hair

37   *The scientific method requires a summary like E=MC²*

'OK,' says John. 'This idea; are we calling it dual-nature theory?'

'You called it that, yes, I like it.'

'Are we serious about it?'

'Well, I don't see any flaws in it, at least not yet.'

'Not yet, no,' he says. 'So what exactly are you saying? I'd like to go over it again to remind myself.'

I think for a bit. 'OK, well here goes,' I say. 'It's a theory of human behaviour which says lots can be explained if we recognise that all cooperating animals have two modes of behaviour; as individuals and as teams.'

'Right, well the scientific method says that once we've described the theory, which can be difficult, then we have to check it for logic, consistency and common sense. And finally we have to try it out against real life. That means seeing does it work. It means making predictions and testing them in experiments. It's rather like designing a new aeroplane; first on paper, then in a wind tunnel and finally seeing will it fly.'

'Actually,' he continues, 'I don't think it's going to be quite enough just to say that we have these two modes of behaviour, you'll need to be more precise than that. Remember how Einstein boiled his theory down to $E=MC^2$.'

So I gather myself and try again. 'From beehives to wolf packs and from church choirs and political parties to industrial conglomerates, every cooperating group is a quasi-living organism with a quasi-mind of its own, and is totally amoral. Morality is simply the language of cooperation, it regulates the behaviour of individual group members, but not of the group itself. That OK?'

'Well you haven't said anything about the prime motivator or propensity. You see it all needs to be set out in detailed logical steps so that sharp-eyed critics have something to get hold of. Descriptions won't do, they'll need explanations.'

'Oh dear, that means I'll have to reconstruct and summarise everything we've been saying so far, a bit like answering an exam question.' Then I remember: 'Well, actually, I've jotted quite a lot of it in my sketchbook as we've gone along.'

'Thought you had.'

38 Roundstone to Leenane. *Dual-nature theory in twelve logical steps*

I wake early. We're in Roundstone. The early morning mist rekindles my childhood memory of idyllic Connemara days.

I make a cup of tea and inspiration gathers as I start summarising dual-nature theory in my sketchbook. By the time John gets up I've roughly scribbled it all out ready for polishing.

Before setting off I put on sun-cream for the first time since we left Cork. What a bit of luck that after all that wind and rain we should have such wonderful weather during this Connemara section of our trip.

We buy our lunch supplies at Ferrons Stores and cycle on westwards.

Sounding like a tour guide I point out various of my childhood landmarks to John as we ride along. When I was little we spent our summer holidays in Connemara, so I know it well.

Dogs Bay is where a boy can catch a bucket-full of prawns, crabs, little fish and tiny exotic squid around the rocks on the incoming tide, and where the sand is clean and white, and alive with grey shrimps and flatfish.

There's the haunted wood.

And the rock hole where if there is a gale blowing at a certain stage of the tide, the waves make a shuddering explosion like heavy artillery fire that can be heard a mile away, even in a high wind.

The road curves round to the north-west and we pass through the area of a thousand small lakes with the sea on our left.

The Coral Strand. John has a swim

A few miles beyond Ballyconneely we come to the Coral Strand. The entire beach here is broken coral, the biggest pieces are two inches long with branches. From a distance it looks like pink sand.

I've always believed there is a big coral reef just out to sea here which produces the stuff. Well there has to be doesn't there; perhaps a colony of coral that floated up on a particularly warm swirl of the Gulf Stream ten thousand years ago and uniquely established itself here. Or maybe it took root from the coral necklace of a drowning sailor off the Spanish Armada. But sadly it seems the truth is more mundane. In his otherwise lovely book *Connemara*, Tim Robinson says it comes from a type of seaweed which is quite common around these parts.

I do wish he hadn't said that.

John has a swim and marvels at the coral. I do a watercolour.

We cycle on past a granite monument on a granite hilltop. It commemorates the safe arrival of Alcock and Brown who in 1919 landed nearby, having successfully flown non-stop across the Atlantic for the first time in human history. They can't have had a very comfortable landing amongst all those rugged rocks.

View from Cullen's Bistro coffee shop in Clifden

At midday in glorious hot sunshine we arrive in Clifden, the capital of Connemara. It's a bright and breezy market town with two main shopping streets at right angles to each other.

Squabbling seagulls congregate where the town dump used to be; on the shore right behind the houses. The gulls probably remember it with nostalgia. Now it's a helicopter pad.

At one end of Clifden the street slopes steeply downhill. The place is jammed with cars and tourist coaches. Being an old market town, the streets are extremely wide and most cars are parked nose-in to the pavements. There are lots of pubs.

We stop for coffee at Cullen's Bistro coffee shop.

Cullen's Bistro coffee shop is a few doors up from Stanley's the men's outfitters and fishing-tackle shop. Over coffee I tell John about Stanley's in the old days.

Just after the war when things were hard to get and the shops only sold 'utility goods', Stanley's used to be two separate shops side by side. One shop sold men's clothing and fishing tackle. It was popular with rich Irish-Americans over on holiday, or on army leave. The other shop sold exotic items which Mr Stanley got these wonderfully generous Americans to part with, things like Texan hats and boots, Parker pens, biros, fancy belts, Pfleuger-geared barrel-spinning fishing reels, fixed-spool spinning reels, novel fishing lures, unusual rainwear, beautiful penknives, and even cartoon magazines. Mr Stanley believed in barter and was very persuasive. His American goods shop was a great success. And of course as children we loved to gaze at these marvellous luxuries. They told of a rich and fabulous civilisation on the other side of the Atlantic, and they got this message across with a gripping intensity that today's museum curators can only dream of.

On our right as we leave Clifden there's a big grey church. It's very imposing; set back off the road at the top of a steep bank. For years there was a huge cattle-grid right below the entrance steps. This grid must have been at least seventy-feet wide. I used to imagine sheep wandering in on market days and eating the flowers around the altar and cows strolling about leaving cowpats down the aisle, until one

View of Main Street, Clifden

day the priest lost his holy patience and got the Bishop of Galway's permission to have the cattle grid installed. It has gone now, which just shows how much Clifden has grown over the years; the church used to be on the edge of town; now it's surrounded by workshops, houses and shops.

The road takes us through low hills for a while. We wind in and out of small valleys. Then we skirt round the head of Streamstown Bay; a thin four-mile-long inlet of the sea. Lovely name; Streamstown Bay. There never has been a town here, so it's an arm of the sea named after a town, which never existed. There was once a Streamstown House but that's long gone.

Then in hot sunshine we climb up on to higher moorland covered in turf bog. As the road curves round to the north-east we get the most wonderful panoramic views mainly of blue mountains and distant horizons. You can see Tully Mountain to the north. Then sweeping round to the right: Mweelrea Mountain in the far distance, the mountains between Kylemore and Lough Fee, then the whole magnificent mass of the Twelve Pins, and behind and between these we get glimpses of Bengorm, the Leenane mountain where the pucai gave me the idea of this trip, Devil's Mother Mountain which used to be called the Devil's Balls, and the Maam Turks. It's a blue-sky, heart-stopping sight; small beer perhaps to a Swiss, a Californian or a Nepalese, but to a Connemara lover on a beautiful day like this it's the nearest thing to heaven.

We sweep down into Moyard, with its abundance of old sycamore trees and montbretia. The sycamores have moss on their branches and in this bright hot sunshine they give a cool shade. The coast here can often be ferocious and wild; the storms and lashing rain can go on for days making it hard for trees to get established, and the seedlings that do appear get eaten by sheep. The tree that seems to cope best, and can be found growing where all the rest have given up, is the sycamore. It adapts to the prevailing wind like a tough old lady tilting her umbrella into the rain.

The other thing that grows in luxurious profusion here is the rhododendron. The lovely rhododendron is scornfully referred to as *Ponticum* by the horticulturally knowledgeable. For some reason they hate it. Whenever you ask them to say why, they bluster all sorts of angry reasons none of which really add up. I suspect it's too successful for them.

Straight on we go; through Letterfrack, and then through rhodo-dendron woods. The road goes between steep mountainsides. This valley must have been carved out by the melt-water when a lake further inland drained out to sea as the last ice age receeded.

Soon we get to Kylemore Abbey. It's a Victorian building set back dramatically among magnificent pine trees on the far shore of a small lake at the foot of the steeply wooded mountainside. It looks like a medieval castle that you might see on the Rhine. Here in Connemara it's quite a surprise.

Then there's more water. Flashing in the sun; it's Kylemore lake which fills the inland end of the valley between the two mountains. The road winds around the shore. For much of the way it is overhung by wind-battered beech trees which have seen better days. They grow on the bank between road and water. Looking between their trunks you can see across the lake to the Maam Turk mountains which are about five miles away.

It's half-three so we stop for lunch on the bank in the shade of a beech tree. It's a dazzling afternoon, with the sun sparkling up into our eyes off the lake. I do a watercolour while John goes in for a swim.

Swimming, drawing, fishing and lunch on Kylemore lake

While he's swimming John finds another freshwater sponge, same as the one he found in the Lauragh River and again it's evidence of the absence of pollution.

Then we have our lunch; another delicious sun-warmed, mix 'n' squash picnic.

Three pucai are dancing in the afternoon light. They're in the sun against the backdrop of Diamond Mountain on the other side of the lake. Now you see them, now you don't. They're rising and falling like mayfly.

It's a perfect afternoon.

Looking at my sketchbook, I say: 'Early this morning I did a summary of dual-nature theory as you suggested.'

'Oh good. Lets have it then.'

'There are twelve statements in all; a bit like lecture notes. Shall I read them out?'

Pucai over Kylemore Lake. The dazzling sun is right behind them.
Now you see them, now you don't

'Yes go on.'

I clear my throat:

'1   The laws of natural selection say that there is nothing which sets humans apart as separate from all other animals. Humans are indeed unique, but so too is every other animal.

2   The cooperating animals include ants, dolphins and hyenas. None of these can survive unless they cooperate. Meaning, get together in groups to perform the tasks of life: eating, sheltering and breeding. The same goes for humans.

3   Evolution has no purpose; like the flow of water poured on to land it just floods forward where opportunity allows. Light waves present the opportunity which allowed the evolution of sight, and sound waves of hearing. The effectiveness of cooperation is a similar opportunity.

4   Cooperation is a very effective life strategy, conferring big survival advantages over non-cooperating species. Without self-denial, cooperation would be impossible. But selfishness, the prime motivator, which is vital in the game of natural selection, directly opposes self-denial.

5   In order to function in working groups, cooperating vertebrates have evolved genetically inherited propensities for rules of self-restraint. The social insects: ants, termites, wasps and bees do it differently; they have achieved cooperation by evolving caste systems. Slime moulds and corals do it differently yet again.

6   In cooperating vertebrates the rules of self-restraint must be both flexible, meaning adaptable to environmental changes, and selective, meaning obeyed or ignored according to instant circumstances. Genetically evolved propensity plus learning, or nature plus nurture, enables this.

7   We humans refer to this propensity and the codes of behaviour it generates as ethics or morality. Contrary to the teaching of Bentham, Kant, Mohammed, Christ, Plato and Moses, morality cannot be defined as an absolute for all people at all times. It is the flexible, selective language of human self-restraint. It is the language of cooperation.

8   Morality is like language. In both cases the rules are adaptable and selectively used. And in both cases the skill is enabled by genetically evolved propensity. We are not born with a language,

ready-made like fingers and toes. We are born with a propensity or predisposition to learn, communicate and teach any human language. The same, in their own culture, goes for dolphins and hyenas.

9   Morality is simply behaviour which enables cooperation. Game theory and gene thinking do not explain the evolution of morality.

10 Now if you think about how cooperating groups themselves behave, the truth about human nature becomes clear. These groups include tribes, hunting troops, armies, football teams, business corporations and universities. They act as organic units; they are discrete quasi-living organisms.

11 Furthermore the tribe usually replaces the individual as the unit of natural selection. It is usually better for the future of one's personal genes to be an average member of the fittest tribe than the fittest member of an average tribe. The same goes for lions, dolphins and hyenas.

12 These groups are units, separate organisms, and in many ways they behave as such. This behaviour is totally amoral. Natural selection says it has to be. The propensity for rules of self-restraint simply doesn't apply at group level. Groups are collections of individuals. They are not sexually reproduced and cannot inherit anything genetically. In times of prosperity human groups may and, by mutual inclination, often do behave morally. But when the chips are down they are totally amoral and selfish. This is ordained by the process of natural selection.

'And that's it. Except to say that I don't believe any one of these statements is original. Though they may not have been assembled or thought through like this, and though some may still be controversial, most are well supported by scientific research.'

'Well done,' says John. 'I'd like to read it carefully in a quiet moment, but it sounds good. It could be a big one.'

Much as we'd like to, we can't stay here all day. It's after four and we'd better get going. It's still about ten miles to Leenane and there could well be a B&B problem. So we collect our things, load our bikes, and we're off again.

First we go on beside the lake then the road rises along the edge of a pine forest on the right.

As we climb up on to higher moorland we come to a little modern church on the left. Its delightful name is the 'Church of Our Lady of the Wayside'. The design copies an intermediate stage of the paper-folding you did when making a water-bomb at school. But I expect the architect would prefer us to use the word origami in our description; sounds more ecclesiastical than water-bomb.

We cross three miles of turf bog with outcrops of granite. The mountains are all around us now, going blue into the distance. It's a rare and truly splendid sight – rare because they're usually shrouded in clouds.

We swoop over little rivers, freewheeling down off the moorland to the shore of Killary harbour.

In fact this isn't a harbour at all. It's an arm of the sea which comes inland between steep two-thousand-foot mountains; a bit like a minor fjord. It's ten miles long and mostly about half a mile wide.

There is a huge ugly looking mussel fishery here, occupying maybe a thousand acres of water. The unit of fishing is a thick rope which dangles vertically in the water from a buoy. Mussels attach themselves to the rope and when they have grown big and fat the rope is simply hoisted out and the unfortunate creatures are harvested.

Having heard so much about the life history of a salmon I can well imagine that a mussel's is equally wonderful. But we don't have a mussel expert with us, and that's probably a good thing, otherwise there'd be so much to discuss and complain about that we'd never get anywhere.

The road sweeps along the shore under the Leenane Mountain, rounds a final bend, and we are in Leenane. It's a compact little two-shop, two-pub village where a river comes down to the sea. Here the traffic coming round one side of the mountain from Clifden meets the traffic coming round the other side from Galway and they both go off north towards Westport.

Leenane

We stop for a pint at Hamilton's General Stores.

The people of Connemara are charming and the scenery on a good day is breath-taking. The one and only reason why it isn't overrun by world tourism is the weather. It can rain and blow a gale for days on end at any time of the year. For true believers that's part of Connemara's appeal: The drinking, the storytelling and music, and the fishing too, are much better when it's raining. And there's no risk of sunburn or marketing overload.

Jam is preserved in sugar, lively old ladies are preserved in gin, prehistoric mosquitoes are preserved in amber and the spirit of Connemara is preserved in rain. The same must be true of Assam; maybe the two should be twinned.

While we're having our Guinness in Hamilton's I tell John about the owner, Eddie Hamilton. Eddie must be eighty now but he's still sharp as a tack. He built himself up from scratch. In his heyday he controlled or influenced everything that went on in the village. A fine man, Eddie, much loved by those who appreciated him and reluctantly admired by the few who didn't.

For many years after the war his combined shop and pub supplied everything the locals needed, from lavatory paper to coffins. The most sophisticated item you could purchase there was a salmon. He never had any salmon – didn't sell them at all. But next time you went in, there would always be one waiting for you. 'Ah well now ye see,' he'd say, with a naughty grin and speaking very fast out of the corner of his mouth, 'ye just came by at the psychological moment.'

Eddie also operated the village petrol pump, right outside his shop. He financed the local fishermen who netted salmon in the Killary. And he brokered the sale and purchase of property and concessions. He was, in fact, the local gombeen man; but a benevolent one.

Some of the stories that are told in the two pubs in Leenane, Hamilton's and Gaynor's, are hilarious.

One, about the films that have been shot here, is more like a saga than a story. It can go on a long time and different people are recognised as the lead tellers of different bits of it. If they happen to be in the bar at the time they are automatically given the floor for their bit of the saga, even if others present know it well.

In about 1975 a film called *Sinful Davy* with John Hurt as the youthful star was being shot out towards the mouth of the Killary. The chosen site was referred to as 'Location' and is still called that today, even on modern tourist maps.

During the shooting the directors and film stars spent a lot of time on the phone to America and other distant places. Film people are like that. This was long before the mobile phone was invented and all the calls had to go through the Leenane Post Office telephone exchange. Sheilagh Walsh, the postmistress, used to tell about how she connected these world-famous names to each other through her ancient little hand-operated, plug-connecting switchboard.

She used to say, 'Oh, I'm a wizard at international calls.'

Did she ever listen in? 'Sure you couldn't help hearing the chat sometimes,' she'd say. 'You'd be surprised at the goings on.'

But she never told.

Though she may not have divulged the secrets of film stars, Sheilagh had ample opportunity because *The Field* was filmed in Leenane some years after *Sinful Davy*. It starred John Hurt again, also Richard Harris. The script called for a lot of rainy scenes, and it so happened that the filming took place during a particularly wet spell.

Sheilagh's description was legendary. To get the authentic effect, she explained, they had to hide the tarmac so they put down straw, hay and farmyard manure in the village street. But unfortunately, though it was a wet summer and seemed to be raining all the time, it never actually rained when they were filming one of the many rainy scenes, so they had to use a rain machine almost all the time. This was basically a huge sheet with holes in it rigged up overhead between gantries. Gallons and gallons of water were pumped up from the little river and poured on to the sheet. That apparently is how film people make rain.

Locals were roped in as extras, including Binagh, the sixty-year-old prototype hippie. She came along with her goats, geese and her one cow.

Well, what with the rain machine and the real rain, and the straw, hay and manure, and with the multiple re-takes involving the actors and film crews, and with all the onlookers of course, the street became an absolutely terrible mess. People walked it into the houses on their boots. 'It even got in the beds,' said Sheilagh.

The film stars, directors, and important people stayed in smart places some miles away, like the Renvyle Hotel and Rossleague House. The more junior ones were put up in the B&Bs and in village houses all round Leenane.

The locals were agog at the goings on. The bed swapping and sneaking in and out at all hours was a real eye opener to this clean-living, God-fearing, little country village.

And of course every clandestine visitor walked more of the mushed-up hay, straw and manure into the bedrooms. Sheilagh said that when the whole thing was over it took them weeks of washing bedclothes, carpets and floors to get the place clean again.

When my wife and I visited them a year later, Eddie's wife Nancy said, 'Sure the place isn't clean yet.'

The film was eventually released and, of course, we looked out eagerly for the street scenes and for Binagh's goats, geese and cow. There was a good scene in Gaynor's pub, which had been specially rebuilt for the purpose. It has since been renamed the Field. Eddie featured briefly outside his shop in a raincoat three sizes too big for him. The film crew must have thought he looked like a quaint little peasant, but the joke was on them; little did they realise he was richer by far than any three of them put together.

The scene with Eddie outside his shop was retained in the eventual film, but nearly all the other street scenes had been cut out. I mentioned this later to Eddie's brother, John-Francis, who laughed and said, 'And after all that mess and trouble.'

Margaret Joyce too remembers it all vividly. 'Oh my God!' she says, 'Don't remind me.'

Sheilagh herself is ladylike and impeccably mannered, which makes her stories all the funnier. Another one is about John-Francis and the very grand lady from Limerick who was on holiday locally. The happy-go-lucky John-Francis was as irresponsible and easy-going as his elder brother Eddie was alert and business-like.

The very grand lady from Limerick comes into the shop, out of the pouring rain, and asks for pink lavatory paper. The schoolgirl serving her says: 'We're out of pink I'm afraid, madam, there's only the white left.'

But the very grand lady kicks up a dreadful fuss saying she has told Eddie several days ago that she has to have pink and that he promised he would have it for her.

Another schoolgirl hears the fuss and says, 'I think I saw some pink up there in the store yesterday.'

The store is where the big items are kept: turf briquettes, Kosangas cylinders, turf-cutting spades, coffins, drums of creosote, bales of wire, salmon nets – that sort of thing. The trouble is it's twenty yards up the road and none of the girls want to go out in the pouring rain. Suddenly they are all very busy behind the cash till serving customers.

So John-Francis who is drinking at the bar in the back of the shop is fished out and told to go out and get the pink lavatory paper. The rain is bucketing down but the grand lady can't wait. He grumpily grabs a newspaper off the counter, holds it over his head and out he goes.

When he gets back, soaking wet, he puts the pink paper on the shelf where the lavatory paper is kept and is amazed to find that there was white paper there all along.

He's furious. 'What did ye want to send me out in the pouring rain for when there was some here all along?'

He gets even more angry when the girls whisper at him to calm down and be quiet because the lady has to have the pink, and she's standing right there. 'Ssssh!' they say. 'The white won't do.'

'Well there she has the pink now,' says John-Francis in a loud voice, 'and I hope her arse knows the difference.'

Silence falls as we gaze out of the pub window. Bengorm mountain rears up about half a mile away across the tidal waters of the Killary. The summit is out of view, cut off by the top of the window frame. 'Isn't that a wonderful sight,' says John.

After a good night's sleep in Margaret Joyce's B&B farmhouse we set off again.

Looking down Glenagevla to the head of the Killary,
Bengorm mountain behind.

40 Peter Mantle. Black Oak Inn, Newport. *Even Oxfam and the John Lewis Partnership are amoral. Bureaucracy links corporations to evolutionary biology*

Yesterday's glorious weather has been blown away. It's quite warm and there's not too much wind but the rain is coming in again off the Atlantic. When it's raining the mountains disappear, and when it isn't we can see the next downpour driving in towards us. Normal Connemara rain in fact.

The Delphi fishery with its two lovely lakes, Finn Lough and Doo Lough, is at the foot of the mountains on the other side of the Killary, about six miles from Leenane. Peter Mantle, who manages the fishery, is a big voice in the battle now raging at national level between the traditional salmon fisheries and the new fish farming conglomerates. John readily agrees when I suggest that we call in to see this high-profile campaigner.

We've already heard from various people about the heated argument now gripping the country. There are headlines in the newspapers, graffiti on roadsides, questions in Parliament.

For as long as anyone can remember there has been hostility between the two traditional salmon fishing interests: the upper-class anglers fishing in rivers and lakes and the working-class net fishermen operating in the estuaries. They've been bitter enemies. Explosives used – mostly but not always – for poaching fish came into the stories told; people got killed occasionally.

Then in recent years along came the big industrial conglomerates: companies like Booker McConnell, Unilever, Guinness and Carrolls. They set up enormous submerged cages in bays and estuaries all round Ireland for rearing salmon. There is a big installation right here in the Killary alongside the mussel farm, and equally sinister looking.

A few years later after a drastic decline in the fishery catches, an unholy alliance was formed between these two sworn enemies; the upper-class anglers and the working-class netters. They furiously blamed the big food conglomerates. A high-profile court case about it all has been raging in the press for several years. Feelings are running high.

'There you go,' says John. 'I've seen it again and again; typical ruthless behaviour by the giant corporations, and nobody can stop them; they have too much money. It's always the same. They bribe politicians, their PR departments plant deceitful newspaper articles, they finance universities and pay scientists to do and publish biased research. As I keep saying they're evil.'

I think to myself: 'There it is; that's the Awful Question again.'

Delphi is a gracious fishing lodge fit for an Edwardian earl. While we wait in the hall I take a quick look at the visitors' book. It's full of names one can recognise: politicians, film actors, business tycoons, Formula One drivers.

Peter Mantle eventually arrives from somewhere down the back: clearly a busy man. He's sorting out some problem about tonight's menu as he breezes into the hall with a member of staff in tow. You can tell he is very much mine host at Delphi Lodge. A large handsome charismatic man in his fifties, he sits us down in an elegant reception room with coffee in fine porcelain cups and saucers. We're looking out over Finn Lough, the smaller of the two lakes.

You can see he's foot-tappingly impatient to know what on earth these two scruffy, tone-lowering cyclists have come for.

John, in the quiet voice of the slightly deaf, introduces himself as a salmon biologist, interested to know about the fishing hereabouts and the salmon politics.

Peter Mantle has a confident grasp of the arguments. The scientific, biological, geographical facts and technical terms are at his fingertips. This subject is his number-one priority; he needs no further stimulus. He's off. He's in orbit. John listens as he expertly tells us how lice are killing off the local salmon and trout populations. It sounds nasty; the lice are about the shape and size of a half-used pencil with their mouth at the point. They attach themselves to the fish and suck its blood. If a fish gets several lice it is so weakened that it becomes unable to make the journey upstream to the spawning beds. The cages, Peter Mantle explains, are the ideal breeding habitat for lice; it would be hard to design a better set-up for the gruesome things.

Quite a lot of this is scientific stuff and is way above my head. What little I do understand sounds very convincing to me. I'm impressed.

So I'm surprised, though I should have expected it, when I notice that John isn't quite so sure. Peter Mantle is surprised too. He must have got carried away by his own rhetoric.

John mildly asks some questions about ecology, culverts, farming methods, restocking policy. After a few of these, Peter Mantle's manner becomes much more respectful as he realises that this slightly deaf, quiet spoken, woolly-bearded cyclist knows a lot more about salmon and trout than he had expected. He in turn asks John's opinion on various scientific mysteries and when we leave they are on level terms of mutual respect.

There is to be a big international salmon conference in Galway in a few weeks time. Peter Mantle says on parting that he hopes to see John there. John says he expects to go and will look out for him.

At the next stop I ask him does he agree that it's the cage farming that's to blame. John, the true scientist, says he doesn't know enough about it. He'd like to hear the views of some of his Irish fish-scientist friends first, but his experience tells him that though the lice may be striking the final blow, the problem will have started years before the arrival of cage farming. A lot of harm was done in the period immediately after the Second World War when new farming methods, road widening, the effluent from new factories and hydroelectric schemes did permanent damage to fish habitats. Fishery managers then went and made the tragic restocking mistake which John has already explained to me, where the new stronger fish displace and destroy the original tribes and then, being genetically unfit for their new habitat, they themselves die out. Out of ignorance we have done dreadful damage to the natural ecology of our great rivers, and all in the name of progress.

'We're learning the hard way I'm afraid,' says John ruefully.

'The tragedy; the appalling truth,' he says, 'is that most of the destruction is still going on today. The knowledge is now widely available. There is a solution to practically every harmful policy or development, be it roads, industry or agriculture. These solutions would cost a little more, but public opinion would back them.

'It's the same throughout the northern hemisphere,' he says. 'People are so easily lead. It happens in Canada, Norway, Iceland, Scotland, Ireland, England, Japan, Korea, Russia, everywhere. The deadly combination of greed and corruption enabled by ignorance allows the engineers and politicians to get away with murder.'

The Galway conference might be interesting and he hopes to go, mainly to catch up on who's who in the Irish salmon world. But he expects there to be too many politicians and lobby groups there, people like Peter Mantle, with commercial motives behind their opinions. It's not going to be a purely scientific event; more like a high profile 'get the public educated' media jamboree.

'Could possibly be a waste of time,' he says. I asked him some months later and of course he didn't go.

Doo Lough, the upper lake in the Delphi fishery, lies between Mweelrea, Irish for the black king, at 2,700 ft, and the Sheffry hills at 2,500 ft. Today they climb up steeply into rain clouds which tinge the upper slopes with a lovely dark purple-green colour. The road winds along the shore. Several of Peter Mantle's clients are out on the lake, fly-fishing in pale grey boats.

By midday the road is going up over bare moorland. There's little to see for miles. There are sheep, dry-stone walls, occasional farm-houses, a few clumps of low trees and turf laid out to dry. But quite a lot of the land here is clay and stone instead of the usual turf bog. Perhaps it was once under turf which has since been removed for fuel.

We journey on all day through Louisburgh and Westport until in the evening we get to Newport.

Newport looks nice. There are generous vistas. The town is on both sides of a wide, tidal estuary. This is the Newport River. A handsome and massive stone bridge crosses the estuary connecting both sides of town.

I bet there's local one-upmanship about which side of the bridge you were born on.

'And then of course she went and married someone from north of the bridge.'

'Well, it only goes to show . . . '

We find a room on the south side in the Black Oak Inn. It's not a B&B. More like a small hotel or restaurant with rooms. It looks down on to a quayside and across the broad river estuary. In the bar lounge there are some magnificent stuffed pike in glass cases. This is a similar establishment to that appalling place we stayed at in Glengarriff, but it's a great deal nicer.

We shower. Then we go down for a pint in the lounge bar. We sink into huge leather armchairs and after a comment or two we sit in silence partly because the armchairs are so huge that when you are comfortably slumped in one it's difficult to see out. The tired cyclist's sore bottom craves a huge armchair. We're knackered as usual.

I doze off.

John wakes me. They've told him the kitchen will close soon and it's time we went in for dinner.

'I've been thinking,' he says when the soup arrives, 'about the scientific method and testing dual-nature theory against real life. You are declaring it as a major principle that absolutely all groups are totally amoral, aren't you? So if that can be shown to be untrue, then the theory must collapse, mustn't it?'

'Er . . . Yes.' I'm wondering what's coming next.

'Well, won't most people challenge that? I mean I know I'm always ranting against multi-nationals, but aren't there countless highly moral teams, organisations and even businesses. Look at IBM, M&S and the John Lewis Partnership, at least in their glory days they had reputations for highly moral philosophies. And look at the Anglican church, Medeçins sans Frontières, Oxfam and the Samaritans.'

'Ah yes but you'll find that that's never quite the reality.' I'm at home here. Just as John's element is the water, mine is the world of international business. 'You'll never find a professor of business management who teaches the advantages of truly altruistic moral behaviour in corporate strategy.'

I rattle off my long-held beliefs on all this.

In business-school teaching, where they say 'profit and growth is the name of the game', morality comes a poor second best to winning. The moral loser gets few points. Business schools teach their lessons against an assumed background of fierce competition. The world they inhabit echoes with aggressive cries of 'the bottom line', persuasive, often misleading, advertising, restrictive practices, monopolising attempts, controlled markets, price fixing and spoiling tactics. Of course they don't promote these dodgy practices, heaven forbid! But their case studies demonstrate, in detail, how competitors do it. Which is much the same thing.

Business games are a popular feature of business school teaching, and it's interesting to notice that there are never any prizes for moral behaviour in these exercises. True morality simply doesn't come into the business equation.

The John Lewis Partnership in England is an example of a big business which overtly embraces morality. But even there it is more a matter of corporate style which is well published in their PR material. It's more style than true morality. When John Lewis declines, as it will one day, it will be taken over by a more ruthless regime which will abandon the camouflage of morality. That's what happened to the Co-operative movement in the 1930s; its idealism was unsustainable. The same can be said of Communism in its pure form.

The chief executive whose personal code of morality threatens to hinder the corporation's survival and prosperity will quickly be removed. And whistle-blowers rarely survive.

I finish by saying: 'In business anything goes so long as you don't get caught breaking the law. It's human nature. But I must repeat that business corporations do readily obey the law, especially if it's effective and their competitors obey it too. It is simply that they are amoral.

'I'm not saying immoral here, I'm saying amoral; morals just don't apply. And you have to be careful not to confuse what an organisation is for; its mission, with how it goes about that mission. Never confuse its work, with its ethics.'

'All right,' says John, 'I'll accept that for the moment. Now here's another problem that's been worrying me in case it might bring our theory tumbling down.'

He picks his words carefully. 'It's essential isn't it that we can show a seamless connection between animal and human cooperation?'

'Oh absolutely, yes, otherwise we can't claim to have unearthed the evolutionary origin of morality.'

'So any differences between human and animal cooperation must be differences of degree; not of principle.'

'Er . . . Yes, that's right, amongst the vertebrates anyway. We agreed that the social insects may be different; they may not use morality and punishment for cooperation, but that's probably OK.'

Is he about to reveal a fatal flaw in dual-nature theory? I'm suddenly feeling defensive.

'Of course all vertebrates are very different in their behaviour,' I say, playing for time. 'For instance, elephant cooperation will be very different from hyena or beaver cooperation, but in degree only; not in principle.'

'The problem I've been struggling with,' he says, 'is that I don't see any equivalent in any animal which remotely anticipates or looks like the huge and devastatingly effective organisations which humans achieve. I'm thinking of churches, armies and my great enemy, the big-business conglomerate.'

'Ah! I read something about that many years ago,' I tell him, relieved that I probably have the answer. 'It was about bureaucracy and the Roman army.'

This argument says that a corporation is a confederation of tribes

which is held together by what we call bureaucracy. The corporation
is a uniquely human construction. It only becomes possible when
speech and writing are invented. Cooperating animals form tribes
and platoons but never corporations, because they can't write.
So bureaucracy, far from being a dirty word, thus turns out to be a
rather amazing human development. And much of the time we're
not actually very good at it.

Bureaucracy enables a platoon to be lead by an absent leader who is
often symbolised by a military flag or company logo. The instructions
of the absent leader are conveyed to the platoon by spoken or written
messages. In this way a human corporation is formed by linking
together many platoons into an organisation which is vastly more
powerful than the sum of its platoons. The corporation is still a
true cooperating group; it is still one single quasi-living organism as
described in dual-nature theory. When obedience is denied, or com-
munications break down; when messages don't get through, that
sector of the corporation collapses.

'The Roman army,' I explain, 'was a good example of a corporation.
Roman regiments often met tribes of Celts, Goths and Vandals who
were braver and more ferocious than themselves, but these different
tribes never united properly into corporations, so the Romans were
usually able to defeat them in the end. It was simply that their
bureaucracy was better.'

'Yes I see,' says John. 'And that shows the horrors of human history
to be examples of corporate amorality. Like Nazi Germany, modern
Israel, the IRA, the Spanish Inquisition, the Crusades, the Hiro-
shima bomb, the bombing of Dresden, the international arms trade,
the destruction of salmon habitats and forests, and of course the anti-
social behaviour of most multi-national corporations. They're all just
following the orders of an absent leader.'

'That's exactly right. And this bureaucracy argument is important
because it enables us to link human corporate behaviour with
evolutionary biology, which is a distinct achievement. We can now
replace the dubious concept of corporate evil with a simple bit of
biology. If hyenas could write they'd develop bureaucracy.'

And so the day ends with our theory still intact, and it's time for
bed.

41 Sheep-loading & pucai dream. Journeying on to Ballina, Stick's bar, John's elbow

I'm awake now but a few moments ago I was deeply asleep. In fact I clearly remember the vivid dream I was having. A girlfriend from years ago had a secret identical twin sister who nobody knew about. She had pure white hair and a bright pink dress, but that's the end of it because I'm suddenly woken up. It's a shame really because it was probably going to be a good one.

What wakes me is a dreadful racket going on outside our window. There's a noisy engine and a clanking of metal. It's half-five a.m. I look out and there on the quayside below our window is an enormous lorry.

Nothing happens for a while.

Then along comes a farmer in his Land-Rover pulling a trailer. It's full of sheep. Twenty-five of the bleating animals, I count them, are yanked out of the trailer and bundled up a clattering tin ramp into the lorry. Going to market, I suppose. Their end is nigh.

Trailer-loads of them queue up after that, bleating and stamping. They all get shoved up the ramp into the lorry, which has three decks, one on top of the other.

The noise is tremendous. The lorry keeps a generator throbbing. Farmers shout when sheep escape. Trailers are constantly turning and backing with loud advice. A sheepdog is told to 'get back in the

Newport, sheep–loading started at half-past five

The pucai stealing sheep

car at once'. Land-Rovers are arriving and leaving all the time. Then at regular intervals there's shouting, banging and hammering because something keeps getting stuck, preventing the driver from adjusting the deck heights in order to squash more sheep in.

By quarter-past six the lorry is packed tight. A late arriving Land-Rover is turned away. The lorry departs and peace descends once more. Everything has been cleared away and peering out I wonder if it actually happened at all. Perhaps it was an illusion.

John, of course, sleeps right through the whole performance.

At breakfast I'm still thinking dopily of illusions. John's not down yet. I allow my pen to wander about in my sketchbook. You can do that; it's a sort of doodling. You're in charge but not completely. You're holding the pen of course, but you don't know what the picture or story will be about until the moment of impact as it were. You need to be semi-conscious for this. And having been woken out of a vivid dream at half-five by a sheep-loading concert that's what I am: semi-conscious. Soon the pucai start to appear in my drawing. They're stealing sheep and loading them into a trailer.

John comes down for breakfast.

Then while finishing my coffee I do a calculation. There are 60 times 60 seconds per hour, that's 3,600 seconds. So cycling at 8 mph and pedalling at about one turn of the pedals per second means that

for every mile we do 3,600 divided by 8 pedal turns per mile. That's
450 turns per mile. We've done 545 miles so far. Multiply that by 450
and by this calculation we have done 245,250 turns of the pedals since
Cork. That's a quarter of a million turns.

'Lord almighty!' says John who hasn't woken up properly yet.

'Sorry about that. It was just a minor episode of accountant's disease
that breaks out now and again. Nothing serious. I can usually keep it
under control.'

'Just as well.'

We look at the map. We'll probably spend a couple of nights in
north Mayo, a night in Sligo with our old friends the Kilroys, and
then continue on to Donegal.

We had always expected that on a long trip like this, if our bodies
didn't actually give up, we would eventually settle into a more or less
comfortable state of long-distance hardiness. And that is what now
seems to have happened. We've at last broken through the pain
threshold. That took about two weeks. Now we're not quite so tired at
the end of the day any more. The legs don't ache quite so much when
first asked for an effort. The raw patches under my buttocks caused
by the seams on my Y-fronts have settled down and I now cycle in
'boxer shorts' instead. The one thing that does bother us both, and is
getting progressively worse, is numbness and tingling in the heels of
our hands. At the end of each day this gets painful and spreads into
our third and little fingers. But it's not serious; merely a discomfort.

It's time to pack up and go.

There's a nice lady at the reception desk when we pay our bill at the
Black Oak Inn. She tells us that a couple of weeks ago two ladies aged
seventy-two and seventy-four had stayed here.

'They were cycling all the way up the west coast just like the pair of
ye. They do it every year.' That puts us in our place. We would love to
have met them and swapped stories of the road with them.

We set off around the coast of north Mayo. It's grand and bare with
huge vistas of dark green bogland. The foreground merges feature-
lessly into middle distance and then to far-off hills. There's nothing to
give the eye a measure of receding terrain; no tree, road, house or cow.
There aren't even any signs of turf cutting. It's a huge scene; much
grander than the human scale.

Geographers and ecologists enthuse about the blanket bogs of
Ireland. Well, here you certainly can see what they mean; this really is

a vast, dark green, fourteen-feet thick, giant's bedspread laid down on the land.

For two days we cycle on through this featureless countryside.

We stop for lunch in Crossmolina. The weather is grey and showery so we scout around for a pub. We choose Stick's Lounge & Bar because of its funny name.

Stick's Lounge & Bar is more like a railway carriage than a pub, and it clearly hosted a boisterous party last night. The place is still in a considerable mess. There is a confusion of small uncontrollable children dashing in and out, and three large babies in nappies are rolling about on the floor. The barman, who must be Stick, fires out jokes like a music-hall comedian but we can't understand them. We laugh anyway and so does he.

The landscape is changing now. The vast rolling bogland has gradually given way to moorland pasture. On our right are the Ox Mountains. Hill sheep are dotted about and you can see the occasional clump of trees around a farmhouse.

John's getting a sore elbow which is a little worrying. It isn't the result of a knock. 'Could be gout,' he says, 'or possibly an abscess.'

'Salmonella?' I suggest helpfully. He doesn't think that's funny so he must be in pain.

We find a place for the night in Dromore West. This B&B is not your usual modern bungalow, it's a substantial Georgian farmhouse. The owners, Pam and Ray Tully, make us very welcome.

42 The pucai explained by Pam Tully. John falls. Children dancing. The Unshin River

Next morning I come down to breakfast and find John having porridge.

'Oh good!' I say. 'Porridge'.

'Yes,' says John rather sadly, 'I thought I had ordered bacon and eggs. That's the trouble with being deaf.'

The dining room is full of people mostly in their mid-seventies. It looks like a party of red-necked farmers and their wives on holiday. They are a bit severe and right-wing looking and they speak in broad old-fashioned Ulster accents. We don't get in conversation with them. It's our first real whiff of Ulster. Later I regret not having chatted to them. Prejudice shrivels the mind and is a pernicious blight which

gets in the way of civilised behaviour. I ought to be made to write that
out one hundred times.

John adjusts his bike outside Dromore House B & B

After breakfast John settles down to do some adjustments on his
bike: The gears aren't quite right and the brakes are squeaking. Little
things like that.

There is grunting and muttering. Of course what's not helping him,
poor chap, is that his elbow got worse in the night and is now looking
even nastier and more swollen.

While John is working on his bike I do a sketch of the view from our
window. It's a dull view but dull views can often produce surprising
results. It all depends on the mood that's on you. Not this morning
though: I'm sketching with a dull brain. I start at the top and work
laboriously downwards, hoping for inspiration. Then, out of nowhere,
some pucai quietly appear and in no time at all they strike up a jazz
band. There are six of them. One is dancing and the others are playing
music. There's a marching drum, harp, fiddle, uillean pipes and a post
horn. The music tinkles out in quiet tinny notes; it mingles with the
morning bird-song. The rhythm is spellbinding.

When I've finished the drawing John is still working on his bike. I
find Pam Tully to get the bill. She is intrigued by my sketchbook so I
show her through it.

She's looks at the pucai I've drawn: 'You want to be careful of them,'
she says.

'Actually I'd like to know a bit more about them,' I say. 'I only know
a few odds and ends from childhood and bits I've picked up here and
there.'

'Well nobody knows much about them. Only it's very wise not to annoy them.'

She hesitates, flashes me a suspicious look, then, lowering her voice, she says, 'Well, it's said they can make cows barren and have been rumoured to steal human babies.'

There's another pause, but I keep quiet because there seems to be something more she wants to say.

Then she continues, almost in a whisper: 'They're supposed to be closely related to swallows you know. Well, I used to think it was all fairy stories but one day last year we noticed three swallows' nests in the eaves above a window. We knocked them down because of the mess they were making on the window pane and, would you believe it, the

Traditional pucae jazz festival outside Dromore House B & B

very next day we had three accidents. Honestly, I'm not making it up. The deep freeze caught fire. A plank fell through the window. And the header tank overflowed all over the ceiling and down the walls. Well, this year the swallows have come back and we are definitely leaving them alone. They've built in the same place again.'

I ask her about the spelling which seems to vary.

'Well, you see,' she says. 'the pucai were originally only to be found in Irish literature, you know, written in Gaelic. So in English different spellings are used by different people. In Irish the plural is pucai, and the singular is puca. A bit like the Gardai and Garda. But in English the most usual is pookies, plural, and pookie, singular. Sometimes people use poochai as well. So there you have it now, you can use any spelling that sounds right.'

John has finished adjusting his bike so we load up, say fond farewells to Pam Tully, and pedal off down the road.

As we cycle along it's clear that John is not at all his usual self. His elbow looks dreadful. It's now swollen and sore, and he feels feverish. He would prefer to wait and get it seen to in Sligo this evening. I want him to go to a doctor straight away. Of course he protests that it isn't serious but the worrying thing is the speed at which it is getting worse: like a poison spreading.

We have arranged to stay with Max and Margo Kilroy in Sligo tonight. Max rowed with us at Trinity. He was in the 1952 crew at Henley. He qualified as a vet and has just retired after thirty years in charge of the cattle breeding and artificial insemination centre for the north-west of the Republic of Ireland. He covered the whole of Donegal, Leitrim, Sligo, Roscommon, Mayo and Galway.

Sligo is only twenty-six miles away now and John insists he can get that far. I make the obvious remark that a decent vet like Max will be able to fix him up in ten minutes; probably just saw his arm off and dip the stump in tar. That's the second joke that falls flat. Poor John.

At five to eleven, the time is noted in my sketchbook, we have a dog attack. We are cycling along quietly when suddenly we are nearly savaged. It's a tiny little beast about ten inches long. One of those Yorkshire terrier type dogs, all fluff and teeth. Employing the element of surprise, it comes streaking through the long grass barking a little high-pitched yap. You can see it thinks it's the Red Baron – diving out of the sun, straight for our ankles. We have to accelerate to get away. We imagine it swaggering back to its lookout point thinking: 'Frightened those dozy bastards. Who do they think they are anyway? Pair of scruffy-looking, bare-legged, silly old farts in daft helmets.'

Then at five past eleven: disaster. John falls in the ditch. It's so easy to do; you're going slowly, looking at something, you go too close to a kerbstone, wobble into it and whoops, over you go. The slower you're going the easier it is to overbalance.

This is a distinct low point. He's bashed his sore elbow and stung his bare legs extensively on nettles.

He lies there under his bike and panniers for a minute or two to let the first shock of pain subside. Then I very carefully help him out. While he sits down to recover I do a quick sketch of the painful event.

If it were me I'd be thinking of an ambulance to the nearest hospital at this point. But John is made of cast iron and after a short rest he insists he can make it to Sligo by nightfall.

John in yellow helmet and with very swollen elbow falls in the ditch

So on we go. At about quarter-past twelve we come to a small village called Beltra.

Coffee would be remedial and we notice people outside a little village hall and a sign saying 'Beltra Feis'. I persuade John, who is by now in a feverish trance, that this would be fun to see, and that we might well be able to get a life-saving coffee and rest here.

And so it turns out. We get coffee and homemade cake and there's dancing thrown in as well.

In fact a children's Irish-dancing competition is in full swing. Up on a stage at the far end of the hall they come out in pairs and dance their set pieces to the accompaniment of an accordion.

The accordion is played by a sixty-year-old man sitting to the right just below the stage; his fingers are nimble and his rhythm bounces along. You can tell by the banter that the audience and accordionist all know each other well. Most of the village will be here, especially the parents and schoolteachers.

The competitors are boys and girls aged between five and twelve. They dance with their arms held rigidly to their sides, their legs swinging and kicking, and their black polished shoes twinkling and tapping.

Two twelve-year-old competitors dancing to an accordion at Beltra Feis

Each competitor has a number pinned on their bosom. Some of the older ones contrive a smile but most have the serious look of concentration. The boys wear dark formal suits, some fitting better than others, and the girls are in pretty dresses which all fit perfectly and are decorated with tinsel and ribbons. The audience claps vigorously after each performance.

It's an enchanting event and we feel privileged to be here.

On the way out I bump into a small boy aged about eight or nine. His name is Michael. Number 54 is pinned to his oversized black suit.

'Well, we enjoyed that very much indeed,' I say. 'How did you get on? Did you win?'

'I got two medals,' he says. Then his eyes light up. 'But my best friend got about four.'

We cycle on going east and come to the sea again. Then at about one o'clock we arrive at a place called Ballysadara. It's a small town on the Unshin River.

What's impressive about the Unshin River, according to our map anyway, is that it starts in Lough Arrow and flows north-west for a few miles until it flows into the sea at Ballysadara. There's nothing special about that till you notice that Lough Arrow is separated by about half a mile from Lough Key and Lough Key drains in the other direction: into the mighty Shannon. So a raindrop falling between the two lakes could either flow north-west for 12 miles to Ballysadara or else it could go south for 160 miles and end up in the sea at Limerick.

It's time for lunch. A big pub called the Dun Maeve is right by the bridge. It looks nice in the sun, which has just come out.

I ask the barmaid: 'Will it be OK if we eat our picnic lunch here while we have a pint?'

She says, 'You can have it out the back by the lake if you like.'

'Oh is there a lake here? I didn't realise that.'

She walks out with us and nods at the attractive, fast-flowing, shallow river. 'Lake or river or something anyway,' she says cheerfully.

It occurs to me to mention the drop of rain falling between Lough Arrow and Lough Key but on second thoughts I don't think she'd be interested. She might even become alarmed and call the manager.

John doesn't look well. He inspects his elbow. It's very swollen now, and has gone dark red. I've never seen anything like it before. Must be an abcess. It looks awful. We'd better get it seen to quickly before something bad happens, but he doesn't seem to be as concerned as I am.

While we wait for our pints to arrive he gazes over at the far bank of the Unshin River where there's a brown bird with a white breast messing about in the shallow, fast-flowing water.

'You won't mind if I have a quick flip of the rod will you?'

'But what about your elbow?'

'Oh well, it's only my left arm, I cast with my right so that should be OK.'

John fishing in the Unshin River oblivious of a vicious
abscess in his left elbow, which is now dark red

When the Day of Judgement finally comes, and it's time for us all to march through the Heavenly Gates and join the angels and archangels and all the Heavenly Host, John won't be anywhere to be found – he'll be out fishing.

A shockingly blue kingfisher streaks downstream.

The brown bird splashing about is a dipper. It's feeding energetically on some submerged rocks. You can clearly see it moving about under the water. It has a white breast and you can watch it bracing its wings against the current so that it stays submerged and in place while it pecks with nervous speed for underwater grubs.

The kingfisher flashes back upstream again. Maybe John has disturbed its nest.

Presently we pack up and set off on the final five miles to Sligo. The urgent thing now is to get John's elbow fixed.

We get to Sligo at about four o'clock. John is ailing: his elbow is bad now and he feels feverish.

At this point sod's law strikes again: when we ask the way, we discover that Max and Margo don't actually live in Sligo town. They live twenty minutes out on the Manorhamilton road. Moreover it's sharply uphill.

The final climb is torture for John. But with a great effort of will he forces himself on, and at half-four, at last, we're there.

43   At the Kilroys

They live in a modern bungalow in the grounds of a grand estate. Doonally House has been left empty for many years and you can see from the collapsing roof and big cracks in the walls that it is now sadly beyond repair. In fact it's slowly falling down.

Nearby, arranged in a quadrangle which covers two acres, are the bull pens, stables really, where the stud bulls are housed.

This is the artificial insemination centre. What happens here is that these prize bulls are cheated into ejaculating their semen. It is collected, put into special containers and delivered to farmers all over the north-west of the Republic. The delivery and insertion into the cows is carried out by a team of expert inseminators. Apart from some laboratory equipment and volumes of breeding records and statistics, that's all there is to it. Sounds simple but of course it isn't. It's highly Mendelian, veterinary and Ministry-of-Agriculture-political, and Max has been in charge of the whole operation for the last thirty years. He retired just a few months ago.

After joyful greetings with these very dear old friends we need to get John's elbow fixed as quick as we can.

Max gives it the quick veterinary once-over. You can tell by the muttering and intake of breath that if John were a bull, he'd have him put down on the spot. Instead he phones around for a doctor. He knows them all, but it's now five o'clock on a Saturday evening and it's not easy to find one he trusts. He finally tracks down a lady called Dr Staunton, and drives us over to see her.

I wait in the car outside the doctor's surgery. There's a view of a beautiful lake with a little island. It's lit up in the afternoon sun, so to while away the time I do a drawing of it. Later I'm told it's Lough Gill, and that what I've been drawing is the actual 'Lake Isle of Innisfree' which was immortalised in poetry by W. B. Yeats. 'I will arise and go now . . .' and all that.

Lough Gill from outside Dr Staunton's clinic.
The small island top right is Yeats's 'Lake Isle of Innisfree'.

Dr Staunton diagnoses either an infection or gout. So she has pre-scribed both antibiotics and anti-gout pills, and she tells him he'd better have it seen to when he gets back to Dublin.

'A bit of fast bet-hedging there,' I think to myself. But then I realise I'm being unfair because it's ten times better to have a doctor who admits she doesn't quite know, than one who pretends she does. So we believe her that much more when she rules out broken bones, cancer and gangrene, and above all when she says it's OK to carry on cycling.

We put on our smart clothes. The Kilroys are taking us out to the Bianconni Bistro for dinner. It's Italian, very select and comfortable, and the cooking is excellent.

During dinner John perks up. Is he responding to treatment for either the gout or the abscess? Or could it be the wine and the happy memories of bygone days? There's so much to talk and laugh about that every now and again we have to remember we are in a restaurant and should try to keep our voices down.

Back at Doonally it's a clear dark night. The stars are wonderful. Millions of them. Some are bright and looking close, others faint and tiny. It's an astonishing sight; rare these days except in out of the way places like the west coast of Ireland where clean air comes in off the Atlantic. Max points to a particularly bright star and insists that it's Meir, the Russian space station.

'It's only about 150 miles away,' he says, 'which means it's right over Ireland not over Russia at all.' He goes in and gets his binoculars.

'Here have a look through these,' he says. 'You can almost see its wings.' I try to argue that he can't be right, but fail.

Max will go on at length on any subject in his slow melodious voice. When we were students Max's mother used to say that he talked so much when he was a little boy that she suspected he'd been vaccinated with a gramophone needle. He talks in detail on a broad scale and these days it's hard to get a word in because he too has gone a little deaf.

But he's fascinating to listen to. He ranges over political corruption, union battles, travelling overseas to inspect and buy bulls, mad cow disease, the law of contract, the farmers' co-op, animal feeds, cattle-breeding statistics, and the Larry Goodman meat-subsidy scandal. Max has some wonderful stories about sharp farming practice and colourful rustic characters.

He's going on about how he warned the Ministry of Agriculture months before the meat subsidy scandal broke, but they wouldn't listen. 'Nobody listens any more these days,' he says.

'I know,' says John. 'They don't even hear very much these days.'

'Hmm? What's that you say?' says Max.

When we wake up next morning John feels much better. The pills have done the trick. Which trick, the gout or the abscess? Well, we're not quite sure. Never mind, we are grateful for the cure.

Max is cooking breakfast, and he's talking like a bulldozer again this morning.

In between repeat highlights of how he avoided being fooled by Larry Goodman's fraud he asks me what I'd like for breakfast. I explain that a big cooked breakfast feels like a brick in my stomach during the morning ride, so I'd prefer cereal: 'Muesli,' I say, 'something like that.'

No good. He isn't listening. I get a very big cooked breakfast: egg, bacon, sausage, black pudding, tomato; all fried, and fried bread as well, and hot buttered toast.

John appears in the kitchen and says, 'Good morning.' I have to amplify to each what the other is saying. By now Max is on to crime in the countryside, which according to him has reached epidemic levels, including flagrant cattle rustling. He asks John what he'd like for breakfast.

'What?' says John quietly.

'What would you like for breakfast?' I shout.

'Oh I couldn't eat very much.' He's looking at the mounds of food being produced. 'Could I just have the bacon and eggs.'

'Just the bacon and eggs,' I shout to Max.

Of course John too gets the very big cooked breakfast.

'Oh well, OK!' says John.

Over our huge and delicious breakfasts we have a pleasant hour chatting and gossiping like only old friends can; especially old friends who haven't seen each other for years.

Eventually we say our fond farewells to Max and Margo and vow to meet again soon.

44 On the road to Cavangarden. Ulster looms. *Dual-nature theory answers the Awful Question. The two halves of the theory lock together*

The countryside has changed again. Now we are cycling through the rich green farming country for which Ireland is famous.

Benbulben is the dramatic mountainside just outside Sligo town. As we follow the coast road round under its massive shoulder, I take occasional sideways looks at John to see is he still OK, and he certainly seems to be. Amazing recovery.

At midday we come to the graveyard where the great poet himself, W. B. Yeats, is buried. You can't miss it because he's been turned into a tourist attraction with parking for twenty coaches. There's a huge architect-designed roadside inn with fancy roofing. It's the W. B. Yeats Tavern.

We stop for coffee. The walls are full of W. B. memorabilia: reproductions of paintings and poems, newspaper cuttings and Victoriana. You can see it's not awfully easy to design a theme pub that strikes a spark between tourism and poetry, which are at the opposite ends of the culture spectrum. But they've done their best, you can't ask for more. Anyway the woodwork is nice and the seats are comfy; the waitresses are sprightly and the coffee is good.

'Poets are all philosophers really, aren't they,' says John as he inspects some of the memorabilia. 'They're always going on about the meaning of life and the joys and pains of being human.'

'Yes I suppose they are.'

But offer me a philosophical moment and I'm away . . .

'You know,' I say, 'I think we may have answered the Awful Question almost without realising it.'

'The question we seldom dare to ask because it is so depressing?'

'Yes: If every little child everywhere on earth has learnt right from wrong well before it goes to school, why do we go on polluting and destroying our environment and the habitats of other living things? Why do we routinely torture and bomb each other? And why is there so much evil in the world?'

'And don't forget the salmon.'

'Yes all right. But the point is that when you regard the human as one of the cooperating animals, and you understand the evolution of morality, the answer's obvious. Evil is merely a human moral construction. Nature does not recognise it. Nature has evolved the propensity for self-restraint which enables cooperation. But the concept of morality is a human verbal explanation for the seemingly mysterious workings of this self-restraint, in other words for the workings of conscience.'

'Yes and as you say, being neither flexible nor selective, it's a pretty inadequate explanation at that.'

'Right! So it's quite wrong to apply this inadequate concept to group behaviour. The careless, cruel, destructive behaviour of groups is perfectly natural. Much more basic in fact than self-restraint within teams. The we who behave badly are groups, but the we who say it's wrong, are individuals.

'What cooperating groups do is, by definition, biologically natural; in fact it's essential to their survival and prosperity. Morality is a red herring in this context. And there, I suggest, lies our answer to the Awful Question.'

I sit back, rather pleased with myself.

The voices around us here in the W. B. Yeats Tavern now have a distinct Ulster edge. I listen to their chatter. The gradual changing of the accents is calibrated confirmation that we are moving up the map . . . moving towards Northern Ireland . . .

Northern Ireland, which has awful questions of its own.

'But steady on a minute,' says John. 'Are you saying that the question nobody dares to ask because it's too awful is in fact a non-question, because this bad behaviour is almost always group behaviour, whereas bad is an individual, not a group criterion?'

'Yes.'

'Well then aren't people entitled to say: if it's a non-question no wonder nobody asks it.'

Oh dear! And I thought I was doing so well. Is this a right hook to the ribs? But after a moment's panic I realise it's actually the perfect reply.

'Yes, but it's only a non-question to those few people who like Machiavelli recognise the amorality of group behaviour. To the rest of humanity it is indeed an Awful Question.'

'Yes that's good,' says John after a bit of thought. 'And it helps to confirm the theory.'

We fall silent.

'There's something else here I've been thinking about,' says John.

'It's that the two parts of our dual-nature theory, individual self-restraint and group amorality, lock together and hold each other up in a solid structure.'

'You'll have to explain.'

'Well it's essential to understand how the use of individual self-restraint enables cooperation before you can start to describe the distinctly different nature of group behaviour. But also without recognising group amorality, the propensity for individual self-restraint is an incomplete description of human behaviour. Regarding groups as quasi-living organisms explains why individuals like Hitler and his henchmen are swept along by their own rhetoric. So assembling the two parts into one structure of human behaviour adds strength and validity to the theory.'

I'm impressed. 'Hey! That's how philosophers are supposed to talk, not scientists. Whatever happened to the scientific method? You can't prove that statement scientifically, can you? It's much too woolly. And you claim you're not a philosopher.'

'Oh dear! Sorry about that, I'd better go and wash my mouth out with soap. I was only trying to underline why dual-nature theory is quite a good name for it. Anyway who called it that? Was it you or me?'

'You did. l remember it distinctly.'

After one of those pauses he says, 'I read recently that every good idea goes through three stages. First, nobody listens, second, everybody says it's nonsense, and third, someone else thought of it first.'

TWO

*Northern Ireland,
Applying the Theory –
Sligo to Newry*

45 Belleek border post, Cavangarden. *Northern Ireland illustrates the Awful Question*

We come to a stony river-mouth where people are fishing. We get off at the bridge and join the collection of men gazing into the water. Several big salmon are clearly visible down there.

The road sign says it's the Bundrowse River, but a man with a strong Belfast accent says that's wrong; it's the Drowas River.

'A classic indication of tribal tension,' says John quietly. His elbow is OK but he doesn't want to fish because he says it would be quite pointless casting here.

'Amidst all this concrete you'd never catch a thing.'

But I sense it's not only the dismal human destruction of the riverside habitat which deters him. There's the deeper foreboding that we are now close to the violence and bigotry of Northern Ireland.

We look at the map. It shows that the border crossing is only about four miles across the fields to our right. It's at Belleek, a small town, well known for its museum-quality lacy porcelain.

'Can you imagine it?' I say. 'There's been bombing there recently, so there'll be a fortified border crossing, night patrols in camouflage, evil-looking wall paintings and graffiti everywhere. And amidst these there'll be delicate art shops selling lacy porcelain bowls to well-to-do ladies from Dublin and Belfast.'

'A tank in a china shop,' says John.

The very thought gives me the creeps. I hate it all. I think of the residents living and working here, and the children growing up in murderous tension. My spindly legs tingle with naked vulnerability as I imagine the barbed wire where hedges used to be, and us on our bikes, running the gauntlet between armoured cars; our movements closely watched from slitty-eyed machine-gun posts mounted in eighteen-foot lookout towers. And we pretend we're civilised.

'Hypocrisy!' I say with disgust.

'Actually I'm thinking,' says John, 'this could be a good test of the idea that morality is the language of cooperation.'

I'm instinctively on the defensive. 'How do you mean?'

'Haven't we been saying that morality is the exercise of self-restraint for the purpose of cooperation? Well here we have two sets of church-going people, they both spout morality all day long and yet they can't cooperate. Quite the reverse in fact.'

He's put his finger right on it; the Northern Irish problem is indeed a perfect test for the idea that cooperation is enabled by moral behaviour. But a sense of failure slowly tangles me in its ghastly grip as I realise that although dual-nature theory may demonstrate the inadequacies of western ethics, it's fairly useless if it can't produce an answer for Northern Ireland.

Maybe it's the destiny of mankind that we will never find the solution. Perhaps we're not capable of building long-term strategies into our politics. If so, we'll soon end up annihilating ourselves and many other animals too.

On up the coast we go. In Bundoran we cross the Erne, the big, fast river which drains Upper and Lower Lough Erne and all their inter-connecting maze of lakes and waterways.

We're on the N15; the big main road from Sligo to Donegal. It's not very nice for cycling. Cars go fast and furious, their roar makes it difficult to talk; it's not safe to cycle side by side. The road surface is a flawless high-quality tarmac. It's sunny in the late afternoon, but today it's colder than the usual soft Gulf Stream climate. We have the wind behind us.

At five o'clock we start thinking about a B&B. We had intended to stop earlier; in Bundoran perhaps, to have a light day so that John's elbow can recover. But he's been getting better as the day wore on and amazingly he's now back to normal again. I must remember to talk to my doctor when I get home. 'In cases where you are unsure if it's gout or an abscess,' I'll have to tell him, 'you should prescribe the pills for both and advise the patient to go cycling and fishing for a few weeks.'

We come to a collection of houses in hilly countryside. It's called Cavangarden. We can see no obvious village centre, maybe we're on a by-pass. There are a couple of B&B signs by the roadside. The second one we ask at has a vacancy.

The landlady is a neat and tidy-looking person of about forty-five. She is suspicious and not very welcoming at all; quite cold in fact. But she lets us in and shows us to our room.

We mention the evening meal problem to her: no restaurant nearby, John's elbow, we've had a tiring day; sob-stuff like that.

You can tell from the signs she gives out that this isn't her problem.

But then surprisingly, she relents. Her natural Irish hospitality overcomes her Ulster caution. She and her teenage daughter cook up a spaghetti bolognaise delight; the perfect dinner for a pair of tired old cyclists.

Living so close to the border must make these poor people perpetually nervous. A couple of dishevelled men wearing bushy beards appear on bikes and immediately they are on their guard. IRA bombers? Drug runners posing as cyclists? You could stuff quite a lot into the tubes of a bike frame. If I were a desperado and had to carry out a dangerous mission, cycling would be an excellent disguise.

But you can see that the genuine pleasure mother and daughter get out of being generous, slowly overcomes their suspicions. They sit with us while we eat and are friendly and chatty. The man of the house has been watching TV in their private living room. When he hears us talking and laughing he comes and joins in.

Their slow thaw from nervous caution to charming Irish hospitality is poignant in the extreme. Our hearts go out to these beleaguered people.

We entertain them with highlights of our trip: John's punctured varicose vein. Getting cut off by the tide. The beautiful weather in Connemara. The dancing competition at Beltra.

It turns out that the man of the house is a member of the Gardai. Here on the border for heaven's sake. He is a fit-looking thick-set no-nonsense individual with the local Donegal accent. He's a nice man but you'd want to have him on your side.

Here's a man, I'm thinking, who knows a thing or two about the dark side of human nature. I'd love to get him to talk about it all, but it would be a social offence to try and encourage him to open up. Maybe if we were to stay a couple of nights . . . Anyway we're cyclists not anthropologists.

John says there's a small river nearby; a brook really. He noticed it when we arrived. I didn't see it at all. 'Thought it looked promising,' he says. So after we've eaten, he sorts out his handful of fishing tackle and off he goes.

I go out for an evening stroll with my sketchbook. The light is fading. After a while I come across an empty farmhouse and start drawing it. It looks damp and gloomy. The hall door and ground floor windows have been boarded up and it's overshadowed by a big old sycamore tree with dark, fungus-spotted leaves.

The evening air is still and I'm discovered by midges. They circle above my head like miniature vultures, and they crawl and itch all over my scalp, face and hands. It's a pucai sort of place. But the pucai don't actually appear in my drawing.

Unless . . . I think with a shiver . . . Unless maybe they've turned themselves into these vigilante midges and are trying to drive me away from the dark secrets of the abandoned farmhouse. Perhaps it's a pucai warning to keep away from things it might be dangerous for me to know about. Things like dry rot, witches, giant spiders, buried guns, packages of heroin, bomb-making equipment and the ghosts of past betrayals and revenge.

Abandoned farmhouse under big sycamore tree.
A pucai sort of place

After drawing the spooky – derived from pucai? – place, I respect-
fully back off. I actually walk the first few paces superstitiously backwards keeping a wary eye on the building.

I return to the very clean bungalow where it is hard to imagine
anything much except supermarkets, TV advertisements for corn-
flakes, washing powder and small family saloon cars. What a contrast
between these two houses; the derelict farmhouse and the modern
B&B.

John's still out when I get back. He finally returns as night is
falling. He caught four little brown trout and one bigger one, about
ten inches.

You'd think there might be a conflict in his mind between the
fisherman who thrills to the catch, and the biologist who observes
and preserves. But he says trout are predators and so are humans so
what's the problem? He's got me there.

'Anyway, they're so much more fun than the Newfoundland brook
trout,' he says. 'Much harder to catch.'

'Well, they would be wouldn't they, if you keep putting them back,'
I point out. 'They'll tell all the others.' But it's no good trying fishing
jokes on John; he's heard them all before.

46 Ardara, the two sisters. Fishing quotas, the sketchbook problem

Next morning we say our goodbyes to these nice people, wish them
luck and on we go.

After Donegal our road goes west along the coast for about fifteen
miles. Then it turns up into hills. It's one of those climbs that seems to
go on for ever and ever. But eventually at about a thousand feet the
road flattens out on to a high moor.

At a quarter to three we stop near a small lake for our picnic.

There's a storm on the horizon. It's heading straight for us, but the
sun shines while we eat.

'God's reward,' I say, 'for surviving twenty-five days on the road.'

'Yes, but which God?' says John demonstrating how well he's picked
up the philosophical method.

'Back in Cork I might have answered that, but now I'm a little
confused.'

'In Canada they say, "And dog created man in his own image." '

'Perhaps he'll reveal himself out of those storm clouds when they get here.'

'Or she,' says John.

Picnic lunch looking over a small lake up in the hills between Donegal and Ardara. Artist's feet in foreground

We wind on down into Ardara, freewheeling most of the way, and find a room for the night in Drumbarra House. It's a substantial old farmhouse B&B set back off the road up a steep stony track that winds past barns and farm machinery. Two absent-minded sisters are in charge. They are in their late thirties or early forties.

There seems to be religion in the air; it's in the pictures and arte-facts, but it's hard to categorise. Could it be the paradox of educated Roman Catholic feminism?

Next morning after a good night's sleep and a fine breakfast I sit in the conservatory and look through my sketchbook making diary notes. I try to describe the intriguing, enigmatic flavour of this B&B. It's done out with refined good taste but there seems to be a subtle message about life as well. It's more like advice than religion. I can't quite place its cultural context. A framed text on the wall in the big farmhouse kitchen gives no clue, it reads: 'All things whatsoever ye shall ask in prayer, and believing, ye shall receive,' Matthew 21:22. You can sense a legal mind at work here because that 'and believing' let-out clause makes it a fairly safe thing to say. But who in their right mind would believe such nonsense?

The two sisters are sort of ethereal in a dotty kind of way. You ask them a question such as 'I'd like to call my wife, would it be OK for me to use your phone?' or 'Do you know, is there a bike shop in Ardara?' and there's a long pause before you get the answer. And then, when it does come, it isn't quite yes or no, or even 'I don't know'. So you give up. These two sisters are quite strong characters, each in her own way, and they give off a sort of mysteriously challenging, but eccentric charm.

When John comes down to breakfast I'm just finishing a quick watercolour in the conservatory. I leave my sketchbook open to allow the paint to dry and go in to join him. This of course is slightly risky; the open sketchbook is an invitation to the curious.

Anyway John gets into a discussion with a middle-aged Scottish couple at breakfast about a gigantic deep-sea trawler that is going to fish off the west coast of Africa as soon as it can get its licence papers completed. Meantime it's making money as a tourist attraction called the 'Biggest Trawler in the World'. They've just been to see it. It's moored outside Killybegs Harbour in south Donegal.

John, of course, is in his element. He's fascinating to listen to even if, like me, you've heard it all before. After factory-ship trawling he describes the rather dreadful fishing-quota cycle. It happens repeatedly all over the world wherever there is a big population of edible fish in local waters; like the squid off the Kerala coast of India, lobsters in Maine, cod off Newfoundland, sturgeon in the mouth of the Danube. The list goes on and on.

John describes the cycle. For centuries he says, local fishermen have been harvesting the waters in relative harmony. Fishermen are typically not very good at business, so inevitably one of them, who is more switched-on than the others, does the organising. He sells their catch and keeps the price steady, buys the materials for repairing boats and making nets, and he argues the case for credit to tide them over off-seasons and hard times.

By the mid-twentieth century this has almost always developed to the point where a local businessman owns the nets and boats, manages the bank loans, and generally runs the show in a benign sort of way, just like Eddie Hamilton in Leenane.

Then along comes modern technology in the form of better boats, engines and nets, sonar equipment to find the shoals, bigger catches, specialised credit facilities and international markets. Local government then steps in and rationalises formal fishing areas and sets quotas which are assigned legally to the local fisheries, to these local businessmen – who else?

The businessmen are not slow to realise that these fishing rights, which were once a loose sort of cooperative, have now become legally defined property. Quotas are worth money and they have become the 'owners'. A fishery quota is very similar to building permission. Both are worth lots of money, and both are artificially created by laws to regulate the use of shared scarce resources. Big international food corporations then come along and buy up these fishing quotas.

Very soon the fishery goes into decline due to over-fishing, and the fish population is wiped out. John points out that when the original population has been wiped out, that particular fish species, cod or squid for example, can seldom re-establish itself. This is because the ecological balance ranging from seaweeds and plankton to predators has been permanently altered.

What has happened is that the resource which the local fishermen have been harvesting for centuries has been taken from them by the democratic process of commerce. Their birthright has been turned into quotas and then sold without their permission and without them getting a penny. Worse still; it has then been destroyed for ever. On the Kerala coast of south-west India, where it was the Japanese who 'bought' their quotas, the cry went up, 'We got rid of the British in 1947. Why can't we get rid of the Japanese?'

This perfectly highlights a serious flaw in the modern application of democracy. We all know government is supposed to be according to the will of the people. But that's the easy bit. As the world becomes a global village, a tricky problem is growing: whose will are we talking about here? Which people? Which tribe? There are tribes within tribes, so which tribe are we actually talking about? Democracy is sometimes not so good when it comes to defending people against business corporations.

The two Scots have been listening intently but eventually their eyes start to wander. Then they remember they haven't done their packing yet.

I collect my sketchbook from the conservatory where it's been drying and go on up to our room. On the landing I meet one of the sisters. She gives me a long sideways look. I say something silly like: 'Still raining I see. I do hope the day improves.'

She replies, 'I'd rather you didn't leave your private diary around where people can read it.'

'Oh sorry,' I say, not quite understanding this rebuke. Then it slowly dawns on me that she must be the one who's been looking at it when she shouldn't have. She must have read my candid description of her strange personality.

Shame and disgrace! As soon as I can, I have a look and, yes, there on the page facing the watercolour are the naughty words. I've gone and done it again – the sketchbook trick. It's a classic mistake which has caught me out several times before. The trouble is there's little point in keeping a diary if you can't put down life as you find it. Also you can't close a page till the paint is dry, which on a damp morning like this can take twenty minutes or more. But there's never really a good excuse for giving offence.

'Oh dear, I did get into trouble there,' I say, explaining the incident to John.

'So that's what happened.' he chuckles. 'I thought you were looking a bit sheepish. That'll learn you.'

View from Drumbarra House B&B which, while drying,
led to my disgrace

47 Pink lady on the road to Carrigart. Frank Trufelli. *Dual-nature theory explains terrorism and looting*

For two wet and windy days we cycle through the granite hills and around the rocky coast of Donegal. Past lakes and small farms we go, over rivers and estuaries.

There are mountains in the distance but the Donegal scenery is somehow less dramatic and grand, less inspiring than farther south. There are lots of holiday houses dotted around in isolated, un-planned positions. It's not that they spoil the view: just that they remind one of the struggles which local authorities all over the world have with planning permission. Struggles which it's obvious the Donegal rural council hasn't always won.

These minor quibbles show how we've been spoilt by the grandeur and beauty of Cork, Kerry, Clare, Galway and Mayo; because Donegal is still very lovely; the scenery is wonderfully weather-washed Atlantic and the wild flowers are beautiful. The honeysuckle is lush and plump, so are the montbretia and ragweed. And the mountain ash, John's favourite tree, is thick with bright red berries.

The places we pass through have lovely names: Crolly, Gweedore, Bunbeg, Meenaclady, Gortahock, the Tullahobegly River, Dunfanaghy, pronounced 'Donfunnahi' in an Ulster accent, Portnablagh, and Creeslough.

In Gweedore, where we stop for coffee, we find that Gweedore isn't on our route. We must have taken a wrong turning. Then we're told that no, it's OK, we're not in Gweedore – this is Magharaclougher and we're on the right road after all.

It's the signpost problem again. The biggest ones are brown. They have a Tourist Board logo and say silly things you don't need to know, like 'North-west Passage', that's neither useful nor witty and we all know it's in Canada not Ireland. The place names are mostly in Irish but our map gives them in English. The distances are in kilometres but on our map they're in miles. The roads are usually numbered on the signposts, but on the small roads, which we prefer to take, these usually differ from the map. The numbers must have been changed by central by-law, which hasn't reached out here yet. And finally, quite often some local joker has turned the signposts around. The German army better be careful around here.

It takes us a while to get used to all this but after a while a sceptical, topographical intuition develops in which the signposts, the maps and the terrain are combined into a rough and ready route-finding ability. When that lets us down and we are obviously lost, we ask the way.

At one point we come to a fork in the road and ask a man standing there, 'Is that the way to Carrigart?'

'Well it is,' he says, 'you can get there that way, but it's a hostile road. It's hilly and there are turnstiles.' Turnstiles? we wonder. But there's something menacing in his voice and we don't ask him to elucidate. Instead he recommends a better road half a mile farther on. Not wanting any hostilities, especially so near to the border with Northern Ireland, we take his advice.

We stop for tea at a hotel in Dunglow, a small country town.

Out comes the map. The coast road looks nice, so we plan to follow it up to a place called Kincasslough where we'll hope to find a B&B.

As we are getting back in the saddle outside the hotel a tall, well-dressed lady comes along. She's about to go into the hotel. But first she looks us over somewhat imperiously. To break the spell she casts we ask her if she knows the way out to Kincasslough.

'Oh yes!' she says, very definitely.

This is a bit surprising because she's speaking with an American accent. Actually she's looking very smart, mainly pink with some purple, she's about sixty. It turns out she was born in Ireland but has lived all her life in Florida and she's over with some friends to see where Daniel O'Donnell lives and hopefully to meet him.

Daniel O'Donnell, 'Wee Daniel', as he's known locally, is a melodious singer of traditional and middle-of-the-road songs. He has a soft Donegal accent and he's immensely popular with a huge fan club, especially among the older ladies. They flock to see him from all over the world, including this fine pink person from Florida.

She tells us with a quizzical look, which says we must be pulling her leg or be particularly stupid, that Kincasslough is Daniel's birthplace and he lives there still with his mother and sister when he's not away on tour. I've certainly heard of Wee Daniel, but John is looking bemused so he probably hasn't. I cover up for him with guesswork like 'Oh yes, of course' and 'Isn't his mother a grand old character?'; that sort of thing.

The fine lady from Florida points to the road out to Kincasslough. We say thanks and that we hope she manages to meet the great man, and off we go.

When we get to Kincasslough we find, right enough, that all the B&Bs have been booked up weeks ago by Wee Daniel's fans. Eventually we find a vacancy in Carrigart.

Our old friend Frank Trufelli lives in Portrush, which is about four or five days' cycle-ride away. He too rowed with us at TCD, a sharp-faced good-looking lad who had more poise and polish than the rest of us. He was the one who always got the girls, the bastard. But we were fond of him and his breezy cynical humour. One sort of knew that his success with the girls was more to do with our gaucheness than any deviousness on his part. Neither of us has met Frank since we left Ireland forty years ago.

We telephone him to say he's got to stand to attention when we come through Portrush.

Frank, it turns out, is a keen golfer these days. He has just completed a term as captain of Portrush Golf Club, an international golf links set right by the sea amongst a thousand acres of sand dunes. Unfortunately he won't be in Portrush when we come through because he and his new wife, Alice, are going to Rosapenna to play in a rather exclusive tournament. Only captains and past captains of top-class clubs are invited. The tournament starts tomorrow afternoon. Then they're off to Italy.

How and where to meet is a complicated question because we'll be travelling west to east while they'll be coming in the opposite direction. But when exactly? We finally decide to meet for lunch at a restaurant on the road somewhere between Portrush and Rosapenna. 'You'll see it on the right, you can't possibly miss it,' says Frank. 'Oh no?' we think. But Mrs Doherty, the landlady at our B&B in Carrigart, says she thinks she knows the place. It's generally agreed that we ought to be able to find it.

I've been thinking about John's challenging remark that if dual-nature theory can't explain the terrorism in Northern Ireland then it's not much use. The problem is that we're saying morality is the language of cooperation, and yet here are two highly religious communities, both expert in moral judgement, who are constantly at each other's throats.

The answer has been falling into place and sprawling over the pages of my sketchbook.

At lunch near a bridge over the Tullaghobegly River I try it out on John.

'About man's appallingly bad behaviour – you know, crucifying people, ripping up rainforests, and shooting elephants just for fun. I'm thinking particularly about Northern Ireland . . . '

'Yes, tell me.' The sceptical voice.

I'm immediately on the defensive, afraid that the beautiful idea is going to get ripped to shreds. 'Well you're the one who started all this in the first place by fuming against big business. I'm only trying to defend my evil career in industry, after all it seemed quite natural at the time.'

'All right, go on then.'

'Well, the way I see it, dual-nature theory explains terrorism in clear simplicity. Terrorism is generated by the systematic infuriation of a minority group, usually a tribe.'

Pause. 'And that's it?'

'Er . . . yes I think so, but remember that being derived directly from dual-nature theory, this can now claim scientific authority. We're talking evolutionary biology here not morality, fact not opinion. In other words, hard science. So this could greatly improve the effectiveness of public debate.'

'You'd better explain.'

'In every terrorist situation you'll find the infuriated doing the violence; the bombing, hijacking and so on, and the infuriators claiming with outraged rhetoric to hold the moral high ground while refusing to back down on the infuriation. The talk is usually about defeating the cowardly, deceitful terrorists.

'Dual-nature theory shows this rhetoric to be foolish and completely ineffective. It indicates the real issues which need to be thought through. Morality simply doesn't apply in inter-group behaviour. The moral high ground is irrelevant to another enemy. Any attempt at punishment is simply taken as an attack.

'Moreover,' I go on, 'because it is usually the infuriators who started the problem in the first place, and who are always the stronger party. It is always in their power to calm things down by conceding.'

'Yes,' says John, 'and usually in their long-term interests to do so. I suppose it means that England should pull out of the North.'

'It could come to that. However dual-nature theory only says that if – and it's a big "if" – if the Protestant majority really does want peace, then the grievances of the Catholic community should be fully understood and systematically removed. The history of the problem is so deep that this could take several generations. Moral high ground rhetoric, which is such a spectacular part of Northern Irish politics, is a corrosive poison in all this, and it makes us all despair of the chances of a solution.

'There's nothing new in what I'm saying,' I conclude. 'Except for one very important point, which is that a biological understanding of the mess we've got ourselves into may one day give us the clarity of vision to help ourselves out of it. Exactly the same thing applies to the American infuriation of Islam.'

'That's simple and clear,' says John. 'But why couldn't we see it when we were discussing Belleek a few days ago?'

'Well I suppose it was all too emotional, and we haven't yet got the habit of applying the theory properly. We missed the obvious point that Northern Ireland is a classic example of people trying to solve a clash between two groups by applying morality. And that morality has scant relevance to inter-group behaviour.

'I know I keep on saying dual-nature theory makes things simple. What I mean is that it enables you to see a problem in its entirety. For example, it shows that by definition a democracy cannot solve terrorism.

'There have been about ten general elections since I came to England in 1964 and in not one of them has the terrorism in Northern Ireland been a serious election issue. All the main parties agree that the terrorists must be defeated and disarmed, but that never works on its own without the removal of the infuriation. The same goes for international terrorism.

'In a democracy politicians are elected by majority vote. So if terrorism is generated by the infuriation of a voting minority, which as a result becomes a cooperating group or tribe, then democracy has no mechanism for removing the infuriation, because there aren't enough votes to carry the removal through. There are by definition always more votes against concession than for it. Simple maths says democracy cannot resolve terrorism.'

It's a relief to have got that off my chest, and it seems to have John's preliminary approval. We sit on the river bank in silence.

But then I notice John seems to be cooking something up. 'Yes, I see,' he says, gazing at the water. 'We're talking about human violence really, aren't we? Violence which often entails killing.'

'Yes.'

'Well if you take a detached look at human violence; as a biological study, like we're saying, and if you realise that humans have these two quite distinct modes of behaviour, then it's likely that we can explain more than just terrorism. I mean what about other forms of human violence? Murder, for example, also war and looting.'

'Hadn't thought of that,' I say. 'You're right.'

To play for time, but also because I need to, I go for a pee in the river farther downstream.

By the time I return he's sorted things out. 'Here's an example of how a good answer can often solve another question as well,' he says. 'Try this: Murder, terrorism, war and looting – they're grades of human violence. Murder is violence between individual members of the same group or tribe. It's an internal thing; a moral issue properly within the jurisdiction of the tribe's code of ethics.

'Terrorism, as you've just said, is violence by a small group against a larger one which is infuriating it.

'War is violence between two similarly matched groups. We would be horrified to watch another species of animal annihilating its cousins in warfare, yet humans do it all the time.

'But the really interesting one is looting. It's different. It happens when strict discipline is suddenly removed. Like, for example, when a war suddenly stops, or an earthquake leaves a vacuum where there was previously law and order. People then find that their working group has just vanished. Poof ! Like that. The rules are instantly vaporised and they become solitaries. It's every man for himself. When they find themselves disoriented like that, their selfish prime motivators quickly surface. The group or tribe has been eliminated and the self-restraining force of morality is temporarily disabled. There are countless examples of this in history. One of the best known was "La Grande Peur", when anarchy ruled France after the French Revolution.'

'Yes, that's terrific!' I say. 'It shows how dual-nature theory can be used to explain human behaviour. Looting is such a strange thing, I've always thought it was somehow weirdly abnormal.'

'Actually, come to think of it,' says John, 'the way a carnivorous pack animal, like the hyena or lion, switches from disciplined hunting to a feeding frenzy once they've caught their prey looks very like looting. Dual-nature theory explains looting in biological terms by analysing the dynamics of cooperation. It's an extreme example of a switch from group to solitary behaviour; an example of nature's default condition reasserting itself.'

'So would that be a hit for our theory? I mean according to the scientific method.'

'If it could be demonstrated in an experiment, yes it would.'

Suddenly another lady wearing skin-tight shiny purple cycling shorts comes whizzing along the road. We can see her from where we're sitting near the bridge over the Tullaghobegly River. Up over the bridge she comes. We're riveted to the spot. It couldn't be her again, could it? We get a good view as she freewheels down, leaning into the bend at the other end of the bridge. She's down on her lower handlebars, her shapely bottom in the air and a man close behind. But sadly no. She is sporting but she's older and somehow not so purple as the heavenly vision in Kerry.

'Close,' says John, 'but no cigar.'

48 Experienced barmaid, military pee, lunch with Frank,
    'Bowl of Light'. *How we switch between individual
    morality and group amorality, and that this should be
    formally taught in school*

Next day it's raining again when we come to a little place on an estuary
near the head of Lough Swilly. It's called Rathmelton. We need somewhere out of the wet to eat our squashed picnic. There's a big modern
roadside inn on the right, set back off the road, called the Silver Tassie.
Some smartly dressed families are having lunch.

But after a pint of Guinness at the bar we sense there's a problem
about letting us eat here. Eventually an experienced-looking barmaid
talks to the fresh-faced young man who is obviously the manager. She
persuades him we're harmless and we are led away to a table in a far
corner where we have another Guinness and eat our basse-cuisine,
but delicious, meal. Plates and knives and forks are brought and we
hide away the plastic bags and food wrappings.

There's no smoking in the restaurant, and towards the end of our
meal, the experienced barmaid comes over to our little corner to light
up a surreptitious fag and have a chat. When we leave we give her a
big tip, which proves how experienced she is.

Experienced barmaid having illicit fag in the Silver Tassie at Rathmelton

Once back on the road it's not long before the Guinness has worked its way through and we're both desperate for a pee.

We see some landscape-gardened municipal bushes for piddling under. They are by a smart new wall on the corner where we join the main road from Letterkenny to Derry. The wall is grey, topped with white stones. It's eight feet high and there are new buildings behind.

Suddenly coming from nowhere, we hear a man's voice; it's very close. Sounding like a concealed policeman or even a soldier, it says: 'This isn't a public lavatory, move on quickly please.' We're close to the border now and around here the police don't stand any nonsense.

John replies rather bravely, 'Well it is now.'

We cycle off sheepishly, quite mystified because it's impossible to work out where the voice came from. Could it have been a hidden underground gun-post covering this main-road intersection? And were we piddling into it?

The road to Derry then loops round the head of Lough Swilly. You can see on the map that it's tidal, narrow and very long, so the Lough must obviously have got its name on account of the swilly way the tides surge in and out.

We are now on a big main highway. We keep close to the side in single file as the traffic roars past. The wet squalling wind is mostly from behind; it blows us along like discarded plastic bags. The less said about these big trunk roads the better; they're not kind to cyclists.

We find a bed for the night in a little place called Burt. It's a little name for a little place, and it's only three miles west of the restaurant where we are due to meet Frank and Alice for lunch. So tomorrow we can have a lazy morning. That'll be nice.

But of course when tomorrow comes, lazing around feels a bit boring. We're so used to pedalling all day, stretching our legs in the breeze, and the lovely Atlantic scenery that we don't know quite how to spend the time. We fritter it away in a sluggish torpor.

For a while, using the notes in my sketchbook, we review the progress we've made so far with dual-nature theory. Our explanations of bureaucracy, corporate greed and terrorism are surprisingly diverse. They're totally separate topics. This seems to hint that more solutions to political and social problems are waiting to be unearthed. And of course that would help to validate the theory. The more questions that can be explained and solved, the more likely it is that dual-nature theory really does work.

We have coffee and it's not long before we hit on another. It's what I call 'the seduction of morality', and this is how it happens.

John is writing postcards. He's stuck for words, looks out the window and says: 'There's a problem I've been worrying about.'

'Oh dear!' I say. 'Well I do occasionally think to myself that it's got to be wrong. After all, if it's such a good idea why hasn't it been thought of before? It is highly improbable that two old men on bicycles, who know little about either philosophy or genetics should come up with a radically new theory of human behaviour which combines both.'

'Well, here's the problem. If in common with all cooperating vertebrates we have two modes of behaviour, surely we ought to be well aware of the switch from one to the other. It must be happening within ourselves all the time, and yet I can't say I notice it either in myself or in others. I'm talking about the switch from moral self-restraint to immoral group behaviour.'

'That's a tricky one,' I say.

Then I remember the pucai. Perhaps like them it's happening all the time; all around us. Perhaps we just don't normally notice it because it's so natural; a bit like breathing.

'Think of a four-year-old child. Because of its inborn propensity for rules of self-restraint, its loving parents have no trouble teaching it right and wrong. Learning is fun and it quickly gets the message. At this point however it has little experience of inter-group behaviour.'

'Yes, I see what you're going to say,' says John. 'That as soon as it becomes aware of the outside world, it notices the alternative, juicier, illicit fun of collective naughtiness. Hooliganism thrills. It's the story of Selassie again.'

'Right. It makes friends at school and joins groups outside the family, and then inter-group behaviour rears its ugly head and the child is quick to learn the next lesson. Which is that there is a vast difference between the small still voice of conscience, which influences the cooperate-or-split decision, and the compelling thrill of gang behaviour, in which these rules are effortlessly overridden.

'The youngster watches a gang. They're having fun. It longs to join in. It then quickly discovers that those who want to join, but at first don't conform because of innocence or conscience, quickly get bullied into place or rejected. This explains the important, essential and natural purpose of bullying. It isn't just a nasty human trait, it's absolutely vital to group efficiency.'

'Bull's-eye!' says John. 'All cooperating animals do it; you just have to watch the bullying that goes on in a litter of puppies.'

'Bullying and boasting flourish in the jockeying for position as leadership struggles simmer and crackle. The problem of football hooliganism fits neatly into this analysis.' I'm sounding like a lecturer again, it's partly because he is slightly deaf.

'Yes, yes,' says John, 'we all know the laddish, boastful, locker-room banter which effortlessly overrides conscience. I read recently about laddishness amongst senior hospital surgeons which explained why they routinely overlooked malpractice. It was a well-published scandal.'

He's got hold of something, so I stifle a banal comment about operating-theatre humour and wait. He goes on: 'There's a much more deliberate, institutionalised, bureaucratic angle here too. I'm thinking of the Canadian fisheries people I'm perpetually struggling with. They ignored what they knew perfectly well to be best strategy for the cod fishery off Newfoundland. Instead they pursued politically acceptable policies until – surprise! surprise! – the cod were completely wiped out.'

'Right, excellent example,' I say, 'and remember Hitler. The man who has worked his way to the top is always a gifted cooperator and opinion former, and so he feels an overpowering responsibility to do the will of the people, which he himself has helped to mould. And the people around him are eager to follow. As the saying goes: "We were just taking orders." That's how the process welds itself together in an almost religious fervour. And of course that's how the still small voice of conscience is effortlessly silenced, drowned out by the thrill of cooperation. There, happening in front of our very eyes, is the switch from individual morality to group amorality. It's the fervour of team self-belief that does it.'

'That's so depressing,' says John. 'It shows, biologically, how a switch of behavioural mode, so common and effortless that we seldom notice it, enables us to do what moral codes say is appalling, but which in reality is perfectly natural. We've done it countless times in the past and there's nothing to stop us doing it again, on into the future, world without end. It means there'll be lots more Hitlers because it's basic human nature.'

' 'Fraid so.'

'Depressing.'

'Very. That's why it's often best to be a cynic like old Frank, or even a pessimist. Life has fewer disappointments for them.'

'Quite true,' he says.

To change the subject I tell him about the marvellous little novel I read recently called *The Seduction of Morality*. It's by Tom Murphy, one of Ireland's leading playwrights. It's about a New York prostitute who deeply shocks her hypocritical Irish family when she comes home on a visit and they gradually discover what her occupation actually is. Some absolutely hilarious passages beautifully conceal the book's deeper morality.

'That's what we could call it,' he says.

'Call what?'

'We could call the switch "the seduction of morality".'

'Yes, that's good, Tom Murphy's not to know we stole it from him, 'And,' I go on, 'thinking of the switch taking place in children, I bet good schoolteachers know all about the seduction of morality both intuitively and from experience. I bet they understand and sympathise with what their pupils are going through.'

'You're dead right,' he says. 'And you know what that means?'

'No, what?'

'It means that trainee teachers should be taught it formally so that, alongside sex education, they can explain to their young pupils what's happening to them. Children need to be helped through this period of intense experiment and learning in a socially constructive way. Dual-nature theory should be formalised as a school subject, called "Group Behaviour" or better still "The Seduction of Morality". It's considerably more important than sex education.'

Still having time to kill before setting off to meet Frank, we sketch out the content of these lessons. They would teach that the seduction of morality is an essential part of human behaviour; that tribes and business corporations which put self-restraint above self-interest in their 'foreign policy' will lose out to more ruthless competitors; that the seduction of morality is a switching mechanism which releases the tribe, seen as an organism, from the authority of the still small voice; from the straitjacket of morality. They would explain the natural purpose of bullying in order to channel it healthily. These lessons would teach that society confuses two quite distinct types of law: those regulating individual behaviour and those regulating cooperating groups. The aim would be to turn out socially responsible cooperators.

When it's time to go and meet Frank and Alice the rain has started again. This time it's heavy showers. We wait till one clears and nip off hoping to make it to the restaurant before the next one. Which we do, but only just.

The restaurant is actually a converted church. From the roadside it's a handsome grey limestone building with steeple, stained-glass windows, and heavy oak doors. Inside it's a smart, slightly self-conscious, restaurant.

Before going in we hide behind a buttress, just as it's starting to pour again, to change into long trousers.

Frank and Alice haven't arrived yet. We're shown to a table and sit down to wait for them.

Frank was frequently late for outings. About the biggest crime an oarsman can commit, worse even than catching a crab, is being late for an outing.

When a dignified, slightly portly, grey-haired gentleman in late middle age comes in through the door we realise it's got to be him. But we remember Frank as lithe and slim with jet-black hair.

There's a moments hesitation.

'Christ!' he must be thinking. 'Would you ever look at those two scruffy-looking bearded old wrecks.'

'Late Trufelli, as usual,' we tell him.

After huge hellos all round and handshakes with Alice, the old Frank comes flooding back, and it's with total joy and absolute sincerity that we tell each other, 'You know, it's amazing! You really haven't changed one little bit.' It's lovely to see old Frank again. Alice listens with a wry smile while we remember the rowing and the privileged irresponsible life of the Trinity student in those early post-war years.

We remember David Coffee, a brilliant squash player and cricketer, who after a wild party near Dublin Airport somehow got into the cockpit of a Dakota passenger plane on the runway and, by pulling a lever which he drunkenly thought was the joystick, released its under-carriage mechanism, very nearly destroying the whole plane. Then there was Andrew Bonar Law, who could climb anything. He once stuck a poster right in the centre of the exam-hall ceiling and to this day nobody knows how he could possibly have done it, except him of course.

John and I also did our bit to liven up the town by throwing the

'Bowl of Light', a controversial piece of sculpture on O'Connell Bridge, into the Liffey. John escaped but I was put in jail for the night, and fined £50. That was in 1953. The escapade caught the public mood, which in those austere early post-war years craved a bit of lightness of heart and public mirth. It became known as 'The night they threw the Bowl of Light in the Liffey'. Articles about it appeared in all the newspapers for months afterwards. Excited letters to the press were printed. Some said it was just a student prank, others that it was disgraceful behaviour; one letter-writer, a retired Irish army major, said I should be flogged in public. People found Protestant *v.* Catholic angles. The sculpture was made of plastic and was widely disliked, so some praised our disgraceful behaviour as an artistic gesture on behalf of the aesthetes versus the philistines. John and I said nothing, and the 'Bowl of Light' was never found or replaced.

Photo of John and me with very large Garda officer taken in 1953
in O'Connell Street, Dublin, about half an hour before
we threw the 'Bowl of Light' into the Liffey

This, I realise, is my chance to ask if Frank knows whatever became of Lexy Cartwright and Jumbo McKee. They were both from Lima-vaddy, not far from Portrush where Frank lives. Their fathers were solicitors who had rival practices in the town, so they had known each other since childhood.

At Trinity, Lexy and Jumbo were two wild lads. Lexy was an all-round sportsman: a talented rugby player, a good oarsman and a great ladies' man. But I had heard that somehow things had gone wrong for him some years after he left Trinity.

Jumbo was a huge bony fellow, and though he was fun and curious about life, he was sort of uncoordinated. We tried hard but could never get him to row properly. He was rather like a large puppy who had grown too fast. He had trouble getting out of bed and kept missing lectures. Jumbo drank rather a lot. Then one term when he went missing we heard that he'd been kicked out of college for not attending lectures. We were allowed to miss quite a lot of lectures but Jumbo, it turned out, had missed them all.

I ask Frank, but he's lost touch with them both many years ago. He says he thinks he heard that Lexy went to the bad and after a time in jail had to go abroad. 'New Zealand, I think.'

Lunch is over all too soon because Frank has to be on the first tee at Rosapenna by three o'clock. He'll doubtless be late, but that doesn't seem to bother him. Dear old Frank; he hasn't changed one little bit.

We wave goodbye to them both and dash smartly back into the restaurant again because there's another lashing downpour. It lasts fifteen minutes.

49 Downpour in Buncrana, high moor, Inishowen Peninsular. *Dual-nature theory survives 'Quis Custodiet?' but doesn't solve it. The Protestant marches*

When the rain blows over we set off again.

Throughout the afternoon we punch into squalls of wind and rain which tear holes in my cheap, flimsy cycling cape. The damned thing gets ripped where it's draped over my brake levers. John is wearing a yellow fishing anorak, it's all wrong for cycling; weighs him down and gets all sweaty inside. We should have brought better rain-gear. Some cyclists have good strong-looking capes, but they don't seem to sell them in any of the shops we pass.

It clears up somewhat as we cycle along.

We are now going due north, pushing on up the Inishowen Peninsular towards Malin Head, the most northerly point of Ireland. The peninsular is bounded by Lough Swilly on our left and Lough Foyle on our right.

We get to Buncrana at about four o'clock. It's another seaside holiday resort. But when we get there the heavens open. We're drenched and get off to shelter under the canopy of a big hotel. The rain bounces up off the road creating a layer of white mist which lies two feet deep on top of the road surface.

As the squall passes over, torrents of water come flooding down the streets of Buncrana. If one of these hits Rosapenna it won't be very nice for Frank's golf tournament.

We're aiming for Cardonagh, which is about six miles south of Malin Head. As we're already soaking wet there's not much point in hanging about, so on we go.

Soon the road climbs up on to a high, barren moor. It's quite a climb but mercifully we now have the fierce wind behind us and when we get to the top there is a tremendous freewheel ride out over the empty landscape. The wind behind must be gale force, and the road has recently been resurfaced, so we absolutely whizz along. I don't think I've ever in my life gone faster on a bike, it must have been 40 mph at times. After that vicious rain it's exhilarating and wonderful; almost like flying: 'Over the hills and far away'.

Finally our wonderful freewheeling spree over the high moor is over. The road has come back down to sea level at Cardonagh.

We find a room in the Oregon B&B. The landlady is called Patricia. She settles us down with a big pot of strong tea and some delicious freshly baked scones with butter.

We check to see did our luggage get soaked in all that rain. But by now we've both mastered the skill of packing everything into plastic bin-liners inside our panniers, so most of our stuff is reasonably OK.

Anything wet, like the clothes we cycled in, gets draped out around the room to dry. I'm glad my wife can't see the mess, or indeed smell it because, naturally enough, as well as the smell of humid well-worn cycling clothes, the squashed picnic food makes its presence known with a promise of gastronomy in store.

We shower and settle down to an hour's reading and sketchbook writing before going out to dinner.

John reading in comfort amongst drying clothing,
equipment and picnic remains

John's now reading *Wildstream: Natural History of the Free Flowing River* by Thomas F. Waters. He says it's a terrific book and quotes occasional passages. They are quite scientific but not too difficult for the layman. It has a lot on ecology and conservation. With a name like Waters, I'm thinking, you'd have to write a book about rivers wouldn't you.

This reminds me of a wonderful book called *The Imperial Animal*, because it's joint authors, amazingly, were called Lionel Tiger and Robin Fox. *The Imperial Animal* made a huge impression on me. I read it in the early 1970s. It was the first time I'd read an explanation of human behaviour which treats mankind like any other animal, and I now realise that ever since reading that book I've been sub-consciously storing away perceptions of human and animal behaviour in the mental compartments it set up for me. And now on this trip these perceptions are all being taken out again and fitted together into what we're calling dual-nature theory.

John puts his book down. 'A behavioural problem has just occurred to me while reading this. It's about the law.'

'The law, yes, that's an angle I'm a bit nervous of.' But then I remind myself that we accountants do tend to have an exaggerated respect for the law.

'In human society,' John explains, 'our tribally-adopted rules of behaviour, our moral codes, are written into law and this law is what controls the amoral behaviour of the subsidiary tribes, families and teams that make up our society. Right?'

'Right.'

'So without the rule of law, these subsidiary tribes with quasi-minds of their own, and with no obligation as discrete entities to behave morally – they would wreck the joint; there'd be anarchy. Is that right? It's the rule of law that enables human society to work, isn't it?'

'Yes, if the law breaks down, so does society.'

'So the problem is who lays down the law?'

'The leadership does it in accordance with the will of the people.' I did economics and political science at Trinity.

'Yes, but you can go higher and higher, right up to international level. If we are to prevent global destruction of the rainforests for example, or of the Atlantic salmon, there always has to be a top authority, a top dog, and what is to stop that person from laying down ignorant, corrupt or evil laws?'

'Yes, that's called the "*quis custodiet?*" problem.'

'The what?'

'We learnt that at college, it's a political-theory exam question: "*Quis custodiet ipsos custodes?*" Who is to control the controller? So far as I know nobody has ever thought of the answer.'

John gets back to his book, but presently he brightens up. 'Actually I don't think this "*quis custodiet?*" problem necessarily destroys our theory. It simply suggests there may be no hope for mankind because we are unable to harness the astonishing mastery our species has achieved through cooperation. We may become extinct, wiped out by the uncontrollable inventions of our own runaway success, but that doesn't mean that dual-nature theory is wrong.'

'Yes, well done! What is it they say? "The operation was a complete success but unfortunately the patient died." '

Gloom settles on our little bedroom.

Our landlady, Patricia, has strongly recommended a nearby restaurant. 'It's called the Tulna-Ri, but everybody calls it Simpsons.'

I choose the lamb chops and get two vast potatoes and braised onion as well. John has the steak with garlic potatoes. We get chatting to Mick Morgan, a Welshman. He has an outsider's view of the tensions up here between Protestants and Catholics. We discuss the strange business of the Protestant marches, the traditional annual street events in which one religious group gets all dressed up, wearing dark suits, medals and bowler hats, and sets off with drums, flutes, banners and flags on a parade whose purpose is the ritual taunting of the other religious group. It's not unlike the New Zealand rugby team doing a harka before the kick-off. But how come a decent God-fearing man with a good job and respectable home-life can switch into a Protestant marcher?

Suddenly I realise that what we're discussing is actually the seduction of morality. Back at home each marcher is an intelligent, polite and well-behaved family man. By what actual process does he change, like the flip of a coin, into an arrogant bully-boy when he joins a gang? I can well remember the days, back in the 1940s, when doctors, solicitors and clergymen, joined in. Even judges did; I know that because my grandfather was a senior judge, and he once took me on a Protestant march. 'This is my daughter Mary's little boy,' he proudly told everyone who knew him.

I try the question out on John and Mick. 'These marches perfectly illustrate our dual nature,' I say. 'One minute we are well-behaved family members, the next we join a bullying, insulting, hooligan gang. The real point here is that both behaviours are perfectly natural.'

Mick Morgan chatting at the bar in Simpsons, Cardonagh

But this must be a bit heavy for pub talk over pints of beer because my words come out sounding as though I'm trying to make a speech.

I soon lose my audience. For Mick the answer is much simpler than that. 'It's obvious really,' he says. 'You first have to decide which side is right and which is wrong. Is it the Protestants with their arrogant "No Surrender" bigotry, or the Catholics who want the whole of Ireland to worship the Pope? Once you have decided that, the rest is easy: you lock up the ones in the wrong.'

And I can tell from John's evasive eye movements that the rising din of pub talk is making it difficult for him to hear what we're saying. He's on some distant continent where there are no politicians, industrialists or engineers and where the salmon leap all day.

Dual-nature theory may go to the heart of our everyday behaviour, but it wouldn't be an easy message to get across in the pubs, on the park benches and in the women's institute.

50 Malin Head, shipping forecast. John swims naked, Inspector of dredging, art talk, disturbed night. *The theory explains team games*

We reach Malin Head at midday. It's the most northerly point of Ireland. Next stop Iceland.

There is a steep climb up to the headland.

Malin Head is a household name because it's mentioned on the radio several times a day as one of the points in the shipping forecast.

There was once a dispute about how to pronounce Malin. In the shipping forecast it used to be with a flat A as in salmon. Then in the 1950s a distinguished member of the Ulster Protestant gentry wrote a letter to *The Times* pointing out that the correct pronunciation is with a long A, sounding like Morelun. The BBC duly complied with this correction. But then some months later somebody else wrote in to say that; yes, OK, the posh may say Morelun, but in the local village of Ballygorman, population fifty, it's Malin; flat A. So that was that, and much to everybody's relief, including of course the shipping navigators and yachting folk, the BBC went back to Malin. Final score: Ballygorman 2 – Protestant Gentry 1

There's a windswept viewing point up here beside some low granite buildings, and there's a big rock with handsomely carved and polished lettering which reads:

Malin Head is the most northerly point in IRELAND. Ten miles offshore is the small island of Inishtrahull. Round Malin Head are well preserved shorelines about 15,000 years old and of great geological importance. The ruined building nearby to the right was formerly a Lloyd's signal tower. Having been built originally by order of The Admiralty around 1805 to report all ships passing along this route.

Apart from the curious punctuation, John spots a problem with this nice little message: Can the well preserved shorelines have appeared, just like that, about 15,000 years ago? And can they really be all that important?

Maybe they did and maybe they are. There are always more questions than answers.

By one o'clock we're getting hungry. It's not actually raining but it's a bit cold and windy so we ask at a charming little roadside pub; would it be OK for us to come in for a pint and eat our picnic. The answer is one word: 'No.' Simple and straightforward but abrupt.

Humiliated, we cycle on till we find a nice lunch spot on the bank of the Keenagh River.

During lunch I ask John. 'Now that we've concocted a theory of human behaviour what do you think of it? Do you think it might work?'

'Well, I'm not up on the latest science involved, but I guess proof would require extensive biological research into the genetic workings of propensity.'

'Oh dear,' I say, feeling way out of my depth.

'However,' he continues, 'scientists aren't totally inhuman, they do accept that the more a hypothesis makes sense the more likely it is to be right. That means the more we can show that dual-nature theory explains the problems and oddities of our behaviour, the more we validate the theory without actually proving it.'

He's saying 'we' again which is comforting. 'You mean we now need to explore the delights and disgraces, the mysteries and mis-demeanours of our behaviour?'

'I'll leave the poetry to you. But you must remember credibility is not the same as certainty.'

'OK, OK.'

After quite a long silence John says. 'Here's a thing about human behaviour. Cooperating animals have athletic competitions; you know, jousting, wrestling and running. But only humans play team games. It would be good if dual-nature theory could explain them; they're such an important part of our lives.'

He's on to something there.

'Remember the Martian in her space ship,' he says. 'She would be intrigued by this curious bit of behaviour. If our theory could explain it, we would gain credibility. People spend an enormous amount of time and money playing, watching and reading about team games, and yet they don't apparently have any survival or reproductive purpose at all. So I suppose I'm saying that any comprehensive explanation of human behaviour must include team games.'

We knock it about a bit and it's not long before we end up with a plausible explanation of the origin and purpose of team games according to dual-nature theory.

First of all there are rules of self-restraint. To be able to play team games, one must recognise and obey the externally imposed rules. As well as these there are also the team's own self-imposed who's–going-to-be-captain and who-plays-where rules, and the unselfish give and take of opportunities.

Secondly the members must be able to communicate.

We agree that rule-making, self-restraint and recognition-plus-communication are the three principal skills required for all verte-brate cooperation. This suggests that humans may get a distinct Darwinian thrill from the way in which team games exercise and sharpen up these skills.

John then speculates as to whether other cooperators have similar methods of practising and honing these skills. Do other animals behave in ways which tingle the same instincts but fall short of organised team games? Do sparrows and meercats have practice warnings of danger, like fire drills in large office buildings? Do lions have practice hunts and do beavers have pretend dam-building sessions? And do the individual animals who are seen to be best at these simulations gain a breeding advantage? What John wants to know is do the ones who shine in practise sessions get the best girls?

Football spectators, we agree, get huge pleasure out of supporting a team. This exercises their instinct for loyalty towards a working group: a club which they play at belonging to and whose success they most urgently desire. Heroes who play individual sports can seldom evoke such a vicarious sense of belonging and loyalty.

Examples of the honing of cooperator skills fall neatly into place. We notch up social memory in rugby, cheater detection in yacht racing, leadership and unselfishness in football, coordinated unison in rowing, and finding the difference between inspired bravery and reckless risk-taking in cricket.

I temporarily divert this collection of evidence with something that has often intrigued me: Why of all the team games we play, do only cricket and baseball have symbolic death as their central feature. Why is there is no other major sport in which the purpose of a team is to kill off the members of the opposing team one by one? We can't think of the answer.

John sums up with a compelling monologue about thrill. He points out that the apparently pointless team games we play give an intense surging thrill to both players and spectators. And this thrill can't be explained as an abnormal stimulation of our animal nature like using alcohol, nicotine or cocaine. It must, he says, be explained somehow by reference to our success as a species.

'So biologically speaking, organised team games are events in which we can safely watch two cooperating groups do battle. They simulate real life and it is plainly obvious that the cooperative behaviour amongst team members is totally different from the competitive behaviour between the two teams. That is why they are so thrilling to play and so compelling to watch. Team games perfectly illustrate our dual nature.'

Sensing nervously that he's about to use the dreadful paradigm word again, I quickly interject: 'But, John, as you yourself pointed out that doesn't prove it scientifically.'

'True, but it's becoming more convincing.'

'Well,' I say, 'there could be a little problem here. I don't think they played team games in the ancient Greek Olympics.'

'Oh dear! Is that right? Bit of research needed there.'

'Yes that could be a fascinating academic study, but I don't believe the answer will upset our theory.'

'Hope not,' says John.

Eventually we load up our bikes and wheel them back to the road.

Five miles later John spots a place to swim. Of course nobody else would even consider it. It's a flat, shallow estuary with a wide expanse of brackish-looking water. Not only that but it's heavily overcast and there's a cold wind. 'It'll only be a quick plunge,' he says, and stripping off, he trots off completely naked across the muddy shore.

While he's splashing about boisterously a lady comes past walking her dog. I give her a cheery 'hello', trying to pretend by my posture and attitude that I've never even met him. But her quizzical look says 'you don't fool me that easily'. Eventually he dries himself on his little towel, dresses, gets back on his bike and off we go.

We cycle on into the afternoon. It's a long straight road that undulates over a sort of no man's land. It's flat but there is no cultivation, or very little; no hedges or fences; no grass or crops. I notice one solitary cow. I guess we must be crossing what was once a vast turf bog which has been stripped bare and drained, leaving stony ground covered in reeds and thorny scrub. This goes on for miles and miles.

At half-five we arrive at Moville which is on the west shore of Lough Foyle. At this point the lough narrows to about half-a-mile wide and dotted lines on the map indicate a ferry at Greencastle four miles farther north. If we can't get across here it means a half-day detour through Derry, right around the shore of this great tidal lough.

We find an attic room in a scruffy little B&B. Then we go to the McNamara Hotel for dinner. The food is wholesome and the service is terrific despite the fact that there must be over forty other people eating here. It's a big old-fashioned dining room and about seven people are serving us all with smooth and expert efficiency.

There's a pretty lady near us with a tattoo on her left shoulder. I do a quick drawing of her. I hold my sketchbook half under the tablecloth trying not to be noticed.

Pretty lady with tattoo dining beside us in the
McNamara Hotel in Moville

But there's a man and his wife at the table next to ours and he's spotted me drawing.

'You did that in about thirty seconds,' he says. 'How do you manage to do it so fast?'

It's irritating to be asked this question all the time, so, bypassing the usual protocols of introduction, I give him the treatment. 'There are several answers,' I tell him rather pompously. 'But the main one is practice. As with many things like playing a musical instrument or riding a bike, practice brings confidence, and confidence eliminates hesitation. What you have to understand is that the gift God gives an artist is not any special talent, it is the pleasure of doing it. Given that, you'll go on until inevitably you become good.'

'Hmm,' he says, 'I could never do it.'

But people seldom get the point here. If I told him obsessive practice would improve his golf he'd get it quick enough. He deserves to be teased in the name of art.

'You should meet my brother Thomas,' I tell him. 'He's drawing all day long: on telephone bills, envelopes, diary and phone-book pages, prescription pads and music scores. If the Devil left his book of evil spells lying around he'd find it full of drawings of little old ladies, car-park attendants and naughty children. God keeps his tablets of stone hidden when Thomas is about. When he was a medical student, a lecturer once noticed him drawing. 'What have I just said, Wilson?' he asked. Thomas looked at his drawing and repeated what the lecturer had said word for word. Afterwards Thomas said: "What he didn't know was that if he had removed my drawing I wouldn't have remembered a thing!" '

We get chatting. The man has just retired from his job as Super-intendent of Dredging in Derry harbour, and with his wife he now runs a B&B. They are here on their thirty-seventh wedding anniversary.

I'd love to hear about the techniques, problems and stories of dredging Derry harbour. He must have fished out some strange and dangerous things in his day. Apart from its importance as a mercantile port, it has been a strategic military harbour since long before King Billy relieved the Siege of Derry in 1689. English troops have poured in and out, many splendid warships, generals, presidents, prime ministers and sometimes even royalty, have visited, and in recent years Derry has of course been the scene of bitter conflicts between the Unionists and the IRA. Superintendent of Dredging in Derry harbour would have been a much more interesting job than being an industrial accountant like me, but I suppose the pay won't have been as good.

Dinner is soon over and sadly we've spent so long telling them about our cycle trip that we don't have enough time to discover his dredging stories.

Our attic room has views on to rooftops and out over Lough Foyle beyond. You can see that this B&B must have been quite nice when it was first established, but that was a long time ago and now it's badly in need of refurbishment.

View out over Lough Foyle from our B&B in Moville. The shore of
Co. Derry, which is in Northern Ireland, is just three miles away

We have a disturbed night. One lot of people on our landing come giggling noisily to bed at half-two. Then at four o'clock another lot leave, heaving and bumping luggage and telling each other to, 'Ssshhh! You'll wake the whole house!' Which is what they do.

The towels are threadbare. The place smells of ripe U–bend and old carpet. The door won't shut, then later it won't open, and there is a notice above the lavatory saying 'Please push handle of toilet up and down three or for times when flushing toilet'.

51 To Drummonds. *Rowing illustrates extreme cooperation and the quasi-living organism. Men, women and social insects' slave castes*

After breakfast we cycle five miles north to Greencastle to see is there a ferry across to Magilligan Point. Some people think the ferry is working, others say it's not. It eventually turns out that a car ferry will soon be operating, but not yet, and certainly not today. Somebody recommends a fisherman so we telephone him but he's about to go to church, then he's going to his mother-in-law's for Sunday lunch and anyway he wants too much money. So we give up and settle for the long inland route via Derry.

While we are still in Greencastle, wandering about trying to get across to Magilligan, our bikes heavily loaded with panniers, picnic supplies and all the other essentials for the journey, we are noticed by a group of Sunday-sport cyclists. There are seven or eight of them, all muscles and dressed in the latest rainbow-flashy, skin-tight cycling gear. They all have streamlined cycling helmets and several are wearing flimsy leather cycling mittens. Their bikes look beautifully lightweight to handle, and fast.

John is over at the harbour wall inspecting the habitat for marine life and I've just come out of a telephone kiosk where I've been speaking to the fisherman about taking us across the water. When they catch sight of me these cyclists look away in embarrassment; I'm a disgrace to their noble sport, which at its pinnacle aspires to compete in the Tour de France one day.

But then, while the others are doing stretching exercises and adjusting their tyre pressures, one of them, a slightly older man, asks me where we are going. 'Cork,' I say with put-on nonchalance. The others hear this and gather round for a chat, their attitude transforming from disdain to respect in a rapid gear change. It's all in the mind, rather like the way a dirty old bottle on a window-ledge in a dusty barn can be instantly transformed from a piece of garbage into a collectible antique.

It's still only eleven o'clock, but they've already come out from

Derry this morning, and expect to whirr right round the whole of the Inishowen Peninsular today. They usually do well over a hundred miles on a one-day outing like this. 'Good Lord Almighty!' we say, 'A hundred miles! That would take us at least three days!' I wish I hadn't swanked about going to Cork and now feel a bit of a fraud. But they, kindly, don't seem to see it that way and we get a wave of fellowship as they mount their bikes and crank powerfully away.

Then we, too, ease into the saddle and glide away with the dignity that befits our age and station in life. We head off south towards Derry.

We stop for our picnic lunch in a deep little lane where the high banks shelter us from the wind.

While finishing lunch we look at the map. We're at a little place called Muff, and we now see that it's right on the border between the Republic and Northern Ireland.

But there isn't any sign of a border-crossing station. No slitty-eyed lookouts, no gun-posts behind barbed wire. No armoured cars. No customs house. Nothing at all, not even an underground bunker to piddle into.

It's all very disappointing; I was looking forward to the opportunity to moan about the obstinacy, suspicion and bigotry of these unfortunate Northern folk and the shocking ugliness of the military presence in their community. Maybe that's all just newspaper fiction and life really is as civilised and normal as many Northerners claim.

We pedal on into the city of Derry, over the bridge, and out the other side. We head west and then north-west into a nasty head-wind. It's wet and this is now a big main road. Cars and lorries come thundering past and envelop us in their spray. We're not so much punching into the cold, wet wind as stumbling along silently, battered and dazed in an endless nightmare.

The road undulates up and down, but mostly up, over bleak hills. Eventually, like wanderers in the wasteland of a medieval saga, we come upon a village called Greysteel.

Amazing! I look twice and yes, that's what it says. A sign reads 'Greysteel. Please drive carefully through village'.

The village is cut in half by the big main road and its thundering traffic.

The sky is grey, so is the tarmac and even the lorry spray. The buildings are grey too. It's as though the place is actually proud of being grey and that's why it's called Greysteel. But who can have given it a name like that, ringing as is does with a sort of fascist clang like the shutting of a prison door? What can they have been thinking of? Why couldn't they have called it Pinkwood or Greenrock? I imagine a sign reading 'Greysteel twinned with Slough' or maybe Goole.

At a pub we stop to shelter from the wind and spray. We ask can they do us a pot of tea. There's a tough ruffian-looking man at the bar. He says no they don't do tea. Bad for his image, I guess, and in fact it would probably give the whole village a bad name if it ever became known that Greysteel had served two cyclists with a pot of tea.

A few miles farther on we come to Ballykelly. There's a grand hotel here. It's called Drummonds. We must be looking pretty awful by now, wet and bedraggled, tired and bearded, but they are very kind to us, and a pleasant girl soon has us installed in huge armchairs in the library. I discretely wipe the gritty wetness off my road-bespattered bare legs lest they dirty the pretty chair-cover. Then she brings a large pot of strong tea and some delicious fresh scones. There is traditional harp music on tape and we sip our tea as elegantly as possible, John's little finger poised naughtily, while gentle airs are being plucked like ripe fruit.

Eventually John breaks the silence. 'Rowing.' he says. 'I've been thinking about rowing.'

'Ah! Rowing. Yes!' I say. 'Our beloved sport. What about it?' Personally I've been thinking about a hot shower and clean dry underpants.

'Well, it just occurred to me that of all the cooperating team sports, rowing is the ultimate.'

'What makes you say that?'

'Well if you think about it the unison required is extreme.'

'That's true.'

'In an eight-oared race,' he continues, 'all members of the crew must be totally engaged and together for every second of the race. Admittedly technique is important, and so of course are strength and fitness. But above all each member of the crew must believe totally in the commitment of every other member. Throughout a race all eight crew-members must be able to row as one, and eventually become physically exhausted as one. There is no opportunity whatever for individual initiative. The crew that best welds itself into a unit has a big advantage.'

'And yet,' I say, 'rowing isn't a spectator sport. To disinterested onlookers it's stunningly dull. Nothing seems to happen, one crew eventually wins and that's that.'

'Yes,' says John. 'And that's precisely it; a good crew is such a well-drilled and uniform machine that there's no individual teamwork to be seen. But as you and I know it's there all right, and in its very purest essence.'

I hadn't thought of it like that before, but of course he's right. The Olympic distance, two thousand metres, takes just under seven minutes in an eight-oared boat. If you tried to go flat out all the way you'd blow up at between four and six hundred metres, so you have to ration out your stamina. In a perfectly judged race, which will include tactical spurts, you must end up totally exhausted at the finish. This rationing out, spurts and all, has to be done by eight people in perfect unison. Other things being equal, the crew that does this best will win. It requires total trust amongst the crew-members. After all: 'If I suspect the guy rowing at three won't go to the very brink of life-threatening exhaustion, why should I?' That means each member must trust each one of the other seven to keep their heads and their discipline and to continue to the point of painful collapse. Mathematically that's twenty-eight two-way trusts.

'Football,' says John, 'has gloriously athletic passages of brilliance, but doesn't need either this totally committed cooperation every single second of the game, or this total trust among team members when all are at the very limit of their endurance. In other words rowing demands more perfect cooperation than any other sport. Any élite-level oarsman or woman, anywhere in the world will tell you that good rowing is one of life's deepest and most transcendental experiences, including sex. And that's because it amounts to total cooperation.'

John's addressing the judge again. 'This cooperative trust, developed in training, is a corporate thing. You can feel it, and you know it's consciously shared. It's extremely powerful and must surely be an essential part of the make-up of every cooperating animal.'

Feeling it's my turn to have a go at the biology, I add: 'Yes, and of course rowing illustrates the idea of the group as a quasi-living organism. Cooperation is central to our success as a species. We have the love of cooperating built into our nature. We invent sports which emphasise it, and we are thrilled just to watch, let alone play them.

We compete for reputations to be good at cooperation. In human courtship, social skill, which is much the same thing as cooperative skill, is high on the list of attractiveness among young suitors. So it builds on itself and the ability to cooperate is improved in our genes by natural selection.'

The question of courtship then brings up a different idea. 'I've been wondering about the differences between men and women.'

'Steady on! Is this going to be politically correct?'

'Maybe . . . ' I say, gathering momentum. 'You see, I suspect team-work is a man thing. Have you ever noticed how quickly most women get bored by it? The effective team has a punchy up and at 'em mood. There's a job to be done and the members are champing at the bit like racehorses lined up at the start. In a good team there is constant competition amongst members to be recognised as the best. They endlessly boast their achievements; often in subtle ways but always as effectively as they know how. There's constant reassessment of ranking in the team hierarchy. Every member does it about them-selves and their rivals. This ranking is according to strength, intelligence, achievement, loyalty, potential, and all the other cooperating behaviour.

'But this fierce jockeying for position must be delicately balanced against and subordinated to the purpose of the team. Ambition mustn't interfere with the self-denying requirements of teamwork. You and I have learnt this at first hand from our careers.

'Now here's the point; I believe women are less able to subordinate this internal competition to the effective pursuit of common goals. Women tend to dismiss men's team-position jockeying as immature and foolish. They have little patience with it and this makes them less effective team players. Women are harder to manage than men. I have watched vendettas amongst women colleagues damaging the per-formance of the organisation they worked for, but I have never seen it between men. When the team is threatened women are less subtle, less flexible than men.

'But,' I go on, 'there's a delightful twist here. Being less impressed with the niceties of this balancing act, women get straight to the point; they slice through the internal politics and therefore, dare I say it, they can often make more decisive goal-setters, better leaders, than men.

'Humans do life's tasks – feeding, sheltering and breeding – in teams. Women make less reliable teamworkers than men. But women are more decisive in a crisis; and finally men are more expendable because only a few are needed for reproduction.'

'Hmm . . . ' says John.

Aware of his biological perspective, I think of ants, wasps and bees.

'In a way,' I say, 'humans almost reverse the roles taken by the sexes in the social insects. In their case sterile females do the work and are expendable. The males are said to be fairly useless, they neither work nor lead, they simply carry male genes, while fertile females do breeding and leadership. In humans, men do the cooperative stuff without which society would collapse but they are expendable; only a few are needed to carry male genes. Women on the other hand are less good at teamwork, but they do breeding and goal-setting. And by the way, I'm not saying men do the drudgery work, what they do is the tasks which require cooperation. There's a subtle distinction there.'

'Yes I like that,' says John. 'But does it add validity to the theory?'

'I'm not sure. It's a perception which the theory offers. It does arise out of it, and it could be delightfully controversial.'

'Yes, that's fun.'

52   Jumbo McKee and Lexy Cartwright

We eventually arrive in Limavaddy in the rain. We are wet and weary and don't fancy cycling all round the town looking for a B&B. So we ask at a pub. A kindly man says he knows the very place. He gets on the phone and books us into the Alexander Arms Hotel, which turns out to be your typical no-nonsense, old-fashioned small-town hotel. It has lots of rooms. There's a large bar decorated with old split-cane salmon rods, gaffes and landing nets. A separate dining room has framed photos of important people, local events and stuffed pike in glass cases. Just right. It smells of that disgracefully promising mixture of turf smoke, wholesome cooking, fag ends and draught beer.

Over dinner we get talking to a man and wife. Remembering Lexy and Jumbo, I ask these two do they live here in Limavaddy? 'Yes,' they say.

Do they happen to know of Lexy Cartwright or Jumbo McKee? I ask. 'No,' says the man.

But then the woman says, 'Wait a minute! Could that be Arthur McKee? He's a well-known solicitor here in town. He was extremely helpful to my sister recently.'

'Well I suppose it could be,' I say.

After a bit of research we find Arthur McKee's home phone number. He's ex-directory but it's him all right. It's Jumbo. We've struck oil!

We've just finished dinner. 'Stay there,' Jumbo shouts down the phone. 'Don't move. I'll be right round.'

He's a huge, shambling, bony man with white hair, a loud voice and a stubbly growth of grey beard. He piles us into his huge, shambling, bony old Volvo and drives a short way out of town. His house is a big traditional Irish farmhouse standing in its own grounds.

The Volvo crunches to a halt on the gravel outside an elegant Georgian front door. In the dark we can make out creepers on the wall and big well-proportioned windows. Clearly Jumbo has come good. He lives here with his second wife, Noola.

They've just finished dinner, so we sit around the farmhouse dining-table drinking wine and talking. There are various attractive daughters and boyfriends in the house, or is it sons and girlfriends? At first they walk in and out, but then, as they realise that their father's colourful past is being unveiled by these two eccentric-looking old cyclists, they all sit around and listen.

Jumbo wants Noola to hear the story of the Bowl of Light. It's been trotted out and polished up several times already on this trip so we are getting quite good at it. Of course the story brings back old memories. There is so much to say that many fruitful strands, funny stories and names from the past come flashing by in quick-fire laughter, but most of them have to be abandoned or we'd be at it for a week or more.

We're keen to know how life turned out for Jumbo over the fifty years since we last saw him, so he gives us a thumbnail sketch.

He did law at Trinity, the plan being that he would then go into his father's firm. But after a year, and repeated warnings, he was kicked out for not attending lectures, for not dining regularly in the college dining hall, a firm rule in those days, and for rowdy drunken behaviour. That was the last we knew of him.

After Trinity he left home and rattled around for a few years trying various careers including the Canadian Mounted Police. He got a shock when they rejected him, so he stopped drinking and took a grip of himself. He went back home, enrolled for a law degree in Northern Ireland and eventually got top place in the final exams.

'I've been a binge drinker all my life, but never really a true alcoholic,' Jumbo says, looking guiltily at Noola. 'I've been off the booze altogether for the last three years now.' She nods in a semi-convincing way. Jumbo on a three-day binge must have been quite something, I'm thinking. We recognised the potential when we were in Trinity.

After qualifying he went into practice here in Limavaddy. He married, divorced and remarried. But Jumbo did well and built up a reputation as an intelligent, open-minded, caring sort of solicitor. He couldn't get on with his father, who obstinately expected him to be a committed Orangeman. Jumbo dabbled in politics and shocked his Unionist family by joining the SDP, John Hume's party, which trod a delicate middle path between the violent Republican factions and the 'No Surrender' Unionists.

And now it's lovely to see that the once hopeless Jumbo, who could never get out of bed, is happy and respected; a delightful shambling character and very much his own man. He's on the brink of retirement after an eventful and successful career.

Jumbo then tells us what became of Lexy Cartwright. Lexy is an Irish nickname, it's short for Alexander. After Trinity, despite his charm and great success with the girls, Lexy went and married a no-good woman. He joined his family's legal practice; also here in Limavaddy. They remained friends and Jumbo saw him on and off over the years. But he noticed that Lexy lived an extravagant lifestyle. He suspected Lexy wasn't always quite straight and tried to warn him. But it was no good and Lexy eventually got caught out.

He had started with various dishonest little legal tricks, mostly at the expense of his clients. Then he was nabbed about a judgment he had won for a client. The amount awarded was £5,000, but he only gave the client £2,000 and kept the rest himself. He had forged a signature, which was spotted because a part of the document was typed where it should have been handwritten. Then there was another incident about a property sale. 'That sort of thing,' says Jumbo. 'Silly little things, and Lexy's tricks seemed almost careless, it was as if the risk thrilled him and he was tempting fate to catch him.'

Each time he was rescued by influential friends and escaped with a caution. But then he went and did it good-oh. Lexy represented a man who had been savagely attacked by the IRA and was left with permanent brain damage. This man was awarded a large sum of money, paid out of government funds. But of course Lexy went and kept most of it himself. A friend of the victim had happened to read about the case in the paper. He joked about how nice it must be to get such a huge sum of money without actually having to work for it. The uncomprehending victim was shown the press report and that led to Lexy's arrest. He was struck off the solicitors' roll and jailed for nine months. Jumbo says he should have got six years. Lexy's no-good woman left him. His name was ruined, and he had to leave the country.

'Of course all that was about twenty years ago,' says Jumbo, 'and I've completely lost contact with him. They say he's now living somewhere in Australia or New Zealand.'

Jumbo agrees with our amazement. But then he looks away and we wonder what's coming next.

'With the wisdom of hindsight you could almost see it coming,' he says. 'It all makes sense when you think about it. It was in his nature all along. His father died when he was little. He grew up to be talented and charming, and was spoilt by his mother. Everything came too easily to him when he was young, and he became selfish, greedy and morally weak. You just didn't pay much attention to that sort of thing when you were youngsters and then Trinity students together.'

That rang a bell with me. Lexy always seemed to have more money than the rest of us.

John then remembers the cruel way he dumped the beautiful high-spirited Molly Murphy. 'She was heartbroken – threatened suicide – when she heard from a friend that he was going out with somebody else. Hadn't had the guts to tell her himself.'

'Typical,' says Jumbo, who hadn't heard it before.

'Also,' says John, 'he was unreliable. While he was rowing in the senior eight we sort of knew he didn't train properly, and he was eventually dropped from the crew.'

Life really is a game of snakes and ladders. Who would ever have guessed that the charming, talented Lexy would end up in a mess and the shambling, hopeless Jumbo would become respected and prosperous, and above all a free spirit in this strife-torn land?

But of course the game's not quite over yet, and for all we know Lexy may well have landed on his feet in New Zealand, coaching rugby and rowing, and living happily ever after. Let's hope so, because we liked him.

The Alexander Arms Hotel is probably known locally as the Lexy. I'm subconsciously turning this over in my mind as we cycle along next morning.

But the saga of Lexy and Jumbo seems more than just a cautionary tale, there's something else here which I can't quite put my finger on.

It's connected with Jumbo realising in hindsight that Lexy had had it in him all along.

Then it slowly dawns on me. Though he mightn't realise it, the same is true of Jumbo; he too had had it in him all along. He was obviously an intelligent boy with a tough, dictatorial father. As he grew up he went through phases of confusion, rebellion, failure and eventually redemption, and being big in body, mind and spirit these phases of Jumbo's life were just as spectacular as Lexy's disgrace.

Jumbo had told us how his father was a fierce, strong-willed and bigoted Unionist. I didn't need any persuasion about that because my own father was one too. My father was a tall man, handsome, talented and witty. I wanted to love him, and later in life, I understood that he too had wanted to love me, but his views were blinkered by anti-Catholic prejudice.

It seems crazy that such a thing could come between a father and his growing son. But to answer his child's innocent questions about life, a man who wants to pass on prejudiced attitudes to the next generation must set up no-go areas where things just have to be accepted without question.

The very best way to make a child rebellious is to confuse it with inconsistent answers and then tell it to accept these as rigid rules.

By the time I came to realise that this was a tribal thing and not personal between us it was too late, my marvellous father and I had drifted apart.

It was quite clearly the same between Jumbo and his own father. As he told us last night, the more he learnt about life the less could he accept the prejudiced, narrow mindedness of his clan, the Northern Irish Protestants. He thought their attitude at times bordered on the fascism which Hitler had taught us all to abhor. So it wasn't surprising that he and his father never really did become reconciled. Tragic but inevitable.

The story of Lexy and Jumbo is much richer than a game of snakes and ladders; it's more like a Greek tragedy.

As Philip Larkin said in his poem 'This Be The Verse':

> They fuck you up, your mum and dad.
> They may not mean to, but they do.

> They fill you with the faults they had
> And add some extra, just for you.

Strong words but true. They were both fucked up by their parents; Lexy by too much indulgence and Jumbo by too much indoctrination. A paradigm indeed. In these troubled times Northern Ireland is a society in which polarisation is hard to avoid.

53 White line. Portrush. Ahimsa. *There is a beneficial symbiosis between the amoral political-party machine and the gutter press*

We cycle uphill for miles and miles. It's foggy this morning with intermittent light rain. The visibility is down to about two hundred yards and we seem to be going through wooded hills. The long grinding climb never seems to end. Then eventually, like Saracens on horseback in a Walt Disney film, we sweep down out of the mist into Coleraine.

At one o'clock we stop for coffee at the York Hotel in Portstewart.

John studying the map in the York Hotel in Portstewart

View of windswept promenade in Portstewart,
with white lines which threw me off my bike

It's warm and wet now. The clouds have lifted a little and the mist-horizon out to sea is about a mile away.

We set off again and just outside the hotel I come crashing off my bike. It happens in a flash.

The road surface is wet and shiny, and before I've gathered speed properly the wobbly weight of my panniers suddenly flips my wheels sideways on a dotted white line. These white lines are road markings and must have been repainted over and over again because they are raised into a lump of paint over half an inch thick. The man who paints them year after year must be proud of his work. It's neat and precise and shines very white. But it's slippery in the wet.

I'm stunned and have grazed my bare leg nastily, and also the palm of the hand I used to break my fall. There's blood all over the place. But thank goodness I haven't hurt myself badly; imagine the funny looks you'd get in hospital if you had to explain that you broke your leg falling off a white line.

We stop for lunch in Portrush. It's a lovely little seaside town and I'd been hoping to have our picnic out on the pier but it's too gloomy and wet so we order fish and chips in the Silver Sands Restaurant instead.

I've been thinking about how wretchedly far our governments seem to fall short of the democratic ideal. So when we've placed our order I try it out.

'Government is all about regulating our cooperative behaviour, so it should be fertile ground for dual-nature theory.'

'Hmm?' says John, who's somewhere else. But I can see he's willing to battle on with it.

'Well, for instance, I'm thinking of the inherent deceitfulness of the party machine and the unholy symbiosis between government and the press.'

'Sounds too deep for me.'

'Well, it's not complicated, it follows on fluently from what we've been saying about the IRA and politicians struggling for the moral high ground. Instead of solving anything their empty rhetoric just poisons the air.'

'Go on then.'

'Well, about the biggest influence on society is the political-party machine, and I've just realised that far from being a social benefactor, dual-nature theory shows it to be an amoral, self-seeking, quasi-living organism just like big business, the army and the church.'

'You mean in the way it interferes with the sacred ideal that democracy is government according to the will of the people?'

'Exactly. The party machine is a world-wide problem in democracies. I don't know enough about it, but I suspect Switzerland is about the only country that's managed to clip its wings.

'Think of a talented youngster in her late teens who wants to go into politics. Long before she's elected to Parliament, she has to join a political party otherwise she has no hope of getting in. The trouble is that as soon as she's elected, she finds that the policies, aims and ambitions of the party effortlessly override those of her electors back home. If there is a conflict, party comes first. It's the seduction of morality again, the corruption of innocence, which, as we've said, is a fundamentally natural biological process. The result is that the government's connection with the will of the people is a flimsy thread at the best of times.

'Should we go to war? Should we apply a death penalty? Or should the auditing profession be truly independent of the firms they audit? Democratic governments routinely refuse to put such questions to the vote or to a referendum. But surely we should be able to pay more respect to the idea of democracy than that?'

'I do agree,' says John, taking up the running. 'Their one overriding purpose is their own survival and prosperity. Good government for the long-term benefit of society comes a poor second to winning the next election. It's staring us in the face. Unfortunately we're so used to populist short-term measures, shameless lies, propaganda and half truths that this gross amorality usually goes unchecked.

'It happens in Canada all the time.' He continues gloomily. 'Of course we're too proud to copy the Swiss, but for starters we could bring in proportional representation of the sort which elects many small parties to Parliament. That would break the grip of the big party machines. Also party funds should be drastically cut.'

'Maybe,' I suggest optimistically, 'maybe one day dual-nature theory will sort all this out. I mean if we could recognise the biological amorality of groups, then we might be able to do something about it. After all this isn't rocket science; it's simple evolutionary biology.'

'I doubt it,' says John. 'People are too short-sighted. I've long believed that the only thing which prevents democracy from destroying itself is fixed terms of office.'

'Yes, I suppose so,' I sadly agree.

At this point our fish and chips arrive, and it's raining again outside.

This interruption reminds me of what I was going to say about symbiosis. 'The gutter press . . . ' I say, 'alongside proportional representation and cutting party funds, that could be another vital curb on the party machine. In fact it could actually be what's saving democracy.'

'The gutter press! Saving democracy? You can't be serious.'

'Absolutely, yes. You see in journalism just as in politics the official purpose is secondary to the real one. Newspapers make most of their money from advertising, but advertising revenue depends on circulation. So good journalism, in other words accurate reporting and intelligent writing, is sacrificed on the altar of advertising revenue. Popular gossipy writing and sexually titillating stories are what attract circulation. "Give 'em a good story, don't let the facts get in the way," says the editor. "Tell 'em what they want to hear."

'The truth as we all know, is regularly mangled and ignored in the interests of circulation. The best trick of all is a big court case in which the outraged superstar sues the newspaper. One's suspicion of collusion is greatly heightened by the way everybody benefits at the expense of the law courts. The superstar gets the publicity she craves, the paper gets extra circulation, the lawyers coin it in and the public get a good story.'

'OK, but how does the symbiosis thing work?'

'Well it's the journalists – the media – and they alone who, by revealing scandals and corruption, keep the party machine in check. Politicians are terrified of journalists. So here we have a weird, socially beneficial symbiosis between two selfish types of corporation, both of which shamelessly pursue goals that are quite different from their publicly and proudly declared purpose in life. Western society depends desperately on the health of this rather peculiar arrangement. It's sort of poetic that the cynical, self-seeking, cigar-chewing editor in his red braces and green eyeshade should turn out to be the knight in shining armour who saves us from ourselves in this way.'

'OK!' says John, 'but does this symbiosis thing confirm dual-nature theory – you know, validate it? Or does it simply follow on as a consequence? I mean is this symbiosis explained by dual-nature theory?'

'Well, let's think . . . maybe not. But I still want to know what it means.'

'Why should it mean anything?'

Typical scientist; they always bring you down to earth.

'I just feel there has to be some significance. Here we have two cynically dishonest, totally amoral, and potentially very harmful cooperating groups which keep each other honest. It seems a weird arrangement. Can it have developed by chance? I don't think so. I sense that in anthropologically-designed laboratory conditions it would always evolve. And yet I'm totally baffled as to what that means.'

'Philosophers,' says John, 'they're always looking for hidden meanings. It's just that we of lesser intellect fail to notice that there usually aren't any there in the first place. That's how most of them earn their living.'

'Well I suppose dual-nature theory can't win 'em all.'

'So let's not worry about it.'

We've finished our fish and chips and are waiting for the bill.

We look out through the rain-streaks on the plate-glass window. Portrush is another classic summer-holiday town whose heyday was in the first half of the twentieth century. It's on a rocky promontory and has a harbour, a permanent funfair and wonderful sandy beaches, swept clean by strong winds and dangerous tides.

There's also a fine golf links where they play international tournaments. This is where Frank Trufelli was recently captain.

My grandparents used to have a holiday house in Portrush. He was a good golfer – my grandfather was – and on his eightieth birthday he went round the course in eighty strokes; a rare achievement which all golfers aspire to, but few attain.

As a child I had many lovely holidays here with my brother and two sisters. The war was on, and we were thrilled once when a German fighter plane, off course from an air raid on the Clyde shipyards, crash-landed on the beach. But we mostly plunged in and out of the waves, played amongst the sand dunes and looked for lost golf balls.

I try to conjure up for John the magic of this lovely little town with its big-buxom-lady-and-thin-little-man vulgar postcards and multi-carriage open-sided tram. Mr Eastwood, who always gave us a cheery wave when he came by in his horse and trap, the corncrakes that craked out their rasping song in Mr Rankin's field, now a housing estate, behind my grandparents' house, and the larks that sang high in the air above the golf links. But all that depends on the sunshine, and there's nothing more dismal than an Irish holiday town when the rain is rolling in off the Atlantic. So my description falters and peters out.

After lunch we cycle round the town the harbour, and promenade. There are not many people about. They must all be indoors keeping out of the rain.

Everything seems a little smaller than I remember it. And the amusements of the twentieth century have given way to those of the twenty-first. The colourful bathing huts and high diving boards on the harbour wall have all gone, so have the kiosks selling kites, hand-held paper windmills and ice-cream. There are no donkey rides on the sands today. And the main street bristles with video shops, scuba-diving and wind-surfing supplies, fast food joints and theme pubs.

We set off again towards the White Rocks and the Giant's Causeway. This is the scenic coast road where the rickety little multi-carriage tram used to go clanking over the points, but the whole place is now enveloped in low driving mist. I'd love to be able to show John how enchanting it all is, but sadly that's not to be. As we cycle away, heads down into the wind, I think to myself: 'Dear old Portrush, that's probably the last time I'll see it before I die.'

In the late afternoon we come to a small place called Lisnagunogue and it's our good luck to get a room in the first B&B we try. It's called Ahimsa and the lady's name is Sheila Reynolds. She gives us the concerned sort of welcome one reserves for the aged, the bedraggled and the lost, which we aren't, not really anyway. Then she sees the bruising and dried blood on my leg from where I fell off the white line this morning, so we give in and play the wounded soldier for maximum sympathy. Actually, I'm only slightly gashed and soon it all washes off and gets covered in elastoplast.

Sheila is slight, grey-haired and lively. 'Ahimsa', she tells us, means non-violence in Sanscrit. It is comfortable, calm and peaceful and there is a faintly oriental smell mingled with boiling fruit coming from the kitchen. She settles us in with herb tea and scones; not quite the pint of Guinness we've been anticipating, but very nice. There are potted plants everywhere.

View from the drawing-room window at the Ahimsa B&B

Sheila Reynolds has charming watercolours on the walls, several are signed 'to Sheila' by personal friends, and most are views of this rocky coast. They include the Giant's Causeway with Rathlin Island in the distance, Dunluce Castle, which is gradually falling off its cliff into the sea, the White Rocks and the Glens of Antrim. The pictures in our room are reproductions of Michelangelo's Sistine Chapel ceiling. Sheila teaches yoga, and this is discreetly evident in her Indian ornaments and rugs.

The special thing about this place is that we are truly in her home and it feels a generously offered privilege.

A framed message on the wall reads: 'May all your weeds be wildflowers.' I imagine that especially here in tangled, suspicious Northern Ireland, Sheila, with her yoga lessons, can teach people a lot about life. If she were a man she might have become a bishop, I'm thinking. But she's probably more practical and effective than that because she has the modesty of a woman.

Rather than going out, we have the remains of our mix 'n' squash for dinner, and Sheila makes us a 'vegetarian salad'. Are there salads for carnivores? But we don't dare ask.

Then we make a break for it and go round to the pub for a pint of Guinness. There are a few locals in there watching *Big Brother* on the telly. When they speak it comes like machine-gun fire out of the corner of the mouth. We can't understand what they are saying. It's more a gutteral communication than a language. Perhaps it's Gaelic.

Back in Ahimsa, Sheila is also watching telly. She has an Ulster TV news programme on, which is listing the new bills about to be put before Stormont. One is the Dangerous Wild Animals Bill.

Anything on wildlife always gets John's full attention. 'What on earth can that be?' he says.

Quick as a flash, but so quietly that John doesn't hear, Sheila says 'Orangemen'. I megaphone the answer to him and we all have a good laugh. Some days later we find out that the bill actually deals with monkeys, snakes, tarantulas and pumas, kept as pets but liable to escape.

Looking out next morning, we see it's still damp, the mist closes the horizon down to about a quarter of a mile, there's no wind and it's muggy. There are raindrops on the windowpane.

Breakfast at Ahimsa is 'vegetarian'. Well it would be, wouldn't it. None of your 'full Irish' here. But it's good. The poached eggs on toast are excellent – are vegetarians allowed eggs? And the highlight is the jam she was making last night from blackcurrants a friend had given her.

As we say goodbye I take a good look at this impressively spiritual lady in the clear morning light and I can see that though Sheila is thin and strong, she looks pale.

'Lovely lady, but she needs feeding up,' says John, when we're out of earshot. 'She could do with a big juicy steak, with onions and chips and a pint of Guinness.'

'Exactly what I was thinking.'

The unfortunate thing with lifestyle enthusiasts is that you find yourself listening to their advice but you are somehow banned from offering any of your own in return. You have to bottle up potentially useful suggestions in case they might give offence.

It's been a lovely place to stay and a blessed relief from the ubiquitous Union Jacks and other subtle reminders of the tribal tension up here in the North. One day it'll all clear away like a passing storm and we'll look back and understand that it was an epidemic of 'the seduction of morality' in which deliberately polarised groups turned against each other with deadly intent, while the individuals making up both groups were decent, upright people all along. It's a perfect case study in dual-nature theory.

While we pedal on down the road, I realise that it's the unobtrusive, healing people dotted about the land, brave women like Sheila, who will quietly help the storm to pass. It won't be the politicians or even the bishops. Only very few charismatic people, like Nelson Mandela, can actually afford to take the lead. Most politicians can only take over when a critical mass of people actually want a change.

In a place like Northern Ireland it's the grass roots that determine the politics, and all you can hope for is that in amongst the weeds you will eventually get enough wild flowers like Sheila Reynolds and Jumbo McKee.

54. Glens of Antrim. Marketing and the sex bomb. *Looting illustrates the dynamics of cooperation*

We are now rounding the north-east corner of Ireland, and the next feature will be the Glens of Antrim. They're a succession of pretty little bays and villages under steep hills that drop precipitously down into the sea. I've never seen them and I'm looking forward to cycling through them. After about twelve miles of farmland we get to the coast and there they are.

According to the road signs there are nine glens. And there are two villages, Cusnendun and Cushendall, which are favourite weekend spots for Belfast people wanting a quick getaway. They look lovely, even on a gloomy day like today. But this switchback coast road only lasts for fifteen miles or so and even on a bicycle you are soon out the other end. So many lovely places, so little time to enjoy them all.

The Glens of Antrim – precipitous coast road

These are fierce little hills; no sooner have you got right to the top of one than you rattle back down again to sea level only to have to pedal-grind and handlebar-heave all the way back up to the top again. After an extremely strenuous ride we come to Cushendall.

We stop in Mary MacBride's pub for lunch and a rest. I have the jumbo sausages, peas, chips and braised onion, plus a pint of Guinness. John has the cod and chips, plus the Guinness.

'Well!' he says, 'we've done bullying, boasting and hooliganism, sex education, team games and rowing, and we've done the Roman army and John Lewis. That must be about it. Dual-nature theory rules OK.'

But I'm not so sure. 'I think there's more to be done on looting and the dynamics of cooperation, and I'd like to work out why our dual nature hasn't been noticed before, and to test how it fits into the history of Western philosophy.'

'Oh dear, and here's me thinking we'd finished.'

'Well we have to be true to the scientific method, don't we.'

'Yes I suppose so.' I've got him there.

After lunch we pedal on into the afternoon. The weather has improved; it's still overcast but the misty rain has lifted and you can see for miles. In fact we can clearly see a bit of Scotland now. It's the tip of the Mull of Kintyre and looks much closer than I expected. It's only about twenty miles away according to the map.

After Cushendall the road is flatter. It's a beautiful ride hugging the shoreline, going in and out of inlets, bays and estuaries; under big cliffs and overhangs, and along the promenades of holiday villages.

There's a posh-looking place set back off the road in Carnlough. We wonder if they might give us tea. It's called the Londonderry Arms Hotel.

'I hope they don't mean firearms,' says John.

'Do be quiet,' I tell him, 'jokes like that will get us kicked out.'

We hide our helmets and put on our politest English accents in an attempt to counteract the appalling, tone-lowering appearance of our knobbly knees and scruffy beards. But it's quite OK. We are courteously ushered into an elegant reception room with grand portraits and huge comfortable armchairs. They bring us tea in a large old-fashioned pewter teapot.

I've noticed several times on this trip round Ireland that though scruffy places often balk at letting us in, the classier joints never bat an eyelid. You'd think it would be the other way round.

Soon we come to Glenarm where we spend the night.

Next morning after breakfast I put Timodine cream where my buttocks are rubbed raw. It's sold for hospital bedsores and works well on the touring cyclist's bottom. I also take the Elastoplast off the cut I got on my leg when falling off that white line yesterday. I close my eyes and rip it off in one quick eye-watering movement like my mother used to do. Some hairs stick to the plaster. The main cut is wet with the juices of healing, so it's time to let it dry off in the fresh cycling air.

And off we go.

Scotland is still clearly visible on the horizon. There's a head wind, but the road under the cliffs is lovely, and kind to cyclists.

After an hour's ride along the shoreline we come to Ballygally.

A sign says 'Thank you for driving carefully through Ballygally'. But we didn't, not on purpose anyway.

The promenade in Ballygally

Next there's a settlement which is unfortunately called Drains Bay, and of course the sign on leaving says, 'Thank you for driving carefully through Drains Bay'. Well you would, wouldn't you; so as not to get splashed, and holding your nose too most likely.

These signs are all marketing and no information. They remind me of those telephone answering services: 'if you want a quotation press one, if you want to renew your policy press two, if you want to make a claim, press three . . . ' and so on. Eventually you get to 'for any other service press five'. Five gets you to 'all our operators are busy right now, please hold'. Apparently all this is being done from a distant land where the wages are low, like say Trinidad or the Andaman Islands, and they're probably all on the beach 'right now'. But there's no alternative, you just have to 'hold'. On comes some totally inappropriate music like 'Sex bomb, sex bomb, you're my sex bomb'. You want to tell them your mother is very ill and to ask will your insurance pay up if you cancel your holiday. Sex at this moment is the furthest thing from your mind. But still they've got you; if you don't 'hold' you pay for the call so far, and have to start all over again. Finally the sex bomb gives way to a real person who would of course have the police sent around to your house at the double if you asked them about sex. That's marketing for you.

John lives in St John's in Newfoundland most of the time. The airport is not far from his house. He says you used to be able to ring them up to ask the delay on incoming trans-Atlantic flights. But now that they have a smart new answering service, probably based in the Pitcairn Islands, it's quicker to hop in the car, nip over to the airport and look it up on the electronic noticeboard.

A place called Glynn is next. There is no doubt about the politics in this little community. It's festooned with Union Jacks, and the curbstones are painted alternately red, white and blue. There's a crossroads in the middle of town and in the centre, where there'd normally be a traffic island, there's a big painting on the tarmac. It's a white six-pointed star with a red hand in the middle, and round the outside is written 'Derry, Aughrim, Eniskillen and the Boyne'; these are the names of the battles in which King William defeated the Catholics in the 1690s. Being a road sign one must conclude that it's been put there, or at least approved, by the local council, which is ultimately answerable to the English Parliament in London. So this is an official public taunt, a reminder to the Catholics, lest they forget, that three hundred years ago they were defeated by the Protestants.

The latent threat of terrorism throbs like toothache in the street decorations and the other cultural signals that are all around us, as we pedal along.

Immediately outside Glynn there's suddenly such a steep hill that for the first time in the whole trip so far, and despite my ultra-high old man's derailleur gears, I'm defeated; I have to get off and walk. It's a symbolic reminder that round here, amongst these resolute folk, the watchword is 'No Surrender'. In warfare against ferocious fighters like the Japs, the Afghans or Johnny Turk I'd always want the Northern Irish Protestants on my side. No wonder they produced so many famous British generals including Alexander, Montgomery and Wellington.

By about one o'clock the suburbs of Belfast start to appear, so we stop for lunch on the grassy bank of a nice little reservoir.

'I've been thinking,' I say over lunch.

'Uh-oh.'

'That looting idea of yours was brilliant.'

'What I like,' says John, 'is that it combines solitary, team and group behaviour in one dramatic example.'

'Yes, and also . . . '

' I know what you're going to say,' he interrupts, guessing at my next thought. 'That we really ought to be calling it triple-nature theory because looting shows that we actually have three, not two modes of behaviour. As well as team and group there's also solitary.'

That wasn't actually what I was going to say, but he's right.

'Yes and, in fact, you could probably include herd, mob or swarm, as a fourth mode. But it's the unrecognised difference between co-operating individuals and teams which is unearthing so many explanations of our behaviour. That's the star attraction.'

'OK, I agree,' he says, 'that's the big one, so don't lets adorn it with unnecessary frills. Triple-nature theory doesn't have quite the same impact somehow.'

'No but listen, there's another thing about looting. And this one may complicate things whether we like it or not. I was thinking about it this morning. Looting illustrates how we effortlessly and unconsciously flip up and down between the modes. And, in fact, we behave in different modes almost simultaneously. What I mean is that we probably won't really understand our behaviour if we use static models. We probably need to bring dynamics into it. You know – set the model in motion, give it a good kick and watch what happens.'

'Hmm . . . ' says John.

'After all, we're trying to understand why humans behave so badly. Right?'

'Right.'

'Well to show you've really understood a system or a process, you should be able to predict what's going to happen next. It's like forecasting the weather. They can't really claim to understand the weather until they can forecast it accurately.'

'I don't quite see what you're getting at.'

I must take this carefully because I'm not sure I understand it myself yet.

'The whole thing, human society, is more complicated than one first imagines. Geneticists imagine it as a game of prisoner's dilemma, but it's much more complicated than that. Imagine the busy market square in an Indian town. Many of them will know or at least recognise each other. Just think of the amazing complexity of the interactions between individuals and groups of individuals all mingling together.'

'I was brought up in India,' says John; he's getting restless and I'm having difficulty getting to the point.

'Right, well in this market square the multiple interconnections of individuals and teams, desires and rules are mind-boggling. Furthermore there'll be exceptions to every rule one identifies. And yet there obviously must be social codes otherwise, as you've said, the whole thing, society, would collapse in a chaos of looting.

'Society can be thought of as a pyramid of interacting groups. But it can also be thought of as a pyramid of individuals. These two different ways of thinking of society set up a "now you see it, now you don't" illusion, a bit like the hologram on your credit card which flips backwards and forwards depending on the angle you look at it from.'

'I still don't see what you mean.'

'OK, let's think of the hierarchical structure of a business. It's a hierarchy of teams. The leader of a team is usually also an individual member of the team above. This is what creates the "now you see it, now you don't" confusion, but in real life it doesn't present a problem. The boss treats the requirements or instructions of the higher team as part of the jungle his lower team must operate in. However, when working as a member of the higher team, this person, the boss of a team lower in the hierarchy, has no problem behaving selflessly and trustingly with fellow members of the higher team.'

'That may describe the structure,' says John, 'but it's mighty hard to visualise. But then I suppose so are the relationships in the Indian market square.'

'If you think that's complicated then what about the cooperating relationships between sister or associated groups like other sub-sidiaries in a conglomerate, or other regiments in an army? Here it's even more a case of "so what's in it for us?" Tough discipline from on high is required to push through team-sacrificing policy.

'At this point,' I say, 'the whole set-up gets too complicated for my tiny brain.'

'Glad you said that!'

'Yes, but here's what I'm trying to get at. I'm sorry to have taken so long. I believe all this is greatly simplified if we bring dynamics into it. Real life runs a constantly changing stream of crises through the structure of society. We all want a quiet life so that we can bumble along in our communities living "happily ever after". But in fact we find crises stimulating, and something always seems to disturb the peace. When it does we cooperate to deal with it. The question is "are the stakes at play high, low or medium?" How we cooperate, with what spirit and in what groupings or teams, depends on how high the stakes are perceived to be.

'High stakes include war, plague, famine, flood, drought and fire. Low stakes include littering the place with sweet papers, beer cans, noise, smells and smoke. And there is a smooth gradient between high and low. A general election is somewhere between the two.'

John has the rare ability to stay silent when stray thoughts need collecting. We look out over the reservoir for a few minutes.

Then I go on. 'So let's think of a great crisis like an earthquake, or a crop failure. There are dynamics here in which people unite in ephemeral cooperative groupings which amalgamate up the hierarchy like the upward pulsing neon signs in Piccadilly Circus. Then when the crisis is over these dynamics settle back to calm equilibrium through a series of interconnected feedback loops, until society has separated out again into its natural peacetime groupings.'

I get these words out rather carefully, but I have the uneasy feeling that I'm not really in control of what they mean.

I blunder on: 'What I'm trying to say is that seen from the Martian space ship, human society presents a fluid and constantly changing picture with a bewildering kaleidoscope of inter-acting teams; some are ephemeral, others permanent. Ephemeral groupings have the power to dissolve team boundaries and unite masses of individuals into larger self-conscious, discrete, quasi-living organisms. But this only occurs when the stakes are so high, and create so much social electricity that it surges on upwards amalgamating teams into ever bigger units until the situation is resolved one way or another.'

'That makes sense,' says John. 'You're saying that these pulses of social electricity explain what's actually going on in society. They are what orchestrate the apparently chaotic activity that can be observed on the trading floor of a stock exchange, or in an Indian market square.'

'Yes and don't forget the series of feedback loops through which the community re-establishes a calm equilibrium after the event has been dealt with. This dynamic aspect – the surges to commitment, and the way they cascade through our social structures – needs to be incorporated into any realistic explanation of cooperative behaviour.'

Then I get a flash of inspiration. 'A way of understanding all this is to think of business games or war games. I'm not talking about game theory as in the prisoner's dilemma, I'm talking about the games which are played in business schools and military academies all over the world. They use powerful computers to simulate complicated real-life situations, and during multiple rounds of decision and feedback, not unlike a chess match, they illustrate the probable outcomes of different strategies. These games are terrific teaching aids for businessmen and soldiers. The surge to commitment is similar, and it's a relief to know that even if the dynamics of society may be too complicated for an individual brain, they could theoretically be simulated by methods borrowed from business or war games.

'We could devise a computer arbitrated parlour game, like Monopoly, in which two or more competing tribes deal with a crisis. The winner would be the one whose surges to commitment are the most effective.'

'Tell me again how the surge to commitment works.'

'Well I'm suggesting that individuals have a tentative one-way ratchet built into their natures, like the tiny spines on wheat-ears which work the seed forwards when its surroundings shift. This ratchet ensures that the cooperator is predisposed to cooperate. This, I believe, is achieved by the existence of an on/off switch at the cutting edge where the cooperate-or-split dilemma is resolved. It can switch from on to off and back again in a split-second, but there is no grey area; no "maybe", in between.'

'Is that important?'

'I can't quite put my finger on it, but I think it could be. Geneticists always want to boil cooperative behaviour down to self-interest. They point to things like reputation, fairness, benefits and costs, punishment, compromise, learning, shame, guilt and revenge. I accept their defence that these motives are often disguised and frequently long-sighted. But I just don't see how self-interest can account for the positive aspects: the transcendental thrill or deep satisfaction of fruitful teamwork. I suggest that this thrill comes from the combination of success with the catharsis of committing to abandon self-interest in unison with others. Game theory does not accommodate an on/off switch or, if it does, it cannot explain how it has evolved. I'm suggesting that when this switch is on, there is a reckless sharing of trust, personal advantage and, above all, commitment. There is no continuum between heroism and scepticism, instead there's an on/off switch. The batsman must swipe or duck, if he dithers he'll get hit.

'I'm beyond the outer limits of my understanding here, but I want to say that an on/off switch operates at the cutting edge of cooperative activity, and that cooperation is enabled by a bias to keep the cooperate-or-split switch at on. Evolution, I believe, has developed the thrill which encourages teamwork.'

'That's too difficult for me,' says John.

'For me too. Like I say it's beyond the outer limits of my understanding. Of course that's where all the interesting stuff is.'

'Just out of reach?'

'Yes.'

'Nothing new there,' he says with a sigh. 'The fish that get away are always the most interesting ones.'

55 Violet Scott, Belfast suburbs, nearly lost in Hollywood, most easterly point, Cloghy, camogie girls, horse breeders

On the outskirts of Belfast we have difficulty finding a bed for the night.

We're at last realising that here in the North there are nearly always two quite separate B&B networks. If the first place you ask at is Catholic, then you only get passed on within the Catholic network, and vice versa. You can always tell the difference. The Catholics are usually less neat and tidy, more cluttered with family photos and religious ornaments. And they're chattier, less, how to say it . . . ? Less Protestant.

We get passed round amongst Protestant B&Bs then, without at first realising we've done it, we stumble on the Catholic community. But there are no vacancies there either.

We start getting anxious. Then we notice a sign saying: 'Slievenamara B&B' pointing up a suburban side-track with gardens and a few sheds on either side. It's a small modern bungalow looking down over fields to Belfast Lough. This is the big estuary that brings ships up to the city. We ask at the door and there is room for us.

The landlady is tall and good-looking, with big, wide-open, almost wild eyes and lots of blonde hair. Her conversation is direct, engaged and intense. She seems to live alone. Violet Scott is her name.

Belfast lough from Slievenamara B&B

It doesn't take long to realise she isn't either Protestant or Catholic. She's English, an outsider, which is why she isn't in either network. Catholics and Protestants at least have this in common, they certainly can't trust the English.

I'd love to know how she got here. I bet it's an interesting story. Though she may not be in the first flush of her youth you can see that, like a vintage car, she's certainly got some go in her yet.

Early next morning there are blue patches in the dawn sky, but it's mostly hazy grey with smoke from the chimneys of Belfast.

I creep into the kitchen and make myself a mug of tea. Then I settle down to a watercolour of the sweeping view of Belfast Lough from the picture window in the sitting room. Ships slide by with the comings and goings of commerce packed in metal containers, like huge shoe-boxes, on their decks.

Violet Scott appears in her dressing gown. She likes the watercolour I'm doing and I promise to make her a copy when I get home. We have a chat and I tell her about our cycle trip round Ireland, exaggerating the heroism where possible.

John surfaces. We have breakfast, say goodbye and set off into the smoky landscape of East Belfast. First we pedal through suburbs, then it gets ever more industrial as we pass warehouses, factories, ship-yards and docks. Steam and smoke fill the air. We cross a massive modern bridge across the top of the estuary where the River Lagan pours out into the sea. At this point we go back out along the other shore of the lough, and cycle through the whole dramatic sequence once more. But of course this time it's in reverse: docks are followed by shipyards, then factories and warehouses, until finally we come to suburbs and we're out on the open road once more.

Eventually we approach Hollywood. It's half-eleven.

Just before getting there I have to get off for a pee. John says he'll go on ahead because I go faster than him and I'll catch him up. 'OK!' I say.

I thought we had agreed earlier to look for a place to have coffee in Hollywood. But my memory is hopeless. I can't clearly remember: did we actually say it? On a bicycle it's all too easy to think you said some-thing when you only thought it.

Also even if I did say it, I'm never completely sure what he has understood. This is not just a question of his hearing; it's also that, like many slightly deaf people, he speaks so quietly that often I can't quite hear what he's saying. My hearing is not that terrific either.

While I'm piddling doubt creeps in. If John gets to Hollywood before I catch him up, will he wait for me there or will he cycle on?

This turns into semi-panic when, as I feared, Hollywood does indeed appear before I catch him up. Worse still; the main road by-passes Hollywood. It's easy to go straight on.

No sight of John. Now then. Was I imagining it or did we really say we'd stop in Hollywood? Has he cycled on or turned off into the town? If I take the wrong decision, we could at this point get separated for days to come. I could cycle on looking for him while he's waiting for me in Hollywood, or the reverse; he could be spinning on ahead while I'm searching the town.

Which to do: go on or stop? Eventually I decide to stop.

I search the town. No John to be seen.

'Oh my God,' I think. 'I've taken the wrong decision, and now we'll never find each other again. It'll be a lonely road to Cork.'

But then mercifully, from the middle of town, I see him in the distance down at a second turning off the by-pass. What I've spotted is his bright yellow helmet. I missed him because I'd taken the first turn-off. He's adjusting his bike. Massive relief.

Very silly of him I think, as my panic subsides into anger.

Then I realise I'm quite wrong because, of course, John has intelligently placed himself where he knew I couldn't get past without him seeing me, so he's not in the least bit perturbed. And anyway the whole episode took place in my head. Nothing went wrong at all.

My anger then subsides into embarrassment. Do cyclists keep losing each other like this all the time? Feeling stupid, I say nothing about it.

After coffee in Hollywood we have lunch on some rocks by a sea wall in Donaghee.

Two motorcyclists arrive and they too stop for their lunch. I do a quick sketch of them. We ought to chat to them, but there seems to be an age or a culture gap, and we don't. Silly really.

Two motorcyclists lunching nearby in Donaghadee

There's a seagull watching us. I imagine it saying to itself: 'You see them round here all the time; two old duffers sitting there grumbling about what the world is coming to. Probably been told by their wives to get out of the house.'

Eventually we've finished our lunch. John has completed his inspection of the crabs, sand-hoppers, worms and other little creatures under the rocks, the motorcyclists have gone and the seagull's flown away. So on we go into the grey afternoon.

The scenery becomes shapeless and forlorn. On our left, the sea is grey and on our right, the land is flat and featureless for mile after mile. We pass the occasional little village and there are lots of small houses dotted about and more being built. There are no shops to be seen and no pubs. Where do these people get their food and their laughs? One can't imagine culture or fun getting much of a look-in around here. Occasionally we come across the grim message of the red, white and blue curbstones.

One little place we pass is called Portavogie. There's a big sign saying: 'Portavogie, the most easterly point in Northern Ireland'.

I think to myself, 'Hmm. Northern Ireland bulges out to the east doesn't it? So wouldn't that make it the most easterly point of the whole of Ireland?' Later John says he wondered about that too. We look it up on the map, and of course it is. So what are they saying? The only answer has to be that so far as these people are concerned the South of Ireland doesn't exist, and what's more they never miss an opportunity to say so.

We've been pushing into a medium-strength head wind under low clouds, and then at half-three it rains hard, but not for long. We cycle on through it.

At about five o'clock we stop in Cloghy for a cup of tea at a dim little place called the Red Snapper. It's been a long day and we're still quite a way from Strangford where we're hoping the scenery will improve.

John chooses the tea and a hot dog.

He's in a bad mood which is extremely rare for him. He complains about everything: the nastiness of the hot dog he's ordered, the dinginess of the café we're in, the surliness of the waitress, the wetness and greyness of the weather, his sore bottom, the Cloghy name of this dreary village and much else besides. I have the tea, two sausages and the mushy peas, and just listening to him makes me feel better. As the very Russian borzoi said to the bulldog while they sat in the dog pound in the film *Lady and the Tramp*: 'My friend Gorky, he say, "Miserable being must meet more miserable being, then – he's happy." '

We remount stiffly and head off towards Strangford hoping for nicer countryside and a place to rest our weary limbs.

Portaferry is the small town at the northern side of the crossing to Strangford. It looks nice, but when we get there the little ferry is on the point of departure. Not knowing when the next one will go, or even whether this is the last one of the day, we nip on board.

The only other passengers are a party of twenty schoolgirls. Ten to twelve years old, they are all dressed in their games uniform of shirts and shorts. There is no teacher with them and they mill about giggling and dancing like only schoolgirls can; some are running around in the wet with no shoes on, only thick games socks. Some are in polished black shoes, but most are wearing football boots with studs on their soles. Four of them make a wonderful clackety-clack sound on the steel deck as they do a formal tap-dance. One of the girls tells me they are going to play a camogie match against a school in Downpatrick. The youthful energy and laughter and the noisy dancing take our weary minds off the miserable memory of the afternoon. 'Make sure you win!' we tell them as they clatter off down the gangway. 'We will!' they shout.

The crossing to Strangford only takes ten minutes. When we arrive on the other side we ask at a big nice-looking hotel. It's called the Ciuan Hotel, written in Gaelic script. We must be in Catholic country here. Another clue was that those exuberant girls were going to play camogie, which is the Catholic version of girls' hockey.

But, dammit, they're full up. A young manageress very kindly phones several numbers and eventually finds us a room. She refuses to let us pay for the phone call. 'Ah sure it's nothing,' she says.

But the room is an hour down the road, out in the countryside and there's nowhere nearby to eat. By now I'm completely drained of life and would prefer to go back to Portaferry. John who has rallied somewhat after his 'Red Snapper' depression in Cloghy, disagrees. He would rather not go backwards, he says flatly.

We nearly have an argument. 'But,' I say, 'it's already half-six, and it'll be dark by the time we get there, shower and then cycle out again for dinner. And we've already done forty-five miles today.' Pride prevents me from adding: 'And I'm totally knackered; my heart's about to seize up, my legs already have, and my arse is sore and wet.' But there's no point in having a row, and we are supposed to be cycling round Ireland so I do have to admit that going backwards isn't quite in the spirit of things.

Wearily, wearily on we plod, sore in the arse and forsaken by God. A bit like the ploughman in Grey's *Elegy*, I'm thinking. It goes round and round in my head, obsessively like a hallucination

We're told to follow the signs to Downpatrick. 'The B&B is seven miles, on the left, you can't miss it.' 'Want a bet?' I think to myself.

After what seems an interminable hour we get there. It's called Hillcrest B&B. They are expecting us and at long last the wet, dreary day is over.

Hillcrest B&B is a substantial farmhouse with stables behind and a gigantic ultra-modern tractor in the yard. There are distant views of Strangford Lough.

We ask Mrs Fitzsimons, the landlady, is there anywhere we can go for dinner. She says much the best place is the Slaney Inn, and her husband Francis will drive us round there, it'll be no trouble. That would be extremely kind we say gratefully, but then we realise we wouldn't have our bikes to get back again.

'Would we be able to get a taxi back?'

'Ah, ye don't need to worry about that,' she says. 'Sure they'll drive you back themselves.'

Seems beyond the call of duty but it's usually a social mistake to spurn generosity. So, not knowing the set-up or having the energy to ask, we just go along with it.

At the Slaney Inn we start with foaming pints of Guinness. Then we have a tremendous meal. The main feature is enormous steaks; so big that we can't possibly eat them all. The owner, whose name is Eamon, comes over for a chat. He has heard we are cycling round Ireland.

How did he know that? we ask.

Mrs Fitzsimons told him, he says.

We're embarrassed not to be able to eat all our steak; he might think we didn't like it. 'Oh don't worry,' he says. 'I couldn't possibly eat that much myself. But it's amazing; little old ladies often come in and polish off a whole one, just like that. They eat the meat mainly, sometimes they don't finish all the veg.'

When we ask him, Eamon tells us he's Catholic. 'What about the

Fitzsimonses at Hillcrest?' I ask. 'Yes, Catholics.' 'And the Cian Hotel?' 'Also Catholics.' So this time we've been passed on within the Catholic community.

There are said to be Unionist para-military hideouts in the Mourne Mountains, which are not far away. 'But,' says Eamon, 'there's been very little trouble round here from the Protestants – only one bomb in recent years. There was several lifted up there a couple of weeks ago, about fifteen of them. They put them all inside.'

These people are mad keen horse breeders, and Eamon is very proud that his father bred Slaney Maid, who won at Cheltenham a few months ago and has just won the prize for Ireland's best steeple-chaser of the year. He tells us that Francis Fitzsimons' best horse is called Mandalik, Charlie Swann is his favourite jockey and they are hoping for big things next season. In fact, Francis has just had a hay barn expensively converted into a stable for this fine young horse. Our bikes have been locked up there for the night in amongst Mandalik's bridle, saddle and grooming implements.

Eamon drives us back to Hillcrest. And the day which tested our morale ends on a high note – not exactly a crescendo, more like a gentle Irish lullaby played on the uillean pipes.

Next morning we head off for Newry which is about thirty-two miles away. It promises to be a lovely ride round the Mourne Mountains on the coast road through Newcastle, Kilkeel and Warrenpoint. At Newry the road crosses the border and we'll be back in the South once more.

We flash through Downpatrick like a couple of racers in the Tour de France. Next comes Clough, a very Protestant place with more red, white and blue curbstones and, 'No Surrender' crossroads.

It's coffee time when we get to Newcastle. A big black cloud is threatening ominously. Just as the heavens open we nip into the Shimna Diner: Grills, Restaurant & Coffee Lounge. It's a nice no-nonsense establishment in the main street. People come dodging in, shaking umbrellas. This is just the place to be when it's coming down in stair-rods.

We order coffee and buns. Then John says: 'You know, the more plausible dual-nature theory becomes, the more I agree with you: If it's such a good idea why hasn't it been thought of long ago?'

'Yes, that's a worry, isn't it.'

'So perhaps,' he says, 'we'd better try to work that out before we get much further. If we can't come up with a good answer our theory'll be shot down in flames.'

He's right, and it'll need to be honest thinking.

Soon the downpour outside is over. The really heavy ones never last very long; I suppose God has used all the water he collected up there in the first place. That explanation would please William of Ockham.

We pay at the desk of the Shimna Diner: Grills, Restaurant & Coffee Lounge. And on we go again.

The road gets narrow as it hugs the shore under the mountains. It's dangerous too, with square-arsed delivery vans hurtling past on their urgent errands. On these roads they're more frightening than the big lorries.

At quarter-to-one we stop briefly in Annalong, it's a pretty place. John takes photos of the town and the mountains behind and I do a quick sketch.

We go through Warrenpoint and then, after an interminable seven miles of flat, straight road, along the estuary of the Newry River.

Annalong, where the road follows the shore under the Mountains of Mourne

Warrenpoint from Omeath

At six o'clock we arrive in Newry Town. We cycle around the town a bit and ask a few people, but it doesn't seem inviting and we can't find a B&B anywhere.

So we plod our leaden loaded bikes wearily back out along the estuary again, this time on the South bank. The map says we cross the border somewhere on this road, but disappointingly, as at Muff six days ago, there is no checkpoint or anything at all to jeer at.

After seven more sore-arsed miles we come to Omeath. It's exactly opposite Warrenpoint, which is about a mile away, and an hour and a half ago, across the water.

There's a nice big hotel called the Granvue, and they have a spacious, luxurious room for us with grand heavy curtains, thick new towels and fancy soap.

Next day, before breakfast, I'm in a feeble state of mind wondering is it worth doing a drawing of the view out of the window. Then a woman leads a beautiful thoroughbred mare into the front garden of the house opposite. It eats the grass on the lawn. Fifteen minutes later a man appears and leads the magnificent beast away again.

It's gone, and now the only trace of its visit is a pile of horse dung on the lawn. At least that's proof that I didn't imagine it.

I'm left wondering does the owner of the horse have to pay for the grass it eats, or does the owner of the lawn pay to have his grass cut and fertilised, and how will it do at Cheltenham next season?

No doubt about it, we're back in the Republic.

THREE

*The Grand Scheme of Things –
Newry to Cork*

Judaism, Socrates, Plato, Christianity and Islam have prevented us from noticing our dual nature, and so has the gulf between gurus and teamworkers

'Remember we were worried about why nobody appears to have come up with dual-nature theory before?' says John. 'Well, I've been thinking.'

'Me too; several ideas have been whirling about in my head.'

'OK, you go first.'

'All right,' I say. 'Well, I'm pretty sure great chunks of it actually have been thought of before. For example, I read somewhere recently that an ancient Greek called Anaximander, who was born in 600 BC – that's well over a hundred years before Socrates – put forward an evolutionary theory of animal origins, including man. Apparently we only have fragments of his writings.'

'Phew! I never knew that. That puts Darwin in his place!'

'Well, not quite; Anaximander only hit on the process of evolution. So far as we know he didn't spot the principle of natural slection.'

'Then,' I go on, ' there's my top man, Aristotle; he said there's a golden mean of behaviour, and that we must learn the self-control to follow it. He also said that man is a political or social animal by nature, so it is natural for humans to live in societies and to behave morally towards one another.'

'Well, there you go; that's what I've been afraid of,' says John, who seems to be weakening. 'If dual-nature theory were right, surely someone would have hit on it soon after Aristotle.'

'You'd think so, I do agree. And in fact after Aristotle I can think of several who got close, particularly Machiavelli and J. J. Rousseau. So the question is why didn't society recognise man's dual nature and the fact that morality is a universal social regulator?'

'That's right,' says John. 'So maybe the reason our theory never got off the ground is because it has a fatal flaw.'

'Have faith,' I say. 'Or actually quite the reverse, abandon faith! Because the way I see it, it's the modern religions – Judaism, Christianity and Islam – which have prevented our theory from getting off the ground. The basic principles you and I've been going on about: that man is an animal; that cooperation rather than morality is the key to our behaviour; that morality is flexible and it doesn't apply to groups; these arguments are not acceptable to modern religions.

'We often forget how comprehensively the beliefs of Judaism, Christianity and Islam underlie our daily lives. Certainly in the Christian world these behavioural codes are deeply imbedded in pop music, in the phrases used in the television news, in bestsellers and in the risqué jokes you hear in the office.

'The three religions are very different, of course, but one thing they all have in common is that each has been revealed in a sacred and mysterious bit of magic which asks us to have faith in one absolute God. The logic of dual-nature theory is denied by this absolutism which is so deep in our culture.'

'The power of belief . . . Yes, that's a good argument,' says John.

'But more than that; orthodox religion and government go hand in hand here. Government must have authority. All nations have ruling élites; we call them courtiers or the establishment. They consist of bishops, university chancellors, judges, politicians, scientists, industrialists, journalists and intellectuals. By mutual consent these people ensure that attitudes and ideas, which might encourage sedition, are suppressed.'

'Yes,' says John. 'Look how long it has taken for the equality of women to become accepted.'

'Exactly. So this puts any new thinking through a fine sieve of authoritarian prejudice. Many basic truths are suppressed before they have a chance to be accepted by society. Remember the trouble Galileo got himself into. The implications of dual-nature theory could seriously undermine authority. It is dangerously seditious to point out that morality has to be both flexible and selective, after all morality is the basis of law, and human society depends on the rule of law. So there we have a good reason why dual-nature theory hasn't yet surfaced, and maybe it never will.'

John's now fiddling about with his coffee spoon. He's got something to say but he's too polite to interrupt without first demonstrating that he's been listening.

'So, Tony, you're combining two arguments: that the absolutism of these religions has stifled dual-nature theory, and that the needs of authority have smothered it further.'

'Yes, they are really two aspects of the same barrier, and I believe it explains why the theory has had such huge difficulty breaking through.'

'And there's another thing . . . ' But now I really do have to give way and listen to him.

'The explanation I came up with,' he says, 'is about the gulf that divides gurus and teamers. Let me explain.'

He develops the theme that individuals throw up ideas, and society then adopts as orthodoxy those which are most suitable for its particular purposes. He goes on to point out that one can divide society into gurus who do the thinking, and teamers who do the doing, each having contempt for the other.

Gurus are the brainy ones, singled out early for a comfortable life of thinking, research, writing and being highly respected as experts. They include academics, inventors, artists, doctors and writers. Gurus tend to work on their own rather than in teams.

Teamers on the other hand, are the socially skilled ones. They are not particularly good at school, not because they're stupid; it's rather that bookwork bores them. They are the ones who get a kick out of making things happen. Teamers include entrepreneurs, football managers, administrators and gangsters. Hitler and Napoleon were brilliant teamers. They needed the legitimisation of gurus, but basically they despised them.

John acknowledges that we all have elements of both in us, but says that doesn't destroy the general idea that they're opposites.

'And,' he goes on, 'it could be that this separation has made it extra difficult for gurus, who love theory, to get their paradoxes and speculations accepted by teamers. Because, though gurus design the world, teamers are the ones who rule it, and to do so they need straight uncomplicated answers for the masses. What I mean is that this separation may be another answer to why our theory hasn't been thought of before.'

'Good one!' I say. 'So now if they ask us why it hasn't been thought of before we have three answers: Religion, government and gurus versus teamers.'

'And,' says John, 'don't forget our great hero, Darwin. If it hadn't been for his explanation of natural selection, dual-nature theory would have been unthinkable.'

'Oh absolutely,' I agree. 'Darwin's our main man.'

'And you know,' I've remembered what I was going to say earlier, 'here's yet another sign that dual-nature theory really has been there all along, bobbing just below the surface. It's very simply that ever since ancient Greece, philosophers have always recognised that Ethics and Politics are different subjects. This anticipates dual-nature theory which says that Ethics studies one side of our behaviour – teamwork, and Politics studies the other – group behaviour.'

'QED,' says John.

57 John's friendship, main road, Boyne valley, teenage waitresses in the Black Bull. Meath countryside, roadside rubbish, Olympics introduced

This morning the coast road skirts round the mountain that forms the Cooley Peninsular, geologically a continuation of the Mountains of Mourne.

Carlingford, the next place we come to is very pretty, sitting under its mountain.

The church in Carlingford

Then my blasted chain comes off yet again. I've crept about half a mile ahead of John so when I've fixed the chain and wiped my hands with grass, I wait for him to catch up.

He does lag behind at times. As I watch him come wandering along without a care in the world, I realise that his dawdling is due to his innate disregard for organised progress. I do wish I could be like that. But we're stuck with the personalities God gave us and we just have to settle for what we've got.

However, if you would like to let your mind wander, and maybe find and rearrange buried ideas, my recommendation is that you go cycling with someone like John, if, that is, you're lucky enough to know one.

As we journey on south we start leaving the mountains behind, there won't be any more now until Wicklow, just south of Dublin. Although it's easier on the flat, and you cover greater distances, it's much nicer amongst the mountains.

On we go through Dundalk.

The scenery changes to lowland. It's all fields, hedges and nothing much to be seen on the horizon; perhaps a tractor or a flock of crows.

We've joined the main Belfast to Dublin road, and the fast traffic hammers past once more. We're pulled along in the slipstreams of huge lorries. In the turbulent air you can actually smell the heat of their great engines, like the breath of charging bulls. We cyclists must be irritating to them I suppose. They drive along in competitive bunches. For a while there are none, then several barge along together trying to pass each other. Thank goodness the road is dry, but it's not a good place for cyclists, especially if your chain keeps coming off.

We eventually get to Drogheda where the River Boyne flows out into the sea. The Boyne valley is renowned for its five-thousand-year-old tombs, its seventeenth-century battle, which changed the course of Irish history, and for the tremendous twenty-pound spring salmon that used to be plentiful in bygone years. But by the time it gets to Drogheda the river has turned into a muddy tidal estuary.

We check in at a big anonymous B&B in Drogheda. There's a restaurant opposite called the Black Bull Inn. After a shower and change of clothes we stroll across there for dinner.

We walk in with legs slightly apart like American cowboys. That's not because we're tough guys like John Wayne, ready at any moment to reach for his gun; it's because, like American cowboys, we've got sore bottoms from being on the saddle all day. And we each carry our valuables – money, camera, watercolours and so on – in a strange looking rectangular handbag. This of course is the touring cyclist's detachable handlebar bag, but most people don't know that.

The restaurant is full of people and activity. Several cheerful teenage waitresses are bustling about. Two of them deftly fold napkins into water-lilies as they get a table ready for us.

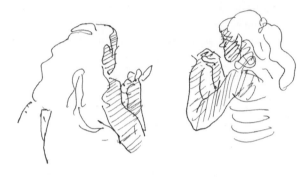

Teenage waitresses in the Black Bull Inn folding napkins
into water-lilies for our table

When we order main dishes from the menu, they say: 'And what'll you have with that, sir?' It's a standard question they've been taught; almost a chant.

'What do you suggest?' says John, playing it safe.

'Well there's fries, wedgies or potatoes, and there's vegetables.'

What, one wonders, can fries and wedgies be if they are not potatoes? It turns out that fries are indeed fried potatoes – chips. Wedgies are sauté potatoes cut in wedges and covered in a spicy sauce which gives them the authentic cheese-and-onion potato-crisp flavour. And potatoes are plain boiled. There's modern culture for you, Irish–American style. We both choose the potatoes

People at neighbouring tables are curious about these two tatty old men, looking weather-beaten and stiff-jointed. Then they see me drawing, but pretending, like you have to, that I'm invisible. That does it; their curiosity overcomes their social reserve, which here in the south is only skin-deep at the best of times.

It turns out that the attractive couple at the table next to us are brother and sister. They're in their late twenties. He's over from

England. Tomorrow they're going to a family wedding and they're both dreading it.

'Aunt Mary is always asking me about girls and contraception. I'm convinced she thinks I'm a poof.'

'And that lecher Declan'll be at the bottle again – Oh God, let's not go!'

Eventually when the teenage waitresses start clearing the tables around us and sorting cutlery, we realise it's getting late. It's time to pay the bill and go back to our anonymous B&B.

Teenage waitresses sorting washed cutlery in the Black Bull Inn

Next morning we take a country road from Drogheda to Dublin airport. It goes over low hills, which are hard work. It's the usual thing; no sooner have you heaved yourself all the way to the top than you've whizzed back down and have to repeat the slog all over again. But we've got used to all that by now and the morning goes by in a pleasant, breezy interlude.

The landscape consists of big untidy cattle farms and large trees. 'Typical county Meath countryside,' says John. The trees are sycamore and ash with a scattering of beech. There's acid yellow ragweed in the scruffy hedges and ditches. Farmers are supposed to eradicate ragweed but they never quite manage it. Crows flap about irresponsibly in the wind, the way crows do in Ireland; they've had plenty to eat, now they're looking for mischief.

The weather is normal for September: cool, dull and grey with medium-high clouds. We cycle over three or four two-hundred-foot hills and from their tops we can see the sea with the Skerries, Lambay Island, a glimpse of Ireland's Eye, and Howth.

When pedalling uphill I go down on to the lower arms of my drop-handlebars to apply the greater effort required. In that position your head is down, looking at the road, so you spend a lot of time gazing semi-consciously at the tarmac and the grass verges. I keep noticing discarded farmers' work-gloves, made of leather, canvas, mixed leather and canvas, plastic . . .

Identifying the different types of glove becomes a sort of game. We've seen so many of these, I'm thinking, that one could make a museum collection. It would display discarded roadside rubbish. This would be sorted into separate glass cases for different regions. Seaside areas would display those small plastic forks that are given out with fish and chips. You see lots of those, also the wooden spatulas that once held choc-ices or lollipops till they were sucked clean. Another common item is the single trainer, never a pair. And of course there are lots of brightly coloured aluminium drinks cans. These glass cases would be sorted into decades. The items representing fifty years ago would be mostly leather, rubber, glass and Bakelite. Today's would be mostly bright-coloured plastics, synthetic fabrics and aluminium. One would contain, very discreetly displayed, a small pair of frilly knickers.

There are the dead animals too. We had lots of mangled rabbits in the West of Ireland, also squashed badgers and birds. Here in Meath it's predominantly dead rats and we've had one very flattened seagull.

The rats surprise me, but then John points out that there's been quite a lot of grain on the roadside, spilt from farmers' tractors. He thinks that's what attracts the rats.

A rather charming feature of roadside wildlife this morning is what John calls 'Woolly Bear' caterpillars. They set out across the tarmac, a perilous voyage indeed for such a small, slow creature. All you can do is wish them luck, and many have nearly reached the other side, so I suppose quite a lot of them do make it. Humans are just as foolhardy. It was in a similar spirit of adventure the South Sea Islanders went out against the prevailing winds and populated the Pacific archipelagos.

After a while we come to Dublin airport, and at half-one we stop for lunch at the Boot Inn. It's near the end of the main runway. In our Trinity days it was a favourite collecting point for parties to the north of Dublin. 'Don't know exactly where the party is,' you'd be told; 'meet you at the Boot at ten o'clock.'

Today is Sunday and the bar is packed with people just out from midday Mass. Most of them are large red-faced men.

Large red-faced men in the Boot Inn

The Olympic Games have just begun in Sidney and some early horse-jumping results are being announced on a big TV screen above the fireplace at the far corner of the lounge bar. People look up at it occasionally but they are not very interested. Their animated chatter drowns out the announcer.

But we're going to have to keep an eye on the Olympics over the next few days because Steve Redgrave, England's great rowing hero, is racing in the coxless four with his crew-mates Matthew Pinsent, Tim Foster and James Cracknell. He has already won gold at each of the previous four Olympics. If he wins for a fifth time it will make him the greatest competitor in Olympic history.

58 Arrival in Dublin, 'Breakfast All Day'. *Marketing is another word for telling lies*

After lunch we reach the untidy outskirts of north Dublin. It's mostly downhill so, over the rooftops, we get glimpses of Dublin Bay and the mountains beyond.

First we go past shabby housing estates and small factories. Then we get lost amongst shabby Victorian houses and shops. Finally we reach the Liffey through the litter of shabby Georgian back streets.

It's somehow depressing to be back in Dublin; sort of an anti-climax. We're at the journey's end before the journey's over. We've still got five or six days to go before we get to Cork and then take the train back to Dublin, so it seems all wrong to be here.

During the ride down to Dublin I'm haunted by the ghosts of the great philosophers of bygone years. Then, as we pass the front gate of Trinity College, with its statues of famous scholars, I remember Miss Ottway Ruthven, our professor of philosophy.

'Wilson!' she says. 'What's this you're saying about the dual nature of human behaviour? An evolutionary theory of morality you say – rather radical, isn't it?' She was always very kind.

Me: 'Well yes, I suppose it is.'

She: 'So how does it stack up against the history of European ethics and political philosophy?'

'Phew!' is my imaginary reply. 'I was afraid you'd ask me that! I haven't worked it out yet.'

I remember that sinking feeling you got when you read an exam question which you knew you couldn't answer. But this one is real;

I'm going to have to grapple with it sooner or later. I'm not going to be able to put it off or, as you sometimes could in exams, answer question no. 3 instead.

Subtle hints of genteel Dublin life: a high-society hotel, an exclusive gentlemen's club, a famous pub, remind us that we're not awfully well dressed. We do hope nobody recognises us as we ride through town wearing our stupid helmets. Word gets around fast in Dublin.

Ignoring the bulk of our panniers, we weave irresponsibly in and out of the traffic, obeying most of the lights and giving self-conscious hand signals, till we eventually arrive at John's rented house on the south side of town.

We shower and put our very dirty cycling clothes into John's washing machine. Then we walk over to a nearby pub for dinner.

Next morning I get an early cup of tea and put the radio on to see how Steve Redgrave did in the Olympics. Being down there in Australia, it's all happening in the middle of the night while we're fast asleep. But it's all right; they won their first heat, beating the Australians, their main rivals, by a length of clear water. So that's OK.

John's still asleep and there's nothing in the house to eat for breakfast. So needing to replace one of my gear levers, which snapped off yesterday, I leave him a note and cycle out to the shops in search of a breakfast café and a bike shop.

Eventually I find Joe Daly's Bike Shop. It's still early but there's a man there already, must be Joe himself. He's opening up the shop and checking the cash till. He can fix it, he says. 'Come back in forty-five minutes.'

There's a Bewley's café across the road that does good breakfasts, so I'm in luck. Bewley's is a well-known and efficient chain of cafés, smart, modern and well designed. But on the way I spot a sign saying: 'Breakfast All Day'.

It's above the entrance to a dingy side-alley.

I'm drawn as if by a magnet to this modest little place. It's not so much the idea of the big blackened frying-pan and the Formica-topped tables with paper tablecloths, as the promise of more down to earth, genuine surroundings.

In Breakfast All Day I'll avoid the plastic smiles and half truths of the marketing in Bewley's café, not to mention the well-dressed clientele and the staff in uniform. Modern marketing with its logos and brand images, is such a turn-off. Much rather the risk of food-poisoning in Breakfast All Day than the certainty of marketing in Bewley's café.

There's a little community of shops up the alleyway: a fruit stall, a health-food shop, Patricia's Books and an empty barber's shop that's boarded up. You can see the tables and chairs through the café window, but it has no name at all. There's a radio on but the place is deserted. Presently a cheerful young lad saunters in from the alley.

'What d'ya want?' he says; his a's pronounced flat, as in rat.

I order egg, sausage, baked beans, bacon, coffee and toast. The door to the kitchen is open and soon I can hear the rattle of pans and the soft thump of a gas stove being turned on.

On the radio a chatty man is doing music and phone-ins. He'll take any calls but the preferred theme this morning is getting up and going to work. 'Many are called but few get up,' he says, but it's an old joke and he goes and spoils it by dragging it out, presumably because he has no callers on the line.

After a while an old man comes in for a coffee. I give him a nod, but he doesn't seem to notice.

But why are these cheap scruffy places so much nicer than your typical Bewley's? I remember the sex bomb in Drains Bay. Marketing shapes us all with a dead hand and turns us into statistics. We're not individuals any more – not people; we're consumers, tourists, viewers, householders and motorists. And of course marketing, the creation and satisfaction of frivolous desires, must take most of the blame for the monstrous over-production and waste of modern industrial society. Marketing is the most deceitful activity of our times and yet instead of tabooing it as lying, we meekly accept the fact that 'Oh well, they all do it'. Somehow it completely evades the discipline of morality; morality simply doesn't seem to apply to the lies told by marketing.

This has to be a prime example of corporate amorality.

Embarrassing products often bring out the most imaginative marketing. The lavatory paper my wife buys has the following message on the wrapper:

ANDREX TOILET TISSUE
Andrex® Toilet Tissue is so soft and gentle against your skin, and now it's even thicker and more absorbent too. Have you tried?

ANDREX WITH ALOE VERA AND VITAMIN E
Andrex® with Aloe Vera and Vitamin E has soft Ripples™ that are

enriched with extracts of soothing aloe vera and vitamin E to give you and your family an extra level of care.

Andrex Moist

Andrex® Moist toilet tissue is the perfect complement to dry toilet tissue, ensuring you feel even cleaner and fresher.

By appointment to Her Majesty The Queen (royal coat of arms). Manufacturers of disposable tissues – Kimberley-Clark Limited, Kings Hill, Kent.

If you have any comments regarding this product, please write to: Consumer Relations Department UKATTW2, Kimberley-Clark Limited, Freepost, 1 Tower View, Kings Hill, West Malling, Kent ME19 4HA, or call us on Freephone 0800 626008 (UK), 1800 626008 (ROI).

I'd love to read their comments register. But let's get this straight. We're talking here about paper supplied for the purpose of wiping your arse® when you have finished the smelly business of defecating. These words about aloe vera and vitamin E have to be total nonsense; the very stuff of music-hall farce; a hilarious joke-poem to the anus. And yet we don't even raise an eyebrow. In the rest of the world people wash their dirty bum with water or wipe it with a leaf. Andrex claim that in the industrial West we all do it with paper and poetry, including, as she's graciously pleased to tell us, Her Majesty The Queen.

Rather a shocking thought that, and I make a mental apology to Her Gracious Majesty®.

But this is not frivolous; it illustrates the power of our taboo about the natural, healthy and daily business of defecation. Isn't it a shame, I think to myself, that we can't apply an equally powerful taboo to the telling of lies and deceitful half-truths in corporate advertising. We shouldn't be surprised; it's merely another illustration that corporations are completely amoral.

But that's not what I'm supposed to be thinking about.

I'm confronted once more by the ghosts of the great philosophers of bygone years.

I know I should tackle this bravely, head-on. But like a coward I toy obliquely with the problem by scribbling an imaginary exam question on the paper tablecloth. The best version reads: 'Relate the

development of European philosophies to their contemporary economic systems, starting with hunter-gatherers.' Playing for time,
I copy it into my sketchbook.

Then I remember that the importance of any philosophy lies in its
influence on the lives of ordinary people. Until it affects the average
family it is an intellectual exercise, a plaything of academics and
brainy, thoughtful people. University and monastic philosophy is
fascinating but to answer this imaginary exam question I only need to
concentrate on the movements which have affected the average
family. This allows me to by-pass great volumes of pure, cerebral,
philosophy about consciousness, truth, existence and causality.
That's lucky, because I do find much of it almost impossible to
understand.

Tucking that promising thought away, I pay for breakfast, collect
my bike from Joe Daly's Bike Shop, and cycle back to John's house.
He's just finished going through the mail and doing a few phone calls,
and he's ready to go. We load up and we're off again, glad to get out of
town.

The sun has come out at last. It's sharp and hot as we bowl along,
and it quickly dries the washed underpants and a T-shirt, which I've
spread out on top of my panniers.

In Bray we buy a choose-your-own-filling sandwich lunch, and at a
quarter-to-two we stop to eat it in a field just south of Greystones.

59 *The history of philosophy has two dimensions: economic development and mode of behaviour*

All morning I've been thinking about that imaginary exam question.
Gratifyingly, things have been materialising and falling into place. So
much so that, as with the seduction of morality and the virtuous
symbiosis of politicians and journalists, which we discussed some
days ago, they seem to confirm the validity of dual-nature theory.

But it's all too easy to be dazzled by one's own ideas, and now
during lunch is a good time to try them out on John.

'If our ideas are any good,' I say, 'we'll want to tell people about
them. But academics will be lying in wait. When they catch us
pontificating with woolly arguments in their chosen territories,
they'll chop us up mercilessly.'

'You're dead right there!'

Lunch in the corner of a field three miles south of Greystones.
Artist's foot in foreground

'Well, with academics in mind, I've devised a philosophical climbing frame which may be useful. See what you think of it. It's a way of relating dual-nature theory to the history of European social beliefs.'

'Phew! There's nothing like a broad sweep.'

'Yes, but I think it can be greatly simplified.'

'Go on then.'

'Well, I start with economics. Many ages of man have been defined, but three main ones stand out: hunter-gathering man, agricultural-city man and industrial man.'

'Yes, OK so far.'

'Next we're saying that the human is a cooperating animal, and therefore like all cooperators, has always had three interchangeable modes of behaviour: solitary, team and group. You'll remember this came into our discussions about looting and about the surge to commitment. So far, we've largely ignored solitary behaviour because we've been concentrating on the workings of cooperation, but for this framework I need to include it.'

'Right-ho. But you ignore mobbing, swarming and herding?'

'Well yes. I do accept that they too are modes of human behaviour, but they seem to be transient sub-modes which don't add to or refute anything we're saying.

'So now,' I go on, 'I'm thinking of a framework which we can erect in two stages. First, we should be able to relate every religious belief and social philosophy of mankind to one or more of these three modes of behaviour. That will give us three great branches of belief. Then we trace these branches through the economic ages of man. It's a 3-D philosophical climbing frame.'

He's listening, so I go on.

'Genetically we've hardly changed at all since the last Ice Age. We've always searched for explanations and solutions, and I'm suggesting that since long before the Ice Ages we've been searching for them from these three different angles: The solitary's angle, the cooperator's and the tribe's.'

'Got any illustrations?'

'I've been thinking about this all morning,' I say. 'First of all, solitaries. For private individuals, wanting, for whatever pessimistic or disaffected reason, an answer to what life's all about and how to live without being dependent on anyone else, there's a big and respected set of what are called consolation philosophies. These include Epicureanism, Hedonism, Cynicism and Stoicism. They also include modern Zen Buddhism and Existentialism. Being personal and introspective, this first great branch of social philosophy is peripheral to dual-nature theory.'

'OK,' says John. 'That's philosophy or religion for solitaries. What about cooperators?'

'Well, there's a huge series of what one could call cooperator philosophies. Anything which tells us how to behave towards other team members is a cooperator philosophy. These, like the Ten Commandments, deal with codes of social behaviour, and rules of morality. "Do as you would be done by", that sort of thing. They advise on how to behave as members of groups. They include Judaism, Christianity and Islam. Political Correctness, now growing spontaneously to fill the vacuum left by the demise of Christianity, may yet develop into a new cooperator philosophy for the industrial age.'

'You like that one, don't you.'

'Yes, I do. And thirdly there are the philosophies or religions governing groups, which include kingdoms, republics, churches and big-business corporations. For these there is the vast body of political philosophies which seek to explain, legitimise and improve the tribe. These include divine kings, secular kings, democracy, utilitarianism, communism, fascism, social democracy and, don't let's forget, business-management theory.'

John listens as I prattle merrily on, my words tumbling out in full flow. He knows there are likely to be false assumptions and illogicalities in all this, but doesn't say so.

'Like I say,' I can feel myself getting pompous but it can't be helped, 'all social philosophies and religions – all beliefs – can be fitted into one or more of these three branches. If you can accept that, then we can trace the development of these three branches through the three ages of man. So now let's have a go at that.'

'On you go.'

'The first age was hunter-gathering man. Unfortunately I don't know enough about the countless philosophies and religions of early societies to distinguish their consolatory, cooperative and political branches. We scornfully belittle the shadowy cartoon-like figures and superstitions of shamanism, witch-doctors, ancestor worship and tribal gods. So I just have to make the ignorant and unsupported assertion that the three branches – the three modes of behaviour – were surely catered for, and that these beliefs must have been nicely tailored to each tribe's particular hunter–gatherer habitat, be it coastal, alpine, desert or rainforest.

'Furthermore, it is highly likely that many hunter-gatherers recognised the dual nature of human social behaviour. I say this because they were more aware of truly being animals than industrial man is. Secondly, the smaller number and size of their cooperative groupings will have made their social structures easier to understand. And finally our dual nature is really pretty obvious once you get rid of all the baggage that comes with modern religion. They didn't have Judaism, Christianity or Islam to blind them.'

'That's a sneaky one!' says John, 'but you're probably right.'

'OK, so I believe primitive superstitions would still be perfectly adequate today if humans hadn't developed farming, cities and writing. The next stage of economic development was agricultural-city man, and from the earliest writing on philosophy and religion we begin to identify the three great branches: consolatory, cooperative and political. They swept shamanism aside because its magic was culturally too simplistic. A farming community with magic as its philosophy is at a survival disadvantage against one using the social cohesion of ancient Judaism.

'Though the dual nature of human behaviour was not promoted as such, it was there under the surface in the ancient Greek Sophists and in Aristotle. They could see very different social philosophies and religions working perfectly well in adjacent city-states. Compare Sparta and Athens for example. They clearly understood the selectiveness and flexibility required when applying the self-restraining rules of morality. In other words, they knew that morality cannot be an absolute. It's astonishing that the ancient Greeks, the ones we call the pre-Socratics, seem to have got it right so long ago. I'm talking 400 BC here.'

'The ancient Greeks never cease to amaze me,' says John.

'Me too, they were fantastic.'

'But then,' I go on, 'Socrates and Plato led us badly astray. They promoted the idea that morality, when we can find it, will turn out to be a pre-existing absolute like $2 + 2 = 4$. This false prediction had two huge political advantages. The first was that it strongly supports the moral codes of self-restraint which enhance cooperation, and thus increase tribal fitness. And the second was that it favoured the ruling class and the church. It enabled the weaving of an authoritarian spell which conferred a spurious authority on the Jewish, Christian and Islamic churches and on the kings – divine mouthpieces of God – who sponsored these religions. Christianity dominated the three branches of European philosophy – consolation, cooperation and politics – from AD 350 until long after the Renaissance.'

'That's good,' says John. 'I can't see any flaws . . . Yet.'

'OK. So then the steam engine is invented. Roll of drums, abracadabra, puff of smoke, enter industrial man. This is the third economic age. Darwin finally loosens the grip of Christianity and the three great branches of philosophy become inadequate because nobody has noticed the dual nature of human behaviour.'

'All three?'

'Yes. I'll take them in turn. First, the private consolation philosophies like stoicism, existentialism and modern Zen Buddhism, do survive intact it's true, but they never were very useful because we are above all a cooperating, not a solitary animal. Existentialists like Kierkegaard and Sartre never really had much impact on society. Second, the dogmas, miracles and absolutism which underlie our cooperator philosophies: Judaism, Christianity and Islam, are shown by science to be absurd. And third, our political philosophy is pathetically incapable of answering the Awful Question. Philosophically speaking we are confused.'

'And you blame Plato for the mess we are in.'

'Yes, or to be fair, I blame his followers. Plato said that ideas, like the invention of the wheel, the arch and the wind-up radio, pre-exist in what he called a parallel universe where they are just waiting for somebody to hit on them. That's a gross simplification of course. This was then built up into the belief, or prediction, that morality will be revealed to be a pre-existing absolute. Plato's followers anticipated the discovery of a morality proof, which has never been found. To me Socrates' and Plato's parallel world of ideas is a true but trivial observation which has been developed far beyond its original usefulness to the point where it is a justification for the concept of God. So monotheism depends on a proof which can never be discovered.

'As I see it, God sits on a donkey and on the end of a stick he's holding out a question in front of its nose, like a carrot. And man is the donkey plodding along trying to get the question. Unfortunately, he's forgotten that he's the one who invented God in the first place.'

'Hmm,' is all John says.

'Well it's a climbing frame.'

'Yes, but you'd like to use it to convince people about dual-nature theory, wouldn't you? You're saying that as we enter the electronic age

we need to get back out of this philosophical blind alley we're in. We need to get back to basics and freshen up the three great branches of social philosophy. And you're saying that possibly dual-nature theory can help?'

'Yes, exactly.'

'People might be more impressed if there weren't so many missing bars in the climbing frame. For example, it ought to be possible to

Panoramic view of the Sugarloaf mountain, Bray Head and Howth, looking north from Wicklow

identify the three branches of philosophy in the superstitions – what a dismissive and arrogant term! – of modern-day hunter-gatherer societies. At the moment we're rather like a pair of archaeologists claiming to know what the lost statue of Athene looked like. It took pride of place in the Parthenon but we've got nothing to go on, only written descriptions, a hand and a bit of her dress.'

He's right of course. I feel both defiant and deflated, because if we're ever to get anywhere with dual-nature theory, I ought to do some heavy research on twentieth-century hunter-gatherer philosophies and religions.

'I've been thinking,' he says. 'Wouldn't it be a major triumph for dual-nature theory if it could explain why the Germans on holiday are renowned for always being the first out of bed, and for putting their towels to bag the best places by the swimming pool. Perhaps we should have a go at that next.'

60 Sudden downpour, hunter-gatherer cows, sacrifice.
Western social democracy, being wasteful and quite far to the left of Aristotle's middle path, is unstable. But how to control the controller?

After lunch we hug the shoreline along lanes and minor roads till we get to Arklow.

It's a lovely ride past Brittas Bay and the Silver Strand. This is caravan heaven – hell to some – where Dublin families come to swim and picnic. The sun goes in and out of the clouds, and you can see for miles.

We spend the night in Arklow.

When we set off again next day, goose pimples spread up my legs, which feel naked in the cold freshness of the morning. Wind and rain showers are in the air.

It's not long before we cycle into heavy rain. It's dramatic: the sky is completely clear from horizon to horizon except for one enormous cloud. It must be seven miles wide. It's ragged at the edges suggesting turmoil, and it's piled high, high up into the sky. Although its underside is low, you can see clear blue to the horizon beneath it. The countryside is flat and our road heads straight towards this theatrical production. Perhaps God's about to scoop us up to Heaven in his huge hand, bikes and all, to tell us off for donkey-talk impertinence.

There's nowhere to shelter and soon it feels strangely warm, so we just cycle on into it. First, there's a battering wind, then some whipping raindrops, then it pours. Of course we get soaked, but it doesn't last long, in fact we come through it surprisingly quickly. He must be after someone else; someone whose sin is greater than ours. After all, there's so much sin around.

The coast road is now flat and featureless and so is the sea. This is big farming country again.

At ten-to-three, when we're about twelve miles north of Wexford, we stop for lunch on a nondescript patch of derelict land. There's a fenced-in electricity sub-installation in the middle, with buddleia and nettles growing through it, and rusting farm equipment in a hedge.

During lunch John says: 'No hunter-gatherers round here any more, I don't suppose; not in this rich farmland. Imagine the fun they'd have picking off one of those wild elephants over there.' He's looking at some cows in the next field.

'Yes and the terrific hooley afterwards. There'd be dancing round the fire, storytelling, singing, drinking and smoking, and the chasing of young maidens through the undergrowth.'

'Disgraceful!' he says.

'Actually I'd love to know more about their religions and philosophies. For instance, what about the origin of sacrifice? I have a theory that sacrificial rituals were repeatedly reinvented in different parts of the world as a way of explaining to the children why their beloved pet calf or lamb has to be eaten. "Why does my Bambi have to be killed, mummy?" the little girl sobs. "Don't cry, darling," her mother says. "How often do I have explain it to you? He's very lucky. This ritual means he's going to Heaven and if you're very good you will go too, one day, and then you'll meet him again." And the idea was built up from there.'

'I'm sure it's all written up in learned anthropological papers,' says John.

'I've been thinking,' he goes on, 'about that framework you were talking about yesterday for the relating of the three branches of philosophy to the ages of man according to the behavioural mode in question. Do you think it could help us to predict the philosophies that may sweep through society in the new electronic age? They say this could become the fourth economic age of man.'

'That's an interesting one,' I say. 'Have you heard of Hegel's dialectic?'

'I think so, vaguely, but tell me.'

'Well, the idea goes right back to our heroes, the ancient Greeks, but it was Hegel who really developed it in eighteenth-century Germany. Actually, I suspect he and Johann Fichte are the ones to blame for their unfortunate swimming-pool behaviour, but that's by the way. Hegel said that political movements don't develop smoothly; they lurch from one extreme to the other, each new idea sweeping clean as it goes.

Marx then vigorously pushed this idea beyond its useful limit to promote socialism. Philosophers often do that.'

'What, push good ideas beyond their useful limits?'

'Yes.'

'They're not the only ones, scientists are at it all the time. Look at Dawkins.'

'Yes well . . . You can see the dialectic in full swing in the upheavals of Fascism and Communism. Nowadays the accepted idea is that this was a classic dialectical opposition between the two extremes of right- and left-wing philosophy. The thinking goes that we've now come to our senses and settled on Social Democracy, which at last occupies Aristotle's middle ground; we've reached equilibrium.'

'Yes; first right then left and finally centre. I can see that's a good explanation.'

'But I'm not so sure about that.'

'Oh dear, I might have guessed it. Why not?'

'Well both Fascism and Communism were highly autocratic. Far from being at opposite extremes, I see them as rivals competing for supremacy at the autocratic end of the dialectical spectrum. If you can accept that, then you realise that Social Democracy doesn't occupy the middle ground at all; it's way over there on the left, opposing autocracy. Furthermore, as the Muslim world keeps telling us, Western industrial society, underpinned by this Social Democracy, is worryingly dependent on the marketing of perpetual economic growth, and on ever-expanding credit. We've got to admit that these are serious flaws. We can absorb them for the moment because of the amazing achievements of science and technology. But we are so extraordinarily wasteful that it can't go on for ever. As somebody said, we have become morally obese on self-indulgent pleasures and drunk on petrol.'

'My point exactly. It can't go on for ever, but it probably won't stop until we've wiped out all the salmon.'

'All right, all right.'

'OK, so what does the dialectic say will happen next?'

'I think the answer's staring us in the face. The hard men will come sweeping down from the hills. These will be people who, starting from behind, can grow faster: the Chinese perhaps, or a unified Africa. It may not happen for three hundred years, but eventually they'll swarm all over us, destroy our water supplies and our pleasure palaces. They'll neglect our roads and aeroplanes, our universities and computer systems. The result will be anarchy for a few centuries and then the whole thing will start all over again. It's happened throughout history, the most famous was the collapse of the Roman Empire.'

'Will the salmon revive?'

'Yes, when our water supplies and hydroelectric installations have been destroyed.'

'Oh yes. Good. That's all right then . . . But seriously can you see any way of preventing this?'

'Well, of course, it would only happen if we allowed ourselves to be taken to the dialectical extreme through foolish over-reliance on the ideal of democracy. But industrial man does seem to be running into danger. Christianity and its assistant, Social Democracy, seem incapable of avoiding it because they ignore the selective and flexible nature of morality. Christianity denies the fact that all group behaviour is amoral.'

'So how can we prevent ourselves from being debauched by the wasteful luxuries of Social Democracy, and then being overrun by the hard men from the other side of the dialectic?'

'I suppose the answer is that we have to learn how to navigate the appropriate mid-channels between the dialectical extremes of political philosophy. It would be a bit like those computer games in which you steer a virtual car round a virtual racetrack. This would mean learning how to position ourselves on that part of the left/ right political spectrum which best suits our internal culture, and our international situation. I mean choosing the most appropriate policies as to peace, external threat, growth or stability, and techno-logical change. And these would alter according to the circum-stances we are in at any particular time. Aristotle said we should study so that we can learn where the Golden Mean is and then seek to follow it. Isn't that beautifully stated!'

'And how would this work in practice? I only ask because it all sounds a bit, you know, utopian.'

'Well, if any group, from small company to nation, finds itself under any sort of threat it should, and usually will, sharpen up the authoritarian aspects of its government. And conversely, when the threat has passed, there is usually benefit to be gained by easing off on the wartime discipline and letting anarchic individuality flourish a little. We do it already but sluggishly, and often after it's too late. Look at how the Afghan nation clings to its hair shirt, and how long it took to respond to Hitler.'

'And you think dual-nature theory can help here?'

'Yes I do, and on several levels. It refutes absolutism which is a main source of inflexibility and polarisation in politics. It exposes the often-deceitful selfishness of corporations, and sub-groups which market over-indulgence . . . '

'Like soft lavatory paper.'

'Right! And it highlights the amorality of the party machine, which puts short-term success before the long-term health of the nation. It underlines the importance of the media in keeping our public awareness honest and free of confusing propaganda. And it shows the importance of effective cooperation in society.

'What I'm saying is that for a healthy society we need to dampen our dialectical oscillations. Navigating along Aristotle's Golden Mean between extremes is the aim. This would require an almost religious understanding of the true nature of cooperation. Such an understanding could arise out of political correctness. And dual-nature theory could give such a movement a good boost.'

'And social democracy you say, is quite far over to the left?'

'Yes.'

'OK, so just to orient myself, could you sketch out a workable political philosophy at the opposite end of the spectrum.'

'Well, think of wartime. The other extreme of the dialectic is quickly adopted when there's an imminent threat of invasion. Also it's not difficult to cook up a workable social philosophy for the hard men from the hills. It would give freedom of action to businesses and similar corporations. But this freedom would be curtailed by a structure of effective legal restraint by trades unions and monopoly commissions, by a free press and ecological "green" concerns. This restraint would be re-enforced by a social ethic, which would be deeply suspicious of corporate amorality. There would be public shame and disgrace, like the medieval village stocks, massive fines, and instant jail for trans-gressing corporate bosses. Self-restraint and cooperation would be idealised, and individualism subordinated to the needs of corporate efficiency. Inequality would be accepted as normal human nature. The poor "who are always with us" would be looked after, but they would not have much of a voice in public affairs. Governments and leaders would be elected in a meritocratic rather than a totally democratic way. Clan leaders and corporate bosses rather than mass-elected representatives would sit in the legislative chambers. Women would have intelligent equality; superior in leadership but subordinate in teamwork. The media would have a very free voice to guard against corruption. The law would be strict. The constitution would prevent the development of strong party machines such as exist in the USA and England today. Governments would have strictly limited terms of office, and dynasties would be made constitutionally impossible.'

I've finally run out of steam, and then of course doubt creeps in.

'I know what you're thinking: The hope that we can steer a middle course between the hard-men philosophy and social democracy is cockeyed optimism.'

'Well there's no harm in working it through,' says John. 'And the big thing it has going for it is the way it's scientifically linked back to our true animal nature: to genetics and evolutionary biology. That's what's new in all this and makes it respectable. Another thing I like about your navigation idea is that it offers a common-sense, rough-and-ready guide. It recognises that when there is a crisis and a surge to commitment we need to steer over to the harder right, and that when the surge dies away, we'll naturally drift back to the left.'

'Yes, and now that globalisation is arriving on the wings of the Internet, we might be able to cook up a universal set of self-restraining codes which will prevent us from blowing ourselves up and poisoning the earth.'

'But hold on,' says John, 'couldn't people say that insisting that people must navigate the mid-channel sounds very much like absolutism?'

'Well not really. First of all, the mid-channel would differ for different nations according to their circumstances, and secondly, remember that absolutism is based on blind faith. What we're proposing is – you've just said this yourself – based on science.'

'OK,' he says, 'that just leaves me with one final problem: how do we stop nations fighting each other, or how do we keep the top nation on the rails?'

Over the past few days we've been worrying about how society can control the foreign policy of the most powerful nation on earth: the Roman Empire for example or the USA or China?

'Yes there it is again, that worrying "*quis custodiet?*" problem. I don't know of any answer I'm afraid.'

It's a sad note to end on. The mundane squelch of reality has settled on us, and the hunter–gatherer's elephants in the next field have turned back into industrial man's grass-processing units.

*Industrial man's grass–processing units in the field opposite a
derelict patch of land where we have lunch*

61 Bloodhounds and cows, pass the parcel at
Wellingtonbridge, Tramore Hotel lunch. *Living
organisms use a three-phase mutually controlling cycle
like scissors, paper and stone. This also applies to quasi-
living organisms like business corporations and nations*

We cycle on into the afternoon.

It's not long before I have to stop for yet another pee; must have done several hundred on this journey so far. As I stand there by a farm gate I imagine a pack of bloodhounds as they follow our piddle-trail. They started in Cork, got into a fight at Puck Fair, met Rover and

Lycaon Pictus, and were chased by Max's bulls. They licked my blood off the white line in Portstewart and, one after the other, they peed into the underground gun-post at Letterkenny. But they're catching up all the time, and now they're only half a day behind. They race along howling and drooling at the thought of marrow-bone of cyclist for dinner. Best not let them catch me. So I hurry up and get back on my bike.

At about half-four we get to Wexford. We're tired and keep an eye out for somewhere to stay the night. Nothing enticing presents itself in this busy city, so we go on through hoping to find somewhere nice in the countryside beyond. But there doesn't seem to be anywhere. No B&B signs to be seen at all.

Eventually, after twenty long miles, we come to Wellingtonbridge. It's getting dark and by now we're very tired. We ask at a pub. Several people join in the discussion. St Jude's is mentioned, but somebody else thinks they don't do B&B any more. Nobody knows for sure. The general opinion is that there might be a place about two miles 'up that little road over there', pointing to a crossroads by a small bridge, Wellington's presumably.

So we go up the little road, our legs now feeling like lead, our arses sore, and night falling fast.

After what seems much more than two miles we decide that now we really are finally and totally lost.

A passing car slows down. The lady driver smiles kindly, almost as though she knows us. She says, 'No you're all right. St Jude's is the next house on the left round the corner.'

The next house has no B&B sign but it is St Jude's. And it's full up. Our hearts sink.

But then the landlady says, 'The Haven B&B is not far and they have room for you. If you like I'll show you the way.'

At this point it dawns on us that the message must have been put out on the bush telegraph back at the pub, and the whole neighbourhood's been alerted: 'Two doddery old men on bikes wandering around looking lost. They're heading for St Jude's hoping to find a bed. Can anybody fit them in?'

Anyway she hops into her car, which is a silver Avensis. I make a mental note of that in case we lose sight of her, and she guides us half a mile through narrow lanes till at last we get to the Haven B&B.

Mercifully they have room for us. Well of course they have. Yet again we've been kindly passed around like a parcel on the B&B network.

By now it's ten-to-nine. Night has fallen. We've done sixty-seven miles today, easily a record so far and we're completely banjaxed.

The landlady's called Nell. She settles us down with a pot of tea, bread and honey, and biscuits. We are much too tired to cycle off again in search of dinner, let alone pedal all the way back up here in the dark, so we supplement Nell's tea with mix 'n' squash leftovers. And tonight we have the luxury of separate rooms.

This is a real old farmhouse. The thick walls in my room slope away from perpendicular where the massive chimney-breast goes up through the ceiling. It's all newly painted and nicely furnished. The whole house has been completely renovated for the B&B trade.

When I wake up next morning my clothes and stuff are strewn all over the floor where I left them last night, too exhausted to tidy things away. But this morning I'm fully restored and ready to go.

A small ferry takes us across the combined estuaries of the Suir, the Nore and the Barrow. John tells me there are two villages farther out along the estuary here. They are on opposite banks. One is called Hook and the other Crook, and that's where the well-known expression comes from. Cromwell, chasing the Irish up the estuary with an avenging fleet, is supposed to have said he'd get them 'by Hook or by Crook'.

My already meagre bladder capacity has diminished worryingly in the last few days. Perhaps it's to do with the relentless pummelling of my saddle. Anyway it's not long before I have to stop once more.

I find a farm gate into a field. Some cows are lying down with their backs to me but I'm spotted immediately. They must have excellent hearing. To them I suppose, this figure in a funny helmet is something unusual. Perhaps it's brought them food. First a few young ones get up with a heave of hind and front legs. To begin with, the older ones can't be bothered, but eventually even they can't control their curiosity and struggle to their feet.

'For heaven's sake,' I want to tell them, 'don't get up. I'll be gone in a minute!'

After standing and staring for a few moments they start ambling towards me. But I've finished before they reach me, and as I depart they're all standing still again. Perhaps they are slightly the wiser; after all, there's not much point getting up for a piddling cyclist, especially if the bloodhounds are after him.

At about half-two we come to Tramore. It's an attractive holiday town sloping down to a small harbour. We go into O'Shea's Hotel to see if they can give us lunch.

They can, but we'll have it in the bar because it's late and they want to clear the tables. John suspects the real reason is that they'd rather not have these two tramps lowering the tone in the restaurant. There's no choice; the only thing we're offered is soup, roast beef and two veg.

I've had an idea: scissors, paper and stone. It's about pre-existing principles, and it came to the surface while we were on the little car ferry this morning.

I'd been looking, in a scattered sort of way, for an answer to the '*quis custodiet?*' problem: who controls the controller? For some reason I was speculating about the slime mould and obsessively trying to connect that with the unholy symbiosis between the political party machine and the media. Connections between apparently unconnected thoughts can sometimes spark off ideas.

Being a cooperative rather than an individual animal, the slime mould is what we've been calling a quasi-living organism. Might it be an evolutionary offshoot of the development from single-cell bacteria to more complex organisms, *eucaryotes* as John calls them? Or is that teleological thinking?

Setting that aside as too difficult, I wondered about how a co-operative organism like the slime mould actually goes the right way. Then I realised that all moving organisms must navigate. They must direct their movements to survive. In other words, they must control themselves.

And, now here's the exciting thought, the slime mould seems to do it not singly, but as a cooperative group.

We're saying that a cooperating group – a tribe say, or a nation – is a quasi-living organism which controls itself, so perhaps by analogy the same navigational control principles as used by bacteria can apply. Perhaps this might be how to control the controller? Is there some pre-existing principle here, something simple like $2 + 2 = 4$, which is available to all life forms? And then I realised; yes of course, that's it. And it connects up with the unholy symbiosis between the political party machine and the media!

While waiting for lunch to arrive I can't contain myself. 'Scissors paper and stone,' I say excitedly.

'You feeling OK?' says John.

I ignore that with maximum dignity. 'You know the game . . . '

'You mean the one where scissors cut paper, paper wraps stone and stone blunts scissors; that one?'

'Yes. You see I think it could be a pre-existing navigational principle and it might help us answer the "*quis custodiet?*" problem.'

I then launch into a torrent of explanation, which is supercharged by the mounting pulse of excitement. I make an effort to take it slowly, and John, kind fellow that he is, listens closely, putting in punctuating mutters. Very few people do actually listen.

'Living creatures,' I say. 'Their prime motivators ask for food, shelter or sex, so they mess about all day looking for these. That's the essence of navigation. They try this, try that, repeat or retreat, remember what happened and try again.

'The navigation systems of all moving life forms probably all follow the same basic principle. And this could well be a three-phase, never-ending cycle in which each phase directs the next, like the children's game: scissors, paper and stone.'

A waiter brings our lunch. 'Thanks very much, that looks nice,' says John. But I hardly notice.

'I searched for similar mutually controlling phases in animal navigation and came up with: Reviews, Decides and Remembers. For example a bear reviews life and finds it's cold and wet. It decides to shelter. It remembers where to shelter for next time.

'This principle has a nice triangular geometry and logic which can be said to be pre-existing in the Platonic sense, like the pre-existing fact that $2 + 2 = 4$.

'There are never less than three steps. The organism can't navigate if it does not complete all three. Two won't do. For instance, it's no good reviewing the situation and deciding what to do, if you don't remember and learn from the result. That's not navigation.'

'No, it's not. I see what you mean,' says John. 'Don't let your lunch go cold.'

'Nor, because life moves on, is it enough to decide what to do and remember the result, if you don't then take stock of your new situation. Taking stock or reviewing, is an essential element of navigation.

'Furthermore, no fourth step is required. Three is enough. A fourth would probably be hopelessly confusing. It would introduce the chaotic possibility of alternative pathways in the iteration of the cycle. This holds true in space as well as flat geometry.'

I pause to eat. The beef is juicy prime cuts off a big leg roasted to perfection this morning. O'Shea's Sunday roast is surely famous for miles around.

After a few minutes I go on. 'If you were designing a robot you would have to make it cycle through these mutually controlling and constantly reiterating phases. And I suggest that you'd end up with three of these phases, not two or four.'

'I like the geometry; it's nice,' he says.

'OK, so it seems possible that from the very beginning life on earth has made use of this bit of pre-existing triangular geometry for navigation. In other words, this geometry is simply another behavioural opportunity provided by the environment. It's even more basic than the opportunities offered by light waves, sound waves and the density of the air, and of course it's much more primitive than cooperation.'

John interjects again. 'Yes I see what you're getting at. This is yet another pre-existing opportunity. That's good.' I think he's interrupting so that I'll get on and eat my lunch.

'Yes, sorry to be prattling on so fast, but the trouble is that an idea like this has so many strands that I'm terrified I might lose one. I find they all crowd into my head at once, not tidily or in proper sequence.

'Anyway,' I go on, 'this three-phase navigation principle can apply to quasi-living organisms: slime moulds, driver-ant colonies and human groups, just as well as it does to individuals.'

'So,' says John, 'your idea is that the paper, scissors and stone principle underlies the navigation, or management, of all human groups.'

'Yes that's it, and industrial corporations may find this three-phase control principle particularly helpful. Business schools and management consultants would have a heyday.

'Furthermore, if I'm right, it follows that every nation's political constitution should use this principle in balancing its powers. Let me sketch out the three elements.

'First of all Review, which motivates and directs Decide, should be represented by the media who, as we've said, are commercially motivated to express the true spirit, the gossip and will of the people in order to sell advertising. This true spirit can frighten a dictator. It's about the only thing that can. The Review set includes the media, the will of the people, trade unions, the court jester, the Internet, the chattering classes, pamphlets, graffiti, satire and the village pump.'

'Decide, which directs and compiles Remember, should be represented by government. Government harnesses the most capable leaders, the ones who can never be prevented from climbing their way to the top of the heap in any society. The Decide set includes the leadership hierarchy, the government, the board of directors, the field marshal, the divine king and the village headman. It also includes action and creation.

'Finally Remember, which directs and constrains Review, should be represented by tradition and culture and its everyday embodiment; the law. The Remember set includes: culture, the law, the church, "the way we do things around here", academia, the rules of morality and the village elders.

'These three elements, media, government and law, should be so balanced in the constitution that any two can combine to override the third. And finally the continual iteration of the cycle should be enshrined as sacrosanct . . . '

'That did all come out in a bit of a rush,' says John. 'But I think I've got it.

'In fact . . . ' he says rather carefully, 'in fact, remember when you talked about how the unholy symbiosis between media and government might be recreated in an anthropological laboratory? I think we were in Portrush at the time. Well, you've just done it! The media are Review and the government is Decide. And as you've just said, Review directs Decide. Life is your laboratory; the court jester overrules the king. Scissors, paper and stone rules OK!'

He then asks, 'Can this solve the *quis custodiet?* problem? Could this three-phase navigation principle rescue us when the situation gets out of hand: when a new Hitler goes mad and threatens the world like in a James Bond film?'

'I don't think anything can save us when things get out of hand. And they often have. For example, in the French Revolution it was the Review element that managed to override both Decide and Remember. With the Incas, it was the Remember element, culture, the priestly caste which dominated both Review and Decide. And of course, the commonest case is where a dictator like Hitler or Stalin manages to subdue both Review and Remember. But I suppose we could claim that in all these cases a properly interlocking, and constantly reiterating, three-phase navigation system would have prevented the nasty situation.'

'Three-phase navigation sounds a bit like the Father, Son and Holy Ghost,' says John.

'Steady on.'

'I'm serious; it might actually explain that weird bit of dogma. You know, the impetuous Son interceding with God the Father on our behalf. God the Father being all powerful and pompous and deciding everything, and the Holy Ghost . . . Well, she's a big woman who acts as referee and keeps the impetuous Son under control.'

'You're right!' I say. 'That would explain the Holy Trinity. At last! As a youngster I always had dreadful trouble trying to understand it and eventually I gave up. But let's be careful; it's important not to do a Plato, or a Wagner here. We have to guard against the temptation to try and extend the principle beyond its useful potential.'

'What do you mean?'

'Well, for example, might it have been possible to harness this navigation principle to prevent the collapse of the cod fisheries off Newfoundland? In other words, could it solve the problems of shared or commonly owned resources? I'm thinking of fishing grounds, hospitals, irrigation systems, schools and the multitude of other semi-public, semi-private enterprises and nationalised industries. But this is tricky stuff, and it could drag the principle into unnecessary controversy. Best leave it for the next bike-ride.'

'Yes.'

I've almost finished my lunch. There's a moment's silence, then John adds: 'And you realise, we're flying on two engines here; this navigation principle is independent of dual-nature theory. If one is destroyed, the other still survives.'

'Yes, that's good.'

'Tell you what,' he says, 'if we called it the Trinity Principle that would be a nice way of saluting Trinity College, Dublin, that wise and broad-minded institution which so generously tolerated our mis-behaviour and launched us on the world.'

'You're right! ' I say. 'That's perfect. Lets call it the Trinity Principle. Game, set and match; scissors, paper and stone.'

62 To Lismore. We meet Norman. *Law making and enforcement should be split in two; cooperator law and group law*

After lunch we pedal on along the coast. Going west now; it's up hill and down dale into a head-wind all afternoon. But there's no rain and quite a lot of sunshine. We go through Fenor, Annestown, Bunmahon and Stradbally till eventually we arrive in Dungarvin and end up in St Anthony's Guest House.

It is now becoming impossible to smother the sad feeling that our great journey round Ireland is more or less over. Tomorrow we'll have a short ride through Cappoquin to Lismore where we've arranged to spend the day with our old friend Norman Gillett who works there as a salmon gillie. Then, for our last day, it'll be a fairly simple thirty-five-mile spin down to Cork.

During the night, on the opposite side of the earth, Steve Redgrave's coxless four were in the the the semi-finals. But the man making our break-fast at St Anthony's Guest House doesn't know the result. His mind is on matters closer to home. 'T'was a wild night,' he says. And indeed water is pouring down the windowpane. Even at half-seven it's still very dark outside.

After breakfast it brightens up. At first there's a spitting wet wind but that soon eases off. The road to Lismore now goes inland through beautiful countryside. We're back in the far South where the climate is wet and mild and the trees and rivers are majestic.

At Cappoquin there are old stone steps going down by the massive old stone bridge over the Blackwater. There's a patch of derelict ground down there, all covered in brambles with buddleia pushing through. The buddleia is in flower. It's pale mauve with little yellow centres, and it's covered with butterflies. You can just see the chassis of an old pram in the rich, damp undergrowth and some hand-squashed beer-cans.

There's a public notice in this wild patch. In big red letters it says. 'Dumping Prohibited – Waterford County Council, Public Health Section'.

Peeing isn't though so, being badly in need yet again, I have a quick piddle there. John picks the blackberries and I wonder how close those bloodhounds are.

We find a place in Cappoquin High Street to have coffee.

John is looking pensive. 'You know, ' he says, ' I'm not so sure that our Trinity Principle will always solve the *quis custodiet?* problem.' We're almost talking a kind of shorthand now. 'We may, as you said, be overreaching the idea's useful application. It might work for James Bond but unfortunately life isn't a Hollywood film. The thing is, I don't think you can ever legislate against the rise of a tyrant. All you can do is to set things up to make it less likely.'

'Well yes,' I say reluctantly, 'I agree. You've got to be right. We've gone and fallen into the ever-open jaws of the overreaching trap. You've fished us out. Thanks.'

'There's another thing,' says John. 'I've been thinking about the law. If we're right, the regulation of society should be split into two separate branches; cooperator law and group law.'

'That sounds like a promising one.'

'It would make things so much clearer for all concerned if the law recognised the two-sided nature of human behaviour. There'd be totally separate courts. Cooperator law would deal with moral codes and individual behaviour: things like murder, theft, deceit, divorce and other misdemeanours which mess up cooperation. Group law on the other hand would deal with conflicts between groups, and between groups and individuals.

'There'd be separate judges, magistrates, barristers and jury systems for each branch. There'd also be quite different punishments and prisons. And, most important, the parliamentary drafting of laws would clearly recognise the difference. That's off the top of my head.'

He's gone a bit cautious. Scientists hate making sweeping generalisations.

'The details would need careful working out, because legislating for human behaviour is so complicated.'

'You're right,' I say, to urge him on, 'and dual-nature theory shows nicely why we find the business of law-making so difficult. How can you hope to make good laws if you confuse two totally different modes of behaviour?'

'Yes, that's what I mean. On the one hand morality, the basis of individual law, can never be an absolute. That's why juries are necessary. But on the other, all cooperating groups are, without exception, amoral. So group regulation based on the assumption of morality is largely ineffective. Group law would include very severe prison sentences for corporate bosses. It would deal with all the harmful tricks groups get up to, including pollution, animal experiments, company law (including tax and contracts), company auditing, monopolies and price-fixing, deceitful marketing . . . '

'Hey and John! – don't forget salmon habitat destruction.'

'Yes, silly me . . . and salmon habitat destruction.'

This reminds us that John's hoping for some fishing at Lismore so we pay up and get back on the road.

At a quarter-to-twelve we get to Lismore and meet up with Norman.

We've stopped for a final pee just before Lismore when a car races past, screeches to a halt, and manoeuvres dangerously backwards towards us. It's Norman.

He says, 'I saw these two old cyclists piddling in the bushes.' He's using what in grammar is called the heroic tense, as though already storing it away for a future story. 'Then I thought Christ! That must be them.'

We try to convince him that as a rule we never, ever, pee by the roadside. It's just that if you're calling on someone it gives a bad impression to say, 'Hello, nice to meet you and can I go to the lavatory?' Wasn't it Dr Johnson who said: 'It's better to travel hopefully than to arrive'? I expect he added, 'and if you should eventually arrive it's best to relieve your bladder first.'

63 With Norman in Lismore. Trucker's Inn.
Fruitful cooperation is the secret of life. Feminism ignores the requirements of cooperation

Norman Gillett, a wiry almost elf-like figure, was at Trinity ten years after John and me. He has a reputation as a superb cox and a delightful rebel. He's one of those old friends you only meet about once a year, but that's been going on for the past forty years, so he is a familiar and treasured part of our life.

Norman did geology and went on to Oxford after Trinity. He coxed the Oxford second boat, just missing selection for the Boat-Race crew due largely to riotous behaviour, learnt at Trinity, but not much appreciated at Oxford. Norman is still remembered in rowing circles for his impish, hell-raising behaviour, but this hides a many-sided personality. By trade he was a successful free-lance geologist working in the oil-exploration business. But his greatest achievement, certainly according to John, is that he has published a book on fly-fishing.

Lismore Castle

Norman has retired from oil exploration and he now spends his summers working as a gillie on the Blackwater, here at Lismore.

With catches averaging around six thousand fish per year, the Blackwater competes with the Moy in County Mayo to be Ireland's most productive salmon river. The regulars who come from all over the world, are mostly rich and famous. They are also expert anglers. The gillies are freelance. As with golf caddies, the system is that they are employed directly by the individual fishermen. There are no middlemen. The gillie relies solely on tips, though there is an informally recognised daily minimum a fisherman is expected to pay. If you want to become a gillie on the Blackwater you just go along and try to build up a reputation and clientele in competition with the resident gillies. You need to be tough; it requires masses of knowledge, personality and persistence.

People who know the set-up are very impressed that Norman has managed to establish himself here, and you can see that he'd be a marvellous companion to have with you on a fishing holiday. He knows the best spots to catch fish at the different times of day, seasons, variations of weather and conditions of river, but he's also a gifted storyteller. Norman has an endless fund of fables and anecdotes from which he can select suitable ones for all ages and conditions of folk. When the fish aren't biting, a well-told story improves the shining hour.

Norman refuses to identify his big name clients, but they include sportsmen, politicians, pop stars, rich aristocrats, multi-millionaires and the young mistresses of Italian property tycoons. One was an American senator who rented the whole of Lismore castle for a week at £1,500 per day. Another was an Italian who brought his own very expensive olive oil and salami; it turned out that he sells it all over the world. 'In England you can only get it at Harrods.'

Of course these two, the salmon gillie and the professor of salmon ecology, both with a taste for Guinness and fun, go spiralling off into the salmon world as soon as they meet. It must have been like this when Stanley met Livingstone. They lapse into a salmonoid shorthand. I try to keep up, but much of the detail escapes me. The main thing is that the fishing is not very good at the moment – nothing new there.

Norman has spare rods, waders and other fishing gear in his car for John, and he's cancelled his clients for the day.

He guides us down to the river bank where we park our bikes under some huge beech trees, dramatically overlooked by Lismore Castle.

I listen to their enthusiasm as they rig up their rods. Then I leave them at it.

John and Norman fishing salmon in the Blackwater

I cycle on into the town for a sandwich and pint of Murphys at the Lismore Hotel. I find a comfortable armchair. It's twenty-to-two and my legs must be wondering why I'm not in the saddle. I review my sketchbook, make a few notes, and very soon I'm fast asleep.

Late in the afternoon the fishermen return. They haven't caught a salmon but that doesn't matter at all. John caught a sea trout and hooked a salmon which got away. He also saw several other salmon. He's delighted with the river. Except for some local farming malpractice, it's the perfect habitat.

Norman tells us that, last night, Steve Redgrave's four won their semi-final heat with ease. The final is tomorrow night. Sonia O'Sullivan, Ireland's great middle-distance runner, also won her semi-final in the Olympic five thousand metres. She looked majestic accelerating down the finishing straight. Sadly, she was then just beaten into a silver medal in the final.

We spend the night at Norman's place.

Next morning the sad truth tolls loud and slow, like the great bell in a French cathedral. This will be our final day, and then there'll be no more to say.

at Lismore. The smudges are from raindrops.

There is a rich mixture of emotions in my soul. I bottle them up as I make myself a cup of tea, the all-purpose answer in situations like this.

When John gets up he, too, is pensive and monosyllabic. Norman gives us breakfast. We chat away till we can't put it off any longer; it's time to go.

Five miles after Lismore we reach Tallowbridge and from there we go for fourteen miles up the valley of the River Bride. It's a peaceful warm morning and this intimate little valley is one of the loveliest of the whole trip round Ireland. Big trees overhang the beautiful sparkling young river for mile after mile.

Eventually at Rathcormack we come to the big trunk road. Lorries, making thudding Doppler sound-effects, pound relentlessly up and down between Dublin and Cork.

Before joining the traffic we stop for lunch at the Trucker's Inn. Huge lorries are parked outside. The bacon and sausages are delicious, the eggs are very fresh and the toilets are spotless.

'Well, it's very nearly over now,' says John, looking at the map. 'Twenty more miles to Cork and that's it.'

'Yes, I've been trying to ignore that, but it can't go on for ever . . . I've been thinking about life. The truth is you and I belong back home in our separate communities; we don't belong together on the road.'

'I know,' says John vaguely. He's looking over at a big lorry driver. The man has a shaved head and is reading a newspaper with pictures of semi-naked girls while he eats his sausage, beans and chips. 'He belongs on the road; do you think he worries about the meaning of life?'

'I think he probably does; more than most actually. We mustn't be put off by his tattoos and his tough-guy haircut. Remember he spends all day in his cab, a long way from home. I know he's got his radio and his mobile, but I bet he does more thinking about the meaning of life than one might imagine. Does he have any choice in the matter or is it all preordained by some sort of everlasting God-like clock which "knows" the future? I think dual-nature theory might possibly be able to answer that one.'

'What, about the meaning of life?'

'Yes – well – no, not exactly. I see that as a trick question; it assumes that life has a meaning in the first place. But why should it? Evolutionary biology doesn't need a meaning for life.'

'OK, I agree with that,' says John. 'The idea of a meaning implies the existence of God.'

Lorry drivers at the Trucker's Inn at Rathcormack

'On the other hand,' I say, 'it does make sense to ask how should I live a fulfilled, good life and be happy? What's the best way to do it? And let's face it, that's the real reason for asking the "meaning" question in the first place. Assuming that our lorry-driver has a choice, should he be lazy or hard-working, honest or deceitful and so on. If you put it like that, and if you accept that human nature has two distinct modes of behaviour, then dual-nature theory has a very good answer.'

'Go on, I'm listening.'

'Well, the first step is simple and bleak: Life has no meaning, only a purpose which is to survive and prosper and to breed. That's it – nothing more. What more can there be?

'The second step is to ask: OK, so how do we do that? Solitary animals, like worms, lizards and tigers, do it on their own. Cooperating animals, like termites and hyenas, survive, prosper and breed in their colonies and troops. It's the same with *Homo sapiens*; to survive we must each do our job as cooperating members of a tribe. As individuals we perish.

'So here's how dual-nature theory answers the question: You are a member of a cooperating species whether you like it or not. But your life is not predetermined. There are big decisions for you to take, and they will help you to determine your own life. They include what country to live in, which groups to join, what job to do and who to marry. You must make friends, cooperate, fit in, understand the rules and obey them as appropriate. Contribute to your family, community, team and country. Join the best working group that will accept you.

'Because you are a cooperating animal, useful contribution to a successful breeding group is the basis of the fulfilled life. But you should be wary of the amorality – of the potential, but not inevitable – nastiness of group behaviour. Things can all go horribly wrong if your chosen tribe is doing anti-social things. So to be able to live a fulfilled good life, you must also understand the answer to the Awful Question. If your generation is unable to put effective legal restraints on corporations, modern technology may do great harm to human populations, to other living things and to the planet. And that's all there is to it. End of speech.'

'Are you saying that all those deep philosophical discussions about reality, predestination, meaning, truth, consciousness and so on, aren't relevant to the question of how to live a good life?'

'Yes, that is what I'm saying. We get along very well without knowing the answers. Does it matter what consciousness is? I don't think the answer will help me to decide how to live life well and whether or not I should commit suicide.'

Now John lights up. 'Mention of suicide,' he says, 'reminds me about the modern anxieties of young men. It seems to me that dual-nature theory might offer comfort to teenage boys suffering under the feminist movement.'

'That would be a good one,' I say, 'if you can pin it up for all to see.'

'Here goes then,' says John thoughtfully. 'Teenage boys are reported to be confused about their role in life. Some become depressed, even committing suicide, taking to crime and behaving like hooligans. They hear the feminist message loud and clear. They get it from the girls at school, from video cartoons and pop music. Basically, for men, it's all over. Men have had their day. They are not going to be needed any more. The human race can and will continue quite happily without men. Men will become redundant. They'll cease to exist. The Y chromosome is withering slowly away.

'Men aren't needed for sex. Girls can do without all that messy urgency with boy's bodies, and anyway, men are very clumsy and bad at it. Men aren't even needed for reproduction; all that's needed is a small quantity of the very best quality sperm. And anyway it's said that science will soon be able to produce female children with no sperm at all. Men aren't needed for protection or in war. In fact there'd be no war, no need for defence, because it's the men who start the fighting in the first place.

'Well,' John continues, 'it's true that the feminist voice has been bottled up and must at last be heard. Men have had it all their own way and have oppressed women for centuries. But – surprise, surprise – feminism tends to get extended way beyond its natural scope. Genetically speaking, men and women complement each other. It's for the benefit of tribal cooperation that women are better at empathy than men, and more caring, articulate, multi-tasking and decisive than men, and that men are more aggressive, better teamworkers and bigger than women. The clincher is that human societies structured on the feminist model would quickly be out-cooperated and out-competed by more conventional fifty–fifty male-female societies. As we've agreed, men make better teamworkers while women are the ultimate deciders.

'So,' John's using his attorney-for-the-prosecution voice again, 'dual-nature theory can do a useful job here in explaining the fallacy of this feminist fantasy. It reminds us that human society is all about cooperation, and that cooperation is enriched by the male and female components.'

'Excellent! That's another goal for dual-nature theory.'

The lorry-drivers are all sitting in an area by the window where three tables have been pushed together. When one comes in through the swing doors he nods to the others before sitting down, nods his order to the waitress without looking at the menu, and opens his paper to catch up with the sports results, and the bare tits and bums. Noticing our bearded, scruffy appearance and animated conversation, these men of the road give us that discreet 'not one of us – thank God' look.

They eat in semi-silence. Most of the drivers are large men, presumably driving large vehicles. They don't seem to know each other and they come and go independently. There are several empty tables, so there is no need for them to sit together, but they do. In fact it's exactly like the members' table in an exclusive Edwardian gentleman's club. I bet there's a pecking order with the fellows driving the square-arsed delivery vans looking up to the long-distance men in articulated lorries.

John's been looking out through the window watching a woman lorry-driver parking her vast fourteen-wheeler, forty-ton articulated beast. 'Watch this,' he whispers, like the commentator in a TV wildlife documentary.

In she comes, barging through the swing door looking for eye contact. The men freeze in a moment of uncertainty.

'Nasty accident back there,' she says.

One of the big men looks up. A van driver wipes the crumbs off a seat for her. She hesitates and then with a faint gesture of acceptance she joins them.

Smoothly folding away the tits and bums pages they all get back to their newspapers. It's pure David Attenborough.

From Rathcormack the road down to Cork is broad, smooth and fast and we feel like sticklebacks caught in the rapids. It's hilly but not hard going, and it's overcast but not wet.

At half-three we arrive at Cork railway station. The journey is over. We've done it; we've cycled right round the coast of Ireland, 1,436 miles in all. It took 43 days.

64 To Dublin. Steve Redgrave wins. *Dual-nature theory explains a surprising number and wide variety of problems about human behaviour. Reintegrating philosophy and science. Harnessing religiosity and PC*

On several recent evenings I've remembered that silly remark by Dr Johnson, about how 'it's better to travel hopefully than to arrive'. Several times I've wanted to get hold of the pompous ass and ask him has he ever arrived wet and tired, with a sore bottom and road grit in his underpants, wondering might there be a bed for the night. But now at last I realise, apologetically, what he must have meant that when you arrive it's all over.

We catch the late-afternoon Dublin express. The train draws powerfully out of town and glides smoothly across the countryside. It doesn't seem to be going particularly fast, but in eight minutes it covers the distance that would take us an hour on bikes.

We're sitting side by side, lost in thought. The seats are certainly a lot more comfortable than a bicycle saddle. In fact they're pure luxury.

For a while we look out in silence as the landscape slides past. Then John says: 'Those bloodhounds never got you.'

'No, they didn't actually. I suspect the pucai protected us. You know, sprinkling pepper to put them off our trail.'

'Just shows,' he says. 'Cooperation may be a powerful pre-existing opportunity but it's no match for magic.'

'Which doesn't exist.'

'Don't you mean pre-exist?'

But before I have a chance to answer he goes on.

'You know,' he says, 'I feel as though we've just finished a human jigsaw puzzle in which separate pieces of behaviour have all been put in place to make a whole picture. And the key to it all has been to recognise our dual nature. Each piece, like the destruction of salmon, is a puzzle or a recurring problem but when you see how they all fall into place, biologically, as aspects of our animal nature, then, somehow there's more hope. At least we're not fooling ourselves any more.'

'Yes,' I say, 'let's see; there's splitting the law into two branches and understanding the origins of terrorism and also of looting, and the evolutionary origins of morality which must be flexible and selective.'

'And the meaning of life,' says John. 'Controlling multinationals, and the advice to teenage boys, also don't forget teaching the seduction of morality in schools. Unfortunately we didn't quite pin down the management of commonly owned resources like the cod off Newfoundland.'

'No, but we've got corporate amorality, the meaning of sport and the thrill of rowing. We've got bullying and the amorality of the party in government . . . How to control the controller was another one that got away.'

'And,' says John, 'we failed to explain German swimming-pool behaviour.'

'Yes, that's a shame.'

Running out of steam, I look up my sketchbooks where I've got them listed.

'Let me see . . . Yes. There's men are teamworkers while women are the ultimate deciders; there's the framework for understanding the history of philosophy, the separation of powers in democratic constitutions, managing a business according to the three-phase navigational cycle, the real meaning of the Holy Trinity, and how to navigate a society between dialectical extremes.'

'That's quite an impressive list,' says John. 'All made coherent by dual-nature theory.'

'The big thing in all this,' he adds, 'is that it's an unbroken thread of evolutionary biology from bacterial self-protection, eating and breeding, right through to human morality. Using the scientific method, it authorises us to chip away at the centuries old encrustations of absolutism, so that at last it's easy to see the fairly simple bones of our true nature.'

'Ah! But what about philosophy?'

'Good question,' he says. I think he's implying that our unbroken thread of evolutionary biology bypasses philosophy; even renders it redundant.

'In fact, John, thinking of my great heroes, the ancient Greeks, dual-nature theory could actually turn out to be neither science nor philosophy, or perhaps both of them.'

'What d'you mean? You've lost me.'

'Well, though Aristotle got there first, it wasn't really until Francis Bacon came along in the sixteenth century that science was recognised as a separate discipline. In ancient times there were many strands of accepted knowledge. You could almost call them common sense. The way I see it, science and philosophy only got split into opposing academic traditions by the fallacy of religious absolutism.

'The split happened when scholars noticed that religious absolutism conflicted with observable facts, such as the earth's position in the solar system, as explained by Copernicus and Gallileo. Since then the science/philosophy split has been reinforced. Philosophy, influenced by Kant, went on for years trying hard to accommodate Christianity. Then, in the twentieth century, it collapsed in a confusion of logic, linguistics and postmodernism. At the same time scientists got too big for their boots with earth-changing advances like jet propulsion, contraception, TV, space travel, genetics and computers.

'The result of this split is that social common sense, which ought to be grounded firmly on the best academic knowledge in all fields, finds itself stumbling over scientific rocks and bogging down in philosophical quicksands.'

'You'll have to explain a bit more. Take it slowly, we've all the time in the world. It'll be a couple of hours before the train gets to Dublin.'

'Thanks, all right then.' I settle back, gathering my thoughts.

'The way I see it, science made these astonishing breakthroughs in the twentieth century, so now we desperately need a clear set of ethical principles to harness them properly. But at the very time when we needed it most, European philosophy went and lost the plot. It happened after the catastrophic failures of Communism and Fascism. The rot started with G. E. Moore and Bertrand Russell's mathematical logic. It then went on via Jewish and feminist studies into postmodernism through Ludwig Wittgenstein to Jacques Derrida, with Sartre's existentialism watching the confusion and saying, 'I told you so all along.' Modern philosophers contribute very little to society; all they really do is to reinterpret the works of dead philosophers, restating open-ended riddles in the context of today, but offering no new solutions.

'It's extremely unfortunate that when we need it most, philosophy is in such a muddle. Just when science presents these vital questions, philosophy goes and drops the ball. Society has been sent round in ever decreasing circles by introspective, nihilistic philosophers searching about for the leading edge. Modern philosophy has zero relevance to the average family.'

'Wittgenstein and Derrida mean zero to me, I do agree.'

'Yes, and yet they are among the most renowned philosophers of modern times. As I see it, as soon as absolutism can be got out of the way, biology and ethics should be merged together again. And the biological fraternity needs to be put back in its place, which is beside, but slightly behind, ethics in protocol ranking. After all, the ethical question: Should we clone humans? is more important, and more difficult, than the biological one: How do we do it? The same goes for deciding the stage at which an unborn baby has human rights distinct from its mother, for genetic engineering of crops, and for many other such quandaries.

'The general public today no longer looks to ethics for the answers; they look to science. And yet there is an uneasy feeling that this is not altogether safe; somehow not correct.'

'Oh no! Not Political Correctness again.'

'Yes, I'll explain why. If you read a novel set in the time of the

Spanish Inquisition you realise, and we tend to forget this nowadays, you realise what a powerful grip ethics, even misconceived ethics, can have on society. Dual-nature theory explains this grip as the genetic propensity to accept social codes of self-restraint.

'What I'm trying to say is that this powerful grip, now lying dormant, could easily be acquired by Political Correctness for the great benefit of us all. After all, what should the rules be if one day science discovers the secrets of limitless energy and everlasting life? We do need the strong grip of ethics to control our newly discovered power. It needs to be as strong as it was during the Spanish Inquisition, under Hitler or in the time of the Pharaohs.'

'So you're saying that if biologists were to recognise the dual nature of human behaviour and the Trinity Principle, then science and philosophy could be reunited to answer many problems of human behaviour? People could be shown the completed jigsaw puzzle?'

'Yes, and if the human tendency towards religiosity can expose the Freudian deceitfulness of marketing and the cult of the individual, and if we can recognise our dual nature, PC might even neutralise the *quis custodiet?* question.'

We go silent; all talked out. Then John lights up again. 'I've been thinking about this for the last day or so. At the moment, fundamentalist Christians are shouting across the water at fundamentalist Muslims. Well, dual-nature theory puts it all in a nutshell: God is the personification of the group mind. It's as simple as that.'

'How do you mean?'

'Well, remember we said that the tribe has a quasi-mind of its own; capable of primitive emotions and thoughts like grief, fear, hysteria, triumph, pride and so on.'

'Yes, go on.'

'Well, everybody is keenly aware of these mass emotions, and once you accept dual-nature theory, it becomes obvious that God is the personification, by the population, of their own group quasi-mind. And smaller groups, like tribes, armies and business corporations, they have their own deity equivalents.'

'Excellent! You've produced a ribbon and tied the parcel with a perfect bow.'

John's scientific training re-emerges. 'But, Tony, we've got to be realistic; it's highly unlikely that two old men on bikes have cracked it.'

'Yes, you're right. But the young can't do it. The rich experiences of life have to be accumulated over a lifetime before one can even recognise the question.

'And you realise,' I say to wind it all up, 'that none of this stuff we've been going on about is either ground-breaking biology or deep-thinking philosophy. It's simply common sense about our cooperative nature. It combines biology and ethics using generally accepted A-level knowledge.'

'For me, ' says John, 'the whole thing is summarised by saying that morality is the language of cooperation.'

After a pause he adds: 'Well, actually, we could even boil that down to one word – cooperation – that's our real God.'

The afternoon Dublin Express finally drifts into the station. We fish our bikes out of the guard's van. After a short trip through the evening traffic, we reach John's rented house in Mount Merrion. We unpack and go out for a final meal in the local pub.

But there's one vital piece of unfinished business. By an almost divine piece of timing, Steve Redgrave is going for his fifth con-secutive gold medal in the final of the Olympic coxless fours in Sydney today. It's due to be shown live on TV at around midnight. So when we get back to his house, we settle down with a bottle of whiskey in John's living room.

There's so much to discuss and remember about the trip that there's too much. We just sit there peacefully watching the telly and muttering occasional trivia.

Me: 'No, I don't think I'll have another, thanks.'

John: 'Really? You sure?'

Me: 'Oh all right then, just one more.'

The build-up to the big race begins. Will the great man do it? You get a sense of people right round the world at this very moment surging to will him on through the telepathic medium of live television. It's truly a global moment.

They're lined up. And they're off! Our boys get a good start. Excitement mounts as they inch ahead over the first five hundred metres. But ominously they don't get away. Their main rivals, the arrogant Australians, are lying second. By fifteen hundred metres, the Aussies have been overtaken by the Italians who are challenging for the lead. Matthew Pinsent rowing at stroke holds the lead – just. This goes on until the last three hundred metres, when the Italians put in a tremendous burst for the line, but Steve Redgrave's four holds them off to win by two thirds of a second. A close and thrilling race.

When I wake up next morning it all sinks in. On the very same day that our cycle ride is over it has been gloriously crowned by Steve Redgrave's win. It's his fifth consecutive Olympic gold medal; and that's never been achieved before by any athlete in the history of the Olympic Games.

66. The pucai and the universe

Now that it's over my thoughts have gone quiet. I remember looking for the Neolithic burial site on the mountainside above Leenane. That's where it all started.

I think about the liberating, mind-expanding, physical days we've spent cycling round my beloved Ireland.

Ireland's like the Bible. I've tried to read it right through several times and always failed. But I've actually absorbed so much about it over the years that when I did finally cycle right round the coast with John, I found that almost all of it was already familiar. Like the Bible, the reality of Ireland has been there all along; in my mind. And now, wherever I may be, I can always close my eyes and put myself back in its valleys, mountains and pubs, wending my way round its beautiful coast.

This raises the very first philosopher's question: what actually is reality? Of course, in reality, dear old Ireland has been there for many millions of years; its waterfalls, woods and glades are always there, regardless of who is cycling past them, and so are the pucai. But part of the reality is also in the imagination, the memory, the mind.

And will you find the pucai in the mind or in reality? The answer is that you'll find them in the West of Ireland, often in the ultraviolet light of dawn or dusk. And like ideas you can't search them out; you have to wait for them to come to you. They are the naughty little flying creatures that hover in the subconscious air between sleep and wakefulness. And if you let them, they'll quietly show you the Universe.